240 Writing Topics
with
Sample Essays

LIKE TEST PREP

ISBN: 1484920562
ISBN-13: 978-1484920565

DEDICATION

To the LIKE Family

Contents

Contents

Contents

Contents

How to Write an Essay: Outline

Outline your argument and ideas in the following way so that you can easily form an introduction paragraph. In order to write an essay in 25-30 minutes, you should train yourself so that you can finish your outlines in 5-10 minutes. Here is how to do so.

Prompt (question): "If you have an opportunity to send your child to study abroad, would you have him/her educated in the US or in your home country?"

1. Argument: I will have my child educated in the United States.
2. Support 1: My child can learn English better.
3. Support 2: My child can experience various languages and cultures.
4. Support 3: My child can play sports.
5. Thesis: Since my child can be better educated in the United States, I will send him/her to study in the United States. (argument+why)

1. Argument: State your argument clearly.
2. Support 1: Give specific reasons and examples.
3. Support 2: Give specific reasons and examples.
4. Support 3: Give specific reasons and examples.

Good writers do not give similar reasons to support their argument. In other words, their three reasons (supports) should be distinguishable from each other.

5. Thesis: Usually a thesis appears in the middle or at the end of the introduction. It has to contain the rephrased main argument (should not be the same as the main argument) + why.

How to Write an Essay 1: Essay Types

In general, there are four types of argumentative (persuasive) essays.

1) experience & example
2) prefer
3) agree/disagree
4) compare and contrast or advantages and disadvantages

With the first three essays, it is easier to write a five paragraph essay.

5 paragraph essay (experience & example, prefer, agree/disagree)
Intro – The paragraph should be at least 3-5 sentences.
Support 1 - The paragraph should be at least 3-5 sentences.
Support 2 - The paragraph should be at least 3-5 sentences.
Support 3 - The paragraph should be at least 3-5 sentences.
Conclusion-The paragraph should be at least 3-5 sentences.

Sometimes it is easier to write a four paragraph essay.

4 paragraph essay (compare and contrast, advantages and disadvantages)
Intro – The paragraph should be at least 3-5 sentences.
Advantages-The paragraph should be at least 3-5 sentences.
Disadvantages-The paragraph should be at least 3-5 sentences.
Conclusion-The paragraph should be at least 3-5 sentences.

How to Write an Essay 2: Introduction

Your outline should easily become your introduction without useless words.

1. Argument: I will have my child educated in the US.
2. Support 1: My child can learn English better.
3. Support 2: My child can experience various languages and cultures.
4. Support 3: My child can play sports.
5. Thesis: Since my child can be better educated in the US, I will send him/her to study in the US. (argument+why)

Remember this? With the above, we can now easily create a complete introduction.

I will have my child educated in the US. <u>There are three reasons for this.</u> First, my child can learn English better. Second, my child can experience various languages and cultures. Third, my child can play sports. Because my child can be better educated in the US, I will send him/her to study in the US.

As you see, I only added one sentence to it. It is <u>underlined.</u> Isn't this simple?

How to Write an Essay 3: Body

All we have to do is to write the support and give specific reasons, details, and explanations.

For example,

①First of all, my child can learn English better in the US than in Korea. ② At school, my child will learn various subjects like Math, Science, Social Studies, Music, and Art in English. ③ Doing so, he/she can talk and write about various topics in English. ④ Then after school, my child will converse with others in English. ⑤his way, he/she will practice conversational English.

To explain, sentence ① is called the "topic sentence" and it contains the most important information. Sentences ②, ③, ④, and ⑤ contains specific examples and details that explain how the child will learn English better. After sentence ⑤, you can write a sentence about your next paragraph. However, this is not required.

Got it? You can write the other two supporting paragraphs the same way. Now, expand the second and the third paragraphs in your own words.

Second of all, my child can experience various languages and cultures in the US. (expand this like paragraph 2 and write at least four more sentences.)
Thirdly, my child can play various sports in the US (expand this like paragraph 2 and write at least four more sentences.).

How to Write an Essay 4: Conclusion

In the conclusion, you have to <u>rephrase</u>, <u>summarize</u>, and <u>conclude</u>. Here, you cannot simply copy the introduction. Instead, be creative.

①US education can benefit my child in many ways. ② My child can master the English language, broaden his horizons, and become more physically strong. ③ Therefore, if I have an opportunity to have my child educated in the US, I will not hesitate to send him abroad.

In sentence ①, I rephrased the <u>main argument</u>.

Introduction -> Conclusion
<u>main argument</u>: I will have my child educated in the US. -> US education can benefit my child in many ways.

In sentence ②, I summarized the <u>supports</u>.

<u>Supports</u>: My child can learn English better. My child can experience various languages and cultures. My child can play sports. -> My child can master English, broaden his horizons, and become more physically strong.

Point 3: I wrote the conclusion by rephrasing the <u>thesis</u>.

<u>Thesis</u>: As my child can be better educated in the US, I will send him/her to study in the US.-> If I have an opportunity to have my child educated in the US, I will not hesitate to send him abroad.

How to Write an Essay: Sample Essay

If I have the opportunity, I will have my child educated in the US. There are three reasons for this. First, my child can learn English better. Second, my child can experience various languages and cultures. Third, my child can play sports. Since my child can be better educated in the US, I will send him/her to study in the US.

First of all, my child can learn English better in the US than in Korea. At school, my child will learn various subjects like Math, Science, Social Studies, Music, and Art in English. Doing so, he/she can talk and write about various topics in English. Then after school, my child will converse with others in English. This way, he/she will practice conversational English.

Second of all, my child can experience various languages and cultures in the US. Unlike Korea, one can experience many different cultures and languages at a very close distance. For example, if my child wants to learn Vietnamese and their culture, he/she can go to the Vietnamese community and mingle there. If he/she wants to try the Italian cuisine, he/she can visit Little Italy. Moreover, there are many different ethnic festivals and ceremonies that my child can visit locally in the US.

Thirdly, my child can play various sports in the US. Unlike most Korean schools, US schools have excellent sports facilities. For example, many schools have swimming pools, football fields, basketball gym, tennis courts, and many others. Moreover, these schools encourage students to play sports. However, most Korean schools do not have such fine sports facilities and they discourage students from playing sports.

US education can benefit my child in many ways. My child can master English, broaden his horizons, and become more physically strong. Therefore, if I could have my child educated in the US, I will not hesitate to send him/her abroad.

> ## Q121. Which season—winter, spring, summer, or fall—is your favorite? Why?

A. Essay Outline

Argument: Summer is my favorite season.
Support 1: I have a lot of free time in the summer.
Support 2: There's more daylight so I can play longer.
Support 3: The summer is always very warm.
Thesis: Because it's easier to have fun in the summer, I like summer the best.

B. Model Essay

I would have to say that summer is my favorite season of all. First off, it means that school is out and I can do whatever I want. Next, it means that there are more daylight hours to enjoy. And thirdly, summer is a time to enjoy being outside in the warm sunshine. Summer is my favorite season of all because of these reasons.

First of all, summer is when school is out and I can spend all of my time playing both outside and in. My parents encourage me to get out in the sunlight as much as possible and this is fine since my friends and I like to go out together and have a good time. We like to go out and go exploring on our bikes, usually through the woods outside our neighborhood. Of course, it rains quite frequently in the summer as well, so we usually try to hang out in one another's houses. We always have a great time together in the summer, because we have all the time we need to have fun.

Another thing that makes summer my favorite season of all is that there's more daylight hours to enjoy. The sun stays out longer, usually sometime after eight in the evening. This means that there's a lot more sunshine to be out in and enjoy while going out and having fun. I can go swimming in the sunlight or just lay and get a suntan, so long as I don't do it for too long, I don't want to get burned. The sun is the reason why we go out and it just means we can be out longer during the summer.

The last reason is that it's the warmest time of year for us and we don't get very much warm weather where we come from. For most of the year, it's usually cool and wet or cold and icy. We only have three months of reprieve from the chill and wet and that is summer. When my neighbors and I want to celebrate the summer, we go out, have barbecues, or just sit and talk outside. This is a good thing to do at night, when the heat of the day lingers in the night air. So the warmth of the summer air is a rare treat for us and we relish it when it comes around each year.

So summer is my favorite season of all because it's the time of year that really puts together everything I like to do and experience. There's no school in the summer so we can really have all the fun we want during the day. There's more daylight during the day so there's more day to enjoy. And the warmth of summer is something we only have a limited time to enjoy throughout the rest of the wetter, colder parts of the year for us. That's why summer is my favorite season.

C. Useful Expressions

1. I would have to say that summer is my favorite season of all.

_____

2. My parents encourage me to get out in the sunlight as much as possible, and this is fine since me and my friends like to go out together and have a good time

_____

3. Of course, it rains quite frequently in the summer as well, so we usually try to hang out in one another's houses.

_____

4. I can go swimming in the sunlight or just lay out and get a suntan, so long as I don't do it for too long.

_____

5. We only have three months of reprieve from the chill and wet and that is summer.

_____

6. This is a good thing to do at night, when the heat of the day lingers into the night air.

_____

7. So the warmth of the summer air is a rare treat for us and we relish it when it comes around each year.

_____

8. So the summer is my favorite season of all because it's the time of year that really puts together everything I like to do and experience.

_____

9. There's no school in the summer so we can really have all the fun we want during the day.

_____

10. And the warmth of summer is something we only have a limited time to enjoy throughout the rest of the wetter, colder parts of the year for us.

_____

Q122. If you could plan the perfect day to spend with your close friends, where would you go and why?

A. Essay Outline

Argument: A perfect day would include an outing to an island close to my town.
Support 1: We can go swimming all day.
Support 2: We can have a big party without bothering our neighbors.
Support 3: We can spend the night stargazing.
Thesis: Because we can engage in many outdoor activities, my friends and I would have the perfect day at an island.

B. Model Essay

There's a lake with an island in the middle of it north of our town, and I would go there for the perfect day, an all day camp out. It's a great place to go swimming because it's deep and cool. It's a great place to have a cookout or picnic because it's far away from the rest of humanity and we don't have to worry about being noisy to our neighbors. And it's far away from the light of houses and the town, so it's a perfect place to go to sleep under the stars. The perfect day for me would be an overnight camp out to that island.

The first reason why I would plan a perfect day on that island is because it's a great place to go swimming with my friends. The lake is nice and deep around where the island is. There's a place where we can dive right in off of a tire swing we put there. The water is cool and we all have a great time splashing around and playing in the water. We always have a great time when we go out there and go for a long swim around that island.

The second reason a campout there would be a perfect day is that we could have as big a party we want without anyone being bothered. We could play our music loudly and dance and sing and no one would threaten to call the police on us. We could eat all the food we brought while we chatted loudly with ourselves and no one we would know would try to crash the party. It would just be me, my friends, some great music, and enough food to last us until we left the following morning. That would make it a perfect day, that we could eat and party without worrying about the neighbors.

The last reason I would consider a campout at that island to be perfect would be that we could fall asleep looking at the stars. In the town where we live, we could never have seen the stars because there were so many houses with lights on. We would also only sleep inside with our parents nearby, so there was no sense of adventure. But on the island, with the town so far away, we can see the night sky clearly. We can all gather together, look at the stars and tell each other our wishes and other personal worries to each other as we drift into sleep. The stars always look beautiful and we feel a sense of peace as we stare up at them from our small island.

So that island in the middle of the lake would be where we would spend our perfect day. It's a great place to swim because it's deep, cool, and we can dive in without getting hurt. It's a great place to have a party and cookout because no one is there to threaten to call the cops or to crash the party. It's also a great place to camp because we can see the stars at night, something we could never do at home. That's why a day on that island would be a perfect day.

C. Useful Expressions

1. It's a great place to have a cookout or picnic because it's far away from the rest of humanity and we don't have to worry about being noisy to our neighbors.

_____

_____

2. There's a place where we can dive right in off of a tire swing we put there.

_____

_____

3. We could play our music loud and dance and sing and no one would threaten to call the police on us.

_____

_____

4. We could eat all the food we brought while we chatted loudly with ourselves and no one we would know would try to crash the party.

_____

5. It would just be me, my friends, some great music, and enough food to last us until we left the following morning.

_____

6. That would make it a perfect day, that we could eat and party without worrying about the neighbors.

_____

7. We would also only sleep inside with our parents nearby, so there was no sense of adventure.

_____

8. We can all gather together, look at the stars and tell each other our wishes and other personal worries as we drift off to sleep.

_____

9. The stars always look beautiful and we feel a sense of peace as we stare up at them from our small island.

_____

10. It's a great place to have a party and cookout because no one is there to threaten to call the cops or to crash the party.

_____

Q123. What is the most frightening experience you have ever had in your life? When did it happen and how did you react to it?

A. Essay Outline

Argument: The most frightening experience was when I had a run-in with a dog.
Support 1: The dog was a terrifying German Shepard.
Support 2: The dog got loose and chased me.
Support 3: I learned why the dog was so terrifying.
Thesis: Although it turned out to be a really sweet animal, the day a dog got loose and chased me was horrifying.

B. Model Essay

I guess the most frightening experience I ever had in my life was when I ran afoul of a neighbor's dog. This was when my neighbor forgot to lock his gate and the dog started to chase me. I couldn't understand why the dog seemed to hate me and I just started running when he came out of the gate. However, it turned out that I shouldn't have been afraid, because he was afraid too. That frightening experience taught me about how I should handle fear and where fear really comes from.

The dog in question was a German shepherd and when I was little, it looked tough, fierce, and very scary. The dog seemed to bark at me every time I walked by, or tried to walk by. At first, it was just startling; I knew that dogs liked to bark at things that are unfamiliar to them. However, after a while the dog would bark and try to jump over his fence, but it was high enough that the dog couldn't jump over. It seemed to dislike me for some reason and I couldn't understand why, so I would start running past the house.

But then one day, I was running past the house and the gate happened to be unlocked. The dog was able to run out of the gate and start chasing me. I ran faster than I had ever run in my life. I was able to run all the way home with the dog catching up. My father was able to run out and shoo the dog away. When he asked me about it, I told him that the dog was always barking at me but this was the first time it had ever chased me. My father decided it was time to talk to this individual.

We went back to the house. I was still afraid but my father assured me that nothing would happen. The dog's owner was an elderly man and it was from him that I learned how the dog was more afraid of me. He had adopted the dog from a rescue shelter. He had been abused by his previous owner, who was currently in jail for that abuse. The man explained that even though the dog, whose name I learned was Charlie, was able to learn to trust him, he was still weary around strangers. He introduced me to Charlie and showed me how I could earn his trust. I let Charlie sniff me and lick my hand, and soon, I was able to pet him. He said that his gate lock was broken and he forgot to take Charlie inside and said he was sorry for that. I said it was okay and I learned that sometimes others can be more scared of us than we are of them.

That experienced taught me about perception and trust. Charlie barked at me because he was afraid of me, and in turn, I became afraid of him. When he chased me, he was just following his instinct. It wasn't until we got to know each other that our fear for each other subsided. Charlie and I became friends and we saw each other frequently until he died. I still miss him, because he showed me that fear is only what we perceive it to be.

C. Useful Expressions

1. I guess the most frightening experience I ever had in my life was when I ran afoul of a neighbor's dog.

_____

_____

2. I couldn't understand why the dog seemed to hate me and I just started running when he came out of the gate.

_____

_____

3. The dog in question was a German shepherd and when I was little, it looked tough, fierce, and very scary.

_____

4. However, after a while the dog would bark and try to jump over his fence, but it was high enough that the dog couldn't jump over.

_____

5. It seemed to dislike me for some reason and I couldn't understand why, so I would start running past the house.

_____

_____

6. I was able to run all the way home without the dog catching up.

_____

7. My father was able to run out and shoo the dog away.

_____

8. I was still afraid but my father assured me that nothing would happen.

_____

9. The man explained that even though the dog, whose name I learned was Charlie, was able to learn to trust him, he was still weary around strangers.

_____

_____

10. When he chased me, he was just following his instinct.

_____

Q124. Should a country's government tell its citizens how many children they can have? Why or why not?

A. Essay Outline

Argument: A government should not tell its citizens how many children they can have.
Support 1: The government would be intruding on the privacy of its citizens by doing so.
Support 2: It's not a necessary step in curtailing a large population increase.
Support 3: A globalized economy will assuage the pressures brought on by today's growing society.
Thesis: Because placing a limit on the number of children a couple can have is an unnecessary abuse of power, a government should not interfere in this aspect of its citizens lives.

B. Model Essay

I do not think that a country should tell its citizens how many children they can have. First off, this is an unnecessary intrusion of the government into people's personal lives. Secondly, the birthrate around the world is dropping on its own, because of the increased freedom of women. And finally, with interdependence made possible by global trade, strained resources can be easily supplemented. So the world has adjusted to allow for more children to be born and to live without fear of starvation.

The first argument against the restriction of children to a certain number is that it is an invasion of privacy carried out by an intrusive government. People already perceive their privacy to be under threat by the enormous amount of security and surveillance in multiple public settings. Coupled with the perception that the government can snoop on anyone that is suspected of being a terrorist, despite what evidence there is to the contrary, this power can be expanded or even abused to enforce the state's own viewpoints or practices upon its citizens, a clear violation of civil rights. The state, if it imposes a child limit on families, can use this surveillance power to intrude on families and take away their children arbitrarily. This is a power that no citizen would ever want its government to have because it leads to tyranny.

The next reason why it's wrong to put an arbitrary limit on the number of children in a family is that the problem it's supposed to solve, overpopulation, is actually being solved on its own. In the developed world, more women are taking control of their lives and their bodies. Contraceptives are now widely available and they're cheap enough for anyone to buy. Also, more women are starting careers of their own and do not have to rely on getting married or having children to secure their futures. The by-product of this is that they're having fewer children than in the past. This means that soon, the birthrate in the developed world will be much lower than that in the underdeveloped world, creating a more balanced population. This coupled with the impending deaths of senior citizens will shrink or stabilize the world population by the middle of the century.

The last reason is that we now have a globalized economy that can relieve the fear of strained resources. A lot of countries have much lower populations than the rest of the world, so they often have a surplus of necessary resources. Those countries with higher populations but with resources not necessary for survival can trade those goods for the surplus goods that are enjoyed by the richer world. This has in fact happened and in the parts of the world with large populations, they are turning themselves around and finding the benefits of trade and raising their quality of life.

So imposing a limit on children is unnecessary and tyrannical because the world is already finding a solution to the problems it's supposed to fix. The power to enforce this law would entail more government spying and curtail people's freedoms. The women of the world are also taking control of their lives and can dictate themselves on how many children to have. Finally, the world has become more open to trade and this has helped alleviate resource strains throughout the world. That's why it's wrong to impose a limit on the number of children families can have.

C. Useful Expressions

1. First off, this is an unnecessary intrusion of the government into people's personal lives.

2. And finally, with interdependence made possible by global trade, strained resources can be easily supplemented.

3. People already perceive their privacy to be under threat by the enormous amount of security and surveillance in multiple public settings.

4. Coupled with this is the perception that the government can snoop on anyone that is suspected of being a terrorist, despite what evidence there is to the contrary.

5. The state, if it imposes a child limit on families, can use this surveillance power to intrude on families and take away their children arbitrarily.

6. The by-product of this is that they're having fewer children than in the past.

7. This coupled with the impending deaths of senior citizens will shrink or stabilize the world population by the middle of the century.

8. This has in fact happened and in the parts of the world with large populations; they are turning themselves around and finding the benefits of trade and raising their quality of life.

9. The power to enforce this law would entail more government spying and curtail people's freedoms.

10. The women of the world are also taking control of their lives and can dictate themselves how many children to have.

Q125. When you begin working, would you rather a) earn a lot of money working in a job that you don't like, or b) earn less money doing something you truly enjoy?

A. Essay Outline

Argument: It's better to do something I truly enjoy.
Support 1: We will inevitably start out making less than we want to no matter the job.
Support 2: We will gain valuable experience that can lead to a pay increase down the road.
Support 3: The more we hate our job, the more unhappy we will be.
Thesis: Working a job we enjoy, although we will not be making as much, is a better decision due to the benefits it gives us.

B. Model Essay

I would probably want to earn less money doing something I truly enjoy. First off, we must all realize that we're going to earn less money at the start. The next thing we need to remember is that the start of work is when you start to gain experience in your chosen field, and that's more important than money. Finally, when we work at jobs we hate, it only leads to depression and/or burnout. It's just a better idea to do the work you love rather than rush into making a lot of money right away.

I think we need to remember that when we're starting out, we're going to make less money than we would like to make or dream of making when we're in school. When we start out, less is expected of us because we do not have the kind of experience that would justify a high salary. We need to earn that expectation and trust by demonstrating that we can do the job we wish to do by doing the support work that goes into the field. Once we prove ourselves for the first few years, then we can expect to move up in salary. So just going after the high salary right away is unrealistic and it shows lack of patience to our employers.

With that start, we gain experience in the field we wish to make a career in. That experience is the currency we have in future job searches. Without experience, employers will not give us a second look if we go in for an application or an interview. So we can give up any thoughts of earning a large salary if we choose to go for the big salary right away and don't take experience into consideration. Gaining the necessary experience is another big reason to choose love of job over desire for money when starting out.

The last thing we really need to consider is that when we perform a job that we dislike, it can lead to depression, burnout, or both. We become depressed when we find ourselves toiling everyday after giving up on our dreams. We can also burn ourselves out after a number of years working at the same job and seeing very little reward in it outside of our bank account. We give up on what we like just so we can go on living, but pretty soon, our salary no longer matters because it goes toward psychiatrists looking for the reason we're not happy. So in this quest for riches, we become less rich inside ourselves and we ultimately give our riches to someone to find the reason we're depressed, even though we know why we're depressed, because work makes us that way.

So it is in our best interest that we choose what we love over what can make us the most money the fastest. It's because the first job we get is the first chance we have to prove our abilities and our worth to the first employers we have. The second reason is that we gain experience when we start out and that has been proven more valuable than money time and time again. And lastly, doing something we hate, regardless of salary, can only lead to depression and burnout. So that's why I would choose the job I love over the job that pays well.

C. Useful Expressions

1. The next thing we need to remember is that the start of work is when you start to gain experience in your chosen field, and that's more important than money.

_____

2. Finally, when we work at jobs we hate, it only leads to depression and/or burnout.

_____

3. When we start out, less is expected of us because we do not have the kind of experience that would justify a high salary.

_____

4. Once we prove ourselves for the first few years, then we can expect to move up in salary.

_____

5. So just going after the high salary right away is unrealistic and it shows a lack of patience to our employers.

_____

6. That experience is the currency we have in future job searches.

_____

7. Without experience, employers will not give us a second look if we go in for an application or an interview.

_____

8. We become depressed when we find ourselves toiling everyday after giving up on our dreams.

_____

9. We can also burn ourselves out after a number of years working at the same job and seeing very little reward in it outside of our bank account.

_____

10. And lastly, doing something we hate, regardless of salary, can only lead to depression and burnout.

_____

Q126. Should students work while they study? Why or why not?

A. Essay Outline

Argument: Students should work while they study.
Support 1: Students need to stop hassling their parents for money.
Support 2: Students need to get used to supporting themselves.
Support 3: Students will gain valuable financial skills by learning to save money early.
Thesis: Students should have part-time jobs while they study to alleviate the burden on their parents and
       themselves.

B. Model Essay

    Students should be able to work while they study. Being a student means that they're often poor simply from the fact that they are still pretty much dependent on their parents for money. A student needs to establish their independence from their families so that they can live on their own in the future. Students also have to build up their savings so that they can live more easily throughout their lives. So we can see that students will need to work so that when they leave school, they can more easily take care of themselves.

    Students are on their own for the first time and as such they're not going to have a lot of money to their name. They usually ask their parents for money if they find themselves broke, something that annoys parents to no end. Parents will insist that they find work because they don't want their kids to come running to them whenever they need or want cash. Parents want their children to learn independence and ought to cut off their kids from what they perceive to be an endless source of spending money. So students will have to start working if their parents wise up and stop giving them handouts.

    The next thing we have to remember is that when students finish school, they're on their own. This means that they're going to have to find their own place to live, buy their own food and medicine, and pay for their own heat, water, and electricity. With a job, they can save that money and put it towards their basic needs after graduation. If they don't save up, they're going to find it very difficult to get out on their own and survive without help and they'll be dependent on their families long after they were to break that tether. So a job is essential for students to establish their independence.

    The last thing that students need to learn is that they need to build up their life savings so that they can live comfortably throughout their lives. Not having this nest egg means that they'll either have to work harder or put off retirement and work longer. Either way, it means that they're not going to be able to live in whatever capacity they desire. But if they start working when they're students, they'll learn how important it is to save up, so that they won't have to work as hard in the future as they do at their first job. So in order to live a good life with few worries and a good lifestyle, they'll need to start saving and they can only do that when they start working. The sooner they start working, the better their savings will be.

    So students should work because it helps them along the path of becoming responsible adults. It weans them off asking their parents for money when they have very little of it. It helps them prepare for life outside of school and their parents' house. Finally, their life savings start with this kind of work when they save up to live the lives they envision for themselves. So I believe that students should work while they're in school.

C. Useful Expressions

1. Being a student means that they're often poor simply from the fact that they are still pretty much dependent on their parents for money.

---

2. Students are on their own for the first time and as such they're not going to have a lot of money to their name.

---

3. They usually ask their parents for money if they find themselves broke, something that annoys parents to no end.

---

4. So students will have to start working if their parents wise up and stop giving them handouts.

---

5. If they don't save up, they're going to find it very difficult to get out on their own and survive without help and they'll be dependent on their families long after they were to break that tether.

---

6. Not having this nest egg means that they'll either have to work harder or put off retirement and work longer.

---

7. Either way, it means that they're not going to be able to live in whatever capacity they desire.

---

8. So in order to live a good life with few worries and a good lifestyle, they'll need to start saving and they can only do that when they start working.

---

9. So students should work because it helps them along the path of becoming responsible adults.

---

10. It weans them off asking their parents for money when they have very little of it.

> **Q127. Which do you think is better for the environment, to build fewer factories or to create more wildlife preservation areas?**

A. Essay Outline

Argument: There ought to be more areas set aside for wildlife to flourish.
Support 1: There are other forms of development that could continue the environmental degradation of our country.
Support 2: Wildlife preserves allow for the continued growth of plants and trees, which clean the air.
Support 3: More wildlife preservations will help solve the very real problem of over-hunting.
Thesis: Because building more wildlife preservation areas will help struggling plants and animals, I believe it is better for the environment.

B. Model Essay

There ought to be more areas set aside for wildlife to flourish to help improve the environment. The first reason is that even with fewer factories, there are other ways development could do harm to the environment. The second reason is that when wildlife preserves are set aside, it allows plants and trees to grow and make the air cleaner for everyone. The final reason is that wildlife preserves allow animals to repopulate without fear from hunters. The need for wildlife preserves should be the top priority for any country seeking to repair the environmental damage that has been done to their land, air, and water.

To start with, even if we stop building factories, there are other forms of development that could continue the environmental degradation of our country. First off, the number of roads that cut through our countryside continues to increase and that means our countryside is not as clean as people thought it to be. Also, farms can degrade the soil and lead to clear cutting for the land to grow food and for animals to graze. And let's not forget all of the new homes people want built out there. Those can also take away from the necessary ecosystems required for a healthy biosphere. So those forms of human habitation also need to be addressed along with factories.

The next thing that must be remembered is that wildlife preserves allow for the continual growth of plants and trees, vital to the cleaning of our air. When preserves are set aside, that means that trees cannot be cut down, so they can go through a natural life cycle which allows them to grow and eventually reproduce. This in turns helps clean the air that has been polluted by the numerous factories that have already been built. Also, it allows for the sheltering of animals that are often under threat from human hunters. These trees are important to our environment, so there should be areas set aside where they stay standing for as long as they are alive.

The third reason also involves hunters and the very real problem of over-hunting. Having wildlife preserves ensures that animals that are under constant threat from overhunting are allowed to repopulate and regrow their numbers. Hunting would be strictly forbidden in these areas and there would be stiff penalties for poaching in the preserves. And with the threat of hunters gone, animals can carry out the cycle of life that is important to their survival and to ours. So the need to protect animals is also an important reason to set aside wildlife preserves.

We should keep in mind that just stopping new factories from being built isn't going to help much without stopping development altogether in many parts of our country. The increase in farms and houses remains a threat to our vulnerable ecosystems and these have to be halted somewhere. The trees need to keep growing so that our air can get cleaner. And animals need to repopulate from overhunting. That's why I feel there should be more wildlife preserves set aside.

C. Useful Expressions

1. The first reason is that even with fewer factories, there are other ways development could do harm to the environment.

_____

_____

2. The need for wildlife preserves should be the top priority for any country seeking to repair the environmental damage that has been done to their land, air, and water.

_____

_____

3. To start with, even if we stop building factories, there are other forms of development that could continue the environmental degradation of our country.

_____

_____

4. And let's not forget all of the new homes people want built out there, that can also take away from the necessary ecosystems required for a healthy biosphere.

_____

_____

5. So those forms of human habitation also need to be addressed along with factories.

_____

6. The next thing that must be remembered is that wildlife preserves allow for the continual growth of plants and trees, which is vital to the cleaning of our air.

_____

7. The third reason also involves hunters and the very real problem of over-hunting.

_____

8. Hunting would be strictly forbidden in these areas and there would be stiff penalties for poaching in the preserves.

_____

9. We should keep in mind that just stopping new factories from being built isn't going to help much without stopping development altogether in many parts of our country.

_____

_____

10. The increase in farms and houses remains a threat to our vulnerable ecosystems and these have to be halted somewhere.

_____

> **Q128. When children misbehave in public places, should parents scold them right away or not?**

A. Essay Outline

Argument: I believe parents need to scold their children right away.
Support 1: Children tend to take advantage of any weakness you show them.
Support 2: By not scolding a child in public, strangers may think you are simply a bad parent.
Support 3: When you scold your child in public, you are showing them that it is never acceptable to behave inappropriately.
Thesis: By scolding a child in public, you are teaching your child a valuable lesson.

B. Model Essay

I think parents should scold their children in public, but only in a soft way. First off, if parents feel too embarrassed to scold their kids in public, the kid will pick up on that and take advantage of it. Secondly, bystanders could see this and think that the parent is weak, particularly in a conservative area where parents have total control over their children. Finally, helping children understand that their actions are unacceptable but in a way that shows that you're a lot more enlightened than those who take a "spare the rod" approach. So gentle scolding in public is certainly a better option than losing face to your child and to on-lookers.

The first thing that all parents need to remember is that their kids will take advantage of any weakness you show when they want to have their way. Children will always demand that they have treats when they go out shopping and parents know that indulgence is never a good thing. However, children are likely to scream and misbehave if they don't get what they desire. If you show a reluctance to scold in public, they're going to continue their negative behavior until they are satisfied that they'll get what they want. Children need to learn early on that they're not going to always get what they want and parents need to be firm in their resolve that they can say "no." Parents must always show firmness to their children, especially in public.

Another thing that people need to remember is that a reluctance to scold in front of bystanders could be interpreted as a sign of weakness. Where I grew up, parents always made sure to scold their children in front of others when they misbehaved. This is because we lived in a very conservative community where parents absolutely dominated their children. There was no coddling or negotiating and, "no" meant "no". Today, it would seem shocking that parents would be so cold towards their children, so a gentler approach should be taken when being firm with children. But anyway you look at it, when people are watching, you must be in control.

The last thing we must remember is that it teaches children that bad behavior is never acceptable, but does it in a socially acceptable manner. When I was growing up, striking one's children was the proper way to get them to quiet down. However, we have learned that this hardly, if ever, teaches the children anything constructive. In fact, parents who take this approach will not only be ostracized by those around them, but it will cause the child to act out even worse because they're reacting to pain. So gentle scolding is preferable, it shows resolve, but it also shows that you are in charge, not your child.

So it is necessary to scold a child in public but in a gentle manner. The child will always exploit parental weaknesses when they're exhibited. People will think that a parent is weak if they don't scold, especially when it's expected. But gentle scolding is always more effective than striking or yelling. So a child should always be gently scolded when that child misbehaves in public.

C. Useful Expressions

1. First off, if parents feel too embarrassed to scold their kids in public, the kid will pick up on that and take advantage of it.

2. Finally, helping children understand that their actions are unacceptable but in a way that shows that you're a lot more enlightened than those who take a "spare the rod" approach.

3. If you show a reluctance to scold in public, they're going to continue their negative behavior until they are satisfied that they'll get what they want.

4. Children need to learn early on that they're not going to always get what they want and parents need to be firm in their resolve that they can say "no."

5. Another thing that people need to remember is that a reluctance to scold in front of bystanders could be interpreted as a sign of weakness.

6. This is because we lived in a very conservative community where parents absolutely dominated their children.

7. Today, it would seem shocking that parents would be so cold towards their children, so a gentler approach should be taken when being firm with children.

8. But anyway you look at it, when people are watching, you must be in control.

9. In fact, parents who take this approach will not only be ostracized by those around them, but it will cause the child to act out even worse because they're reacting to pain.

10. But gentle scolding is always more effective than striking or yelling.

> **Q129. Should students consult their parents about their majors and career or should they consult their teachers and friends instead?**

A. Essay Outline

Argument: Students should avoid consulting their parents about their majors and seek guidance from teachers and friends instead.

Support 1: Teachers and friends have a better idea of your strengths and weaknesses.

Support 2: Parents tend to have an extremely biased point of view concerning their child's future.

Support 3: Teachers have the necessary training to make decisions about their students' futures.

Thesis: I believe students should consult friends and teachers rather than their parents because they are more apt to give better advice.

B. Model Essay

Students ought to consult their teachers or friends about their majors, not their parents. First of all, teachers and friends have seen you study and learn throughout your schooling, either in part or in whole, so they know your strengths and weaknesses better. Secondly, parents tend to be biased towards their own dreams for their children, without regards for their children's feelings. Finally, teachers, as education professionals, have a better understanding of the fields that students consider, and thus can give better advice. So teachers are certainly more knowledgeable than parents about which direction a student's education should take.

Your friends and teachers have watched you progress through your schooling practically throughout your life, and thus know your strengths and weaknesses. If your teachers have noticed your talents in a particular subject, say biology, then they may recommend that you major in biology and become a doctor or scientist. A parent, on the other hand, may hate the biology field for religious reasons and demand that their kids avoid taking biology out of a fear of displeasing their god or gods. This is a clear case of emotional bias conflicting with factual evidence. The teacher never lets such biases get in their way of helping their students become successful and should be listened to more intently.

Another thing that parents tend to be emotional about is their own dreams for their children. Parents like to fantasize about the path their children take along the road of life and they breed and attempt to condition their children through classes, extracurricular activities, and sports. But whether they want to admit it or not, their children have free will, and ultimately, they're the ones who decide which path their children take. This is often influenced by their friends, who join them in their interests, hobbies, and activities. The parents' dreams for their children are just basically the unfulfilled dreams they had for themselves and it's wrong to project that frustration onto their kids. So parents really shouldn't dictate their children's majors when they enter college.

The third thing that we must remember is that teachers are professionals and know more about children's education than parents. This is something that is forgotten by the modern day homeschool movement, which sees teachers as being unnecessary. However, teachers go through many years of training and years of study before they become certified. Part of that learning is knowing how to gauge the interests and strengths and weaknesses of the kids they set out to educate. So they know how to read the abilities of students better than parents.

So parents are not as neutral or qualified as teachers are when it comes to advising students about their majors. Teachers have watched students and their progress for years and even helped them out along the way. Parents often project their own unfulfilled dreams onto their children in order to steer them along the path they wanted to take before, without considering the child's own feelings. Also, teachers are professionals and know more about this than parents. That's why I believe teachers should advise students on their majors, not their parents.

C. Useful Expressions

1. Students ought to consult their teachers or friends about their majors, not their parents.

2. Secondly, parents tend to be biased towards their own dreams for their children, without regard for their children's feelings.

3. A parent, on the other hand, may hate the biology field for religious reasons and demand that his kids avoid taking biology out of a fear of displeasing their god or gods.

4. This is a clear case of emotional bias conflicting with factual evidence.

5. Parents like to fantasize about the path their children take along the road of life and they breed and attempt to condition their children through classes, extracurricular activities, and sports.

6. The parents' dreams for their children are just basically the unfulfilled dreams they had for themselves and it's wrong to project that frustration onto their kids.

7. This is something that is forgotten by advocates of the modern day home-school movement, which sees teachers as being unnecessary.

8. Part of that learning is knowing how to gauge the interests and strengths and weaknesses of the kids they set out to educate.

9. So parents are not as neutral or qualified as teachers are when it comes to advising students about their majors.

10. Parents often project their own unfulfilled dreams onto their children in order to steer them along the path they wanted to take before, without considering the child's own feelings.

Q130. In order to get healthy, should people exercise more or sleep more?

A. Essay Outline

Argument: The most effective way to get healthy is to exercise more.
Support 1: Through exercises, one is able to burn off extra calories that are causing him to be fat.
Support 2: While sleeping, we are sedentary.
Support 3: Exercise ensures that our hearts stay healthy.
Thesis: Exercising increases our health more because physical activity keeps our body in great condition.

B. Model Essay

To become healthy, people need to exercise more rather than sleep more. This is because exercise actually uses energy and thus burns calories. Sleep basically has you not moving and building up energy, so calories become converted into fat while you sleep. And finally, a lack of motion leads to a hardening of blood vessels, which can lead to heart disease. So exercise is a better choice for better health because the increase in motion helps keep your arteries healthy and your fat levels down.

Exercise has been shown to burn calories and this, in turn, burns fat and keeps your weight down. The modern day diet is full of carbohydrates, which we need to produce energy. The problem is people don't do enough physical activity to burn that energy and that gets stored as fat. When we exercise more than we eat, we can burn off that excess energy and lower our weight to healthier levels. This is the reason why so many people get gym memberships, because it gives them the opportunity to burn off that excess energy that they can't burn in their everyday lives. This burning of fat helps us become healthier as we continue to commit to exercising.

Another thing to remember is that we are the most sedentary when we are asleep. Sleep is simply allowing our bodies to go into a relaxed state to the point where our mind relaxes, too. When that happens, our bodies do not move until the time when we are roused from our sleep-state. All during that time, the food that we have yet to digest will convert to energy and get stored in our fat cells until it is needed for activity. So sleep just adds to the fat that builds up from unused energy, while exercise actually uses that energy.

Also, when activity is limited, the arteries that supply blood to our hearts stiffen and harden. When they're hard, the arteries can be more easily blocked by cholesterol and blood clots. This results in a heart attack for anyone who doesn't exercise. This is because exercise can actually make the blood vessels more flexible and thus less prone to blockages and can help clean out the plaque from cholesterol. So our hearts and arteries become healthier as we exercise more because of this flexing and cleaning.

So that's why exercise is better than sleep when it comes to improving one's help. Exercise burns calories and uses the fat stored in our bodies, which in turn, slims us down. Sleep is actually the most time fat has to accumulate in our bodies because it's the longest period of regular inactivity. And exercise can keep our arteries flexible and clean, lowering the risk of a heart attack. That's why I believe that more exercise is a better keeper of health than more sleep.

C. Useful Expressions

1. And finally, a lack of motion leads to a hardening of blood vessels, which can lead to heart disease.

---

2. Exercise has been shown to burn calories and this, in turn, burns fat and keeps your weight down.

---

3. When we exercise more than we eat, we can burn off that excess energy and lower our weight to a healthier level.

---

4. Sleep is simply allowing our bodies to go into a relaxed state to the point where our mind relaxes.

---

5. When that happens, our bodies do not move until the time when we are roused from our sleep-state.

---

6. All during that time, the food that we have yet to digest will convert to energy and get stored in our fat cells until it is needed for activity.

---

7. When they're hard, the arteries can be more easily blocked by cholesterol and blood clots.

---

8. This is because exercise can actually make the blood vessels more flexible and thus less prone to blockages and can help clean out the plaque from cholesterol.

---

9. Exercise burns calories and uses the fat stored in our bodies, which in turn, slims us down.

---

10. That's why I believe that more exercise is a better keeper of health than more sleep.

Q131. If you could give a meaningful gift to a family member, what would it be?

A. Essay Outline

Argument: I would love to give my mother a sapphire pendant if I could give a meaningful gift to someone in my family.

Support 1: My father had given my mother one on their wedding anniversary.

Support 2: I want to replace the lost pendant my mother previously had.

Support 3: The necklace would serve as a remembrance of my father.

Thesis: Due to its familial significance, the gift I would give to a family member would be a sapphire pendant.

B. Model Essay

If I could give a family member a meaningful gift, I would give my mother a necklace with a sapphire pendant. This was a gift my father got her on their 30th wedding anniversary. It got lost once when we were moving house a long time ago. My father died not long after, and that necklace was one keepsake of him I'm sure she wishes she still had. That necklace meant a lot to my mother and even though it probably wouldn't be the same, I would want my mother to have that piece of my father's memory back.

First of all, my father once gave my mother such a necklace for their wedding anniversary. It was just after my father got a big promotion at the company he worked for. He wanted to get her a really special gift and this was one of the first few pieces of jewelry he bought her that wasn't costume jewelry, in other words, it was real and really expensive. It was sort of a reminder to her that she had the right man, someone who could provide for her and bring happiness to her. It was the promise he made to her when they first got married and a symbol that that promise was fulfilled.

The second thing that would make me consider getting her this gift is that it got lost during a move. I knew it was very special to her and it crushed her to find that the movers lost it along with other jewelry she owned. She would ultimately be reimbursed for the loss (it was actually less than the initial value of the necklace), but it could never replace my mother's memories of my father. It tore my mother apart; she cried over the loss of that necklace just as much as she cried over the loss of him. I would like to finally heal that wound after such a long time.

That brings me to the biggest reason I would try to find a replacement necklace like the one my mother lost all those years ago. It was among the last gifts my father ever gave my mother before he died. A month later, he was driving home from work when a tractor trailer plowed into his car. He was killed instantly. I still remember the moment when my mother received that call. Before that moment, I never needed to be a source of strength for anyone, but when she collapsed in agony, I went over to comfort her. She wore that necklace at his funeral and it wasn't long after that we had to move because we couldn't afford to stay there without my father's income. It was on that move that she lost that necklace. When that necklace disappeared, he seemed to disappear forever.

That sapphire pendant was very important to my mother, and I really want to replace it to see her happy again. It was the most expensive anniversary gift my father ever gave her. It got lost during the move we made after he died. And it was the one reminder of him that she had that really meant a lot to her. That's why I would like to get my mother a sapphire pendant necklace.

C. Useful Expressions

1. My father died not long after, and that necklace was one keepsake of him I'm sure she wishes she still had.

_____

2. It was just after my father got a big promotion at the company he worked for.

_____

3. He wanted to get her a really special gift and this was one of the first few pieces of jewelry he bought her that wasn't costume jewelry, in other words, it was real and really expensive.

_____

_____

4. It was the promise he made to her when they first got married and a symbol that that promise was fulfilled.

_____

5. I knew it was very special to her and it crushed her to find that the movers lost it along with other jewelry she owned.

_____

6. It tore my mother apart; she cried over the loss of that necklace just as much as she cried over the loss of him.

_____

7. I would like to finally heal that wound after such a long time.

_____

8. A month later, he was driving home from work when a tractor trailer plowed into his car.

_____

9. Before that moment, I never needed to be a source of strength for anyone, but when she collapsed in agony, I went over to comfort her.

_____

_____

10. And it was the one reminder of him that she had that really meant a lot to her.

_____

Q132. Different students have different learning styles. Some learn best by listening to lectures, some from reading information on their own, and others from participating in group activities, Explain your learning style.

A. Essay Outline

Argument: I learn best through listening and reading.
Support 1: I can retain information better when I read and listen to something simultaneously.
Support 2: I can read aloud to myself and it also helps improve my listening abilities.
Support 3: My fellow classmates also learn best through this method.
Thesis: Because my classmates and I can memorize information best this way, listening and reading simultaneously is my go-to method for learning various materials.

B. Model Essay

If I had to explain my learning style, I would have to say that I'm a read and follow along kind of learner. When I read something that I really want to remember, I often have an audio recording play along with it. I also read the text aloud to myself when I'm in my own room so that I can hear the words I'm reading when there's no audio available. I also follow along as the teacher and other students read the text we're learning at the time. This mix of listening and reading allows me to absorb information more thoroughly than by a single method alone.

When I go out to by learning materials, I usually try to get the materials that come with a complimentary CD or an audio recording. This is so that when I play the recording, I can follow along and help my memory absorb what I'm reading. It's also helpful from an audial standpoint since my hearing has been less than acute because of a childhood illness. I always find that my listening abilities improve when I have a visual reference at the beginning. When I'm able to take away one or the other after the initial go-through, I find that I can actually remember it better. So that blending of the visual and the audial allows me to memorize things right away.

Another way I can blend this audial with the visual is by reading the material to myself out loud. Of course, I always do this in the privacy of my own home, because it would make me look strange. However, I find my own voice to be the perfect substitute for an audio recording should the materials I'm using not have any available. As I've said before, my hearing can often be assisted by my literacy and vision in order to improve my listening capabilities. Reading to myself aloud helps me learn because, like having an audio recording, it supplements my reading and improves my listening.

While I'm in class, we have a lot of read-alongs, particularly in my English and literature classes. I always enjoy these because my teacher and classmates all contribute to my preferred learning style of mixing listening with visual acuity. Many teachers I've talked to agree that this form of study really helps. I've also seen many of my classmates taking my lead and asking for materials with audio compliments to assist in their reading and memorization. So I find people agree that this is the best way to learn various types of materials.

So I try to combine listening and reading in helping with memorization. I always try to buy materials that have an audio recording and book in one package for that end. I also read to myself aloud if I can't find materials related to what we're learning that fits that need. I also enjoy read-alongs in my classes because those give me the most opportunity to learn in my school settings. That's why my method of learning is both reading and listening at the same time.

C. Useful Expressions

1. If I had to explain my learning style, I would have to say that I'm a read and follow along kind of learner.

2. This mix of listening and reading allows me to absorb information more thoroughly than by a single method alone.

3. It's also helpful from an audial standpoint since my hearing has been less than acute because of a childhood illness.

4. When I'm able to take away one or the other after the initial go-through, I find that I can actually remember it better.

5. Another way I can blend this audial with the visual is by reading the material to myself out loud.

6. However, I find my own voice to be the perfect substitute for an audio recording should the materials I'm using not have any available.

7. While I'm in class, we have a lot of read-alongs, particularly in my English and literature classes

8. I've also seen many of my classmates taking my lead and asking for materials with audio compliments to assist in their reading and memorization.

9. So I find people agreeing that this is the best way to learn various types of materials.

10. I always try to buy materials that have an audio recording and book in one package for that end.

Q133. In many countries, obesity in children is an increasing health problem. What do you think are some of the causes, and what are some of the solutions to the problem?

A. Essay Outline

Argument: Due to our inactive and cowardly lifestyle, our children have become obese.
Support 1: Parents are contributing to the problem by being overprotective of their children.
Support 2: Technology allows our children to be entertained for long periods of time without actively engaging in any physical activity.
Support 3: Parents need to ensure that their children are eating a variety of different foods, not just fats and sugar.
Thesis: In order to better the health of our children, our society needs to revamp its view on diet and exercise.

B. Model Essay

The causes of childhood obesity are the result of our less-physical and aversion-to-risk culture that we now live in. We now disallow our children from doing anything on their own because we fear for their safety, so they just stay in their homes for most of the day. We also have distraction devices that keep their focus on things that don't require physical activity. Finally, we don't watch what they eat as much as they should. These unfortunate truths of modern life are making our kids less healthy, less happy, and unfortunately less fit than when we were kids.

One thing that parents have done that led to an increase in childhood obesity is that they don't let their kids out of the house to play because of overblown fears. The biggest of these fears is that they can go out to play and get abducted by a child molester. They fear this because they constantly see stories about this happening on the news or they see it on TV shows about crime. However, if they do the research, there's only a one in 1.5 million chance of a child being abducted by a stranger. So this miniscule fear is not allowing our children to get the fresh air, sunshine, and exercise they need to be healthy, happy, and thin.

The next thing we need to realize is that today, children have distraction devices that can keep them entertained without their input. These include the usual suspects of TV and video games. They also include robotic toys for younger children. They encourage kids to sit and stare for hours on end when they can be spending that time doing real play either inside or out. Electronic gadgets like these are tricking kids and their parents that old-fashioned, physical play is no longer necessary. This, of course, leads to the further fattening of our kids.

The last thing that parents need to start doing is to finally check our children's diets. Today, there is too much processed food and too many kids getting treats at a frequent rate. We need to stop indulging our children like this and we need to read the labels on the food we serve them. We need to watch out for large quantities of sugar and salt in the food we buy at the market and instead include more fresh vegetables and fruits in their meals. We also need to ignore their protests at foods they don't perceive to like; they either eat it or go without. Children will learn eventually that the only options are eating healthy or starvation, and that the latter is less appealing.

So those are what can be done to make our kids less obese and healthier than they are now. We can get them outside again by alleviating our overblown fears of child abduction. We can take away the distraction devices and get our kids to really play again. And we can start monitoring the food we give them and start giving them fresher food again. Not doing these things are the reasons childhood obesity are a problem today.

C. Useful Expressions

1. The causes of childhood obesity are the result of our less-physical and aversion-to-risk culture that we now live in.

2. These unfortunate truths of modern life are making our kids less healthy, less happy, and, unfortunately, less fit than when we were kids.

3. One thing that parents have done that led to an increase in childhood obesity is that they don't let their kids out of the house to play because of overblown fears.

4. These include the usual suspects of TV and video games.

5. They encourage kids to sit and stare for hours on end when they can be spending that time doing real play either inside or out.

6. Electronic gadgets like these are tricking kids and their parents into thinking that that old-fashioned, physical play is no longer necessary.

7. We need to stop indulging our children like this and we need to read the labels on the food we serve them.

8. We also need to ignore their protests at foods they don't perceive to like; they can either eat it or go without.

9. Children will learn eventually that the only options are eating healthy or starvation, and that the latter is less appealing.

10. We can take away the distraction devices and get our kids to really play again.

Q134. Do you think that seeing violence in video games or movies causes people to behave violently?

A. Essay Outline

Argument: The violence in video games and movies does not lead to violent behavior in people.

Support 1: Every society tries to find the scapegoat for the ills of society.

Support 2: Humans have the capability to distinguish between reality and fantasy.

Support 3: We live in a relatively safe society nowadays.

Thesis: Seeing violence in the media doesn't lead to increased violence due to the structure of today's society.

B. Model Essay

I do not think that seeing violence in video games or movies cause people to behave violently. First off, this is a common cry of moral crusaders that has been heard ad nauseum even though the evidence shows that violence is cause by perceived injustices, real or imagined. Secondly, a majority of people can see a difference between what is real and what is fantasy. Finally, real life is a much less exciting place than it's portrayed in movies or video games. People need to realize that the rest of us are smart enough to see that entertainment is not real life.

Every generation, moral crusaders need to find a demon to fight against because of the way the world changes socially. Over the last century, these moralists have railed against comic books, rock music, and rap. Video games are just the latest thing to rile up uptight adults who fear that their children are getting dangerous ideas from the new medium. However, these "dangerous ideas" don't come from video games; they come from a rejection of the parents' worldview that happens with every generation. Violence that happens throughout the world comes from people's anger at the perceived injustices around them. In the past, that came from racial segregation and censorship. Today, it comes from economic inequality and anti-corporatism. So video games provide a convenient strawman to the older power holders so that they can avoid the real issues that cause violence.

We also need to remember that most of us can see a difference between what is real and what is not. If a person is mentally sound, and indulges once in a while in a video game, he will turn off that video game and just go on with his normal life without feeling the need to pick up a loaded gun and shoot the first person he sees. However, this is what the moral crusaders are suggesting: video games create instant murderers. But most video game players are students thinking about their next exam or a regular person who's thinking about what to have for lunch; they don't think about who they're going to kill that day. They play video games to take a break from reality and they return to reality when it's time for them to do so.

We also need to remember that although violence might make for a great news story, it is getting much more rare in the real world, something that people find easy to either forget or disbelieve. But thanks to increased policing and surveillance, crime has become rarer now than it has been over the last hundred years. People don't fret about getting mugged like they did more than thirty years ago and people don't see monsters in their streets or neighborhoods. They also don't carry guns with them everywhere unless they're police officers. The real world is a lot less exciting than video games, and that's the biggest reason why people play video games: because real life gets boring. So everyone knows that video games and reality are different, because reality gets too mundane to cope with all the time, and video games provide an escape from that.

So the moral backlash against video games is another backlash against a popular form of entertainment that goes back nearly a century. It is used to divert attention away from real issues so that there's an easy-to-blame scapegoat. However, the majority of us can differentiate reality from fantasy, and that real life is much more boring than in video games. That's why I don't believe movies and video games make people violent.

C. Useful Expressions

1. First off, this is a common cry of moral crusaders that has been heard ad nauseum even though the evidence shows that violence is cause by perceived injustices, real or imagined.

_____

_____

2. Finally, real life is a much less exciting place than it's portrayed in movies or video games.

_____

3. Every generation, moral crusaders need to find a demon to fight against because of the way the world changes socially.

_____

_____

4. Video games are just the latest thing to rile up uptight adults who fear that their children are getting dangerous ideas from the new medium.

_____

5. So video games provide a convenient strawman to the older power holders so that they can avoid the real issues that cause violence.

_____

_____

6. However, this is what the moral crusaders are suggesting: video games create instant murderers.

_____

7. People don't fret about getting mugged like they did more than thirty years ago and people don't see monsters in their streets or neighborhoods.

_____

8. So everyone knows that video games and reality are different, because reality gets too mundane to cope with all the time, and video games provide an escape from that.

_____

_____

9. So the moral backlash against video games is another backlash against a popular form of entertainment that goes back nearly a century

_____

10. It is used to divert attention away from real issues so that there's an easy-to-blame scapegoat.

_____

Q135. Some children are picky eaters. Do you think parents should force children to eat food they don't like, or should children be allowed to eat only the foods they want?

A. Essay Outline

Argument: Children should not be given the freedom to eat whatever foods they want.
Support 1: Obviously, when given the option, children will pick only tasty foods.
Support 2: We have an obligation to introduce our children to different types of food.
Support 3: Parents need to remain the authority figure in the home.
Thesis: Because it would be disadvantageous to allow our children to eat whatever they want, I believe parents need to regulate their child's diet.

B. Model Essay

As every parent knows, it's important that children get the right nutrition for their development; thus picky eaters present a challenge. However, I do not think children should be allowed to eat only what they want. First off, children will only want what taste good, and that could lead to unhealthy eating. Second off, it can keep kids from exploring new, exciting foods that they might actually like. And thirdly, letting the kids pick their meals too often will take control away from the parents and give it to the kids. So for the sake of kids' health, curiosity, and discipline, parents should force kids to eat foods they don't like.

When children are allowed to choose their own food, they will always pick the tasty options. However, the tasty food will not always be good for them. Many of the foods they choose will be loaded with sugar and fat because kids like sugar and fat. This could possibly add to the increasing problem of childhood obesity. They can also have stomach problems or have weaker bones, muscles, or organs in the future. Parents need to remember that early nutrition is vital to a child's health right from the start.

Another thing we have to consider is that we need to open children's minds to all of the possible foods they might actually like. Picky eaters will often say they don't like something when they've never even tried it, and small children really haven't tried very much. Put the new food on their plate, but only a little, and encourage them to try it. They may see everyone else eating and liking the food and will get curious. If they eat it, congratulations, your child is now a little less picky. If they don't, don't give in to their demands, but don't force them; it's better that they go hungry once or twice before they finally succumb. Keep this approach and pretty soon, they'll be enjoying all sorts of foods that they thought they'd never enjoy. It can really get your kids excited about eating healthy.

We also need to remember that parents should be the ones in charge, not the kids. If parents allow their kids to dictate their meal choices, where does it end? Pretty soon, they'll be demanding their own bedtimes or the times when they control the TV or computer. Children will start running our lives when we should be controlling theirs. Children don't know what's really good for them and it's up to the parents to put them on the right path, no matter how much they complain.

So the control of what food gets put in front of children should belong to the parents, and not the children, because children only care about tasty things and not good nutrition. They'll also be narrow-minded if we don't encourage them to try the things that everybody else eats. Finally, parents need to be firm in their food choices if they want to maintain discipline with their kids. That why I feel that parents should make their kids eat things they refuse to eat.

C. Useful Expressions

1. As every parent knows, it's important that children get the right nutrition for their development; thus picky eaters present a challenge.

_____

_____

2. Second off, it can keep kids from exploring new, exciting foods that they might actually like.

_____

3. So for the sake of kids' health, curiosity, and discipline, parents should force kids to eat foods they don't like.

_____

4. Many of the foods they choose will be loaded with sugar and fat because kids like sugar and fat.

_____

5. Put the new food on their plate, but only a little, and encourage them to try it.

_____

6. Keep this up and pretty soon, they'll be enjoying all sorts of foods that they thought they'd never enjoy.

_____

7. We also need to remember that parents should be the ones in charge, not the kids.

_____

8. If parents allow their kids to dictate their meal choices, where does it end?

_____

9. Children will start running our lives when we should be controlling theirs.

_____

10. They'll also be narrow-minded if we don't encourage them to try the things that everybody else eats.

_____

Q136. Should children be given the freedom to dress anyway they want?

A. Essay Outline

Argument: Children should be entitled to choose their own outfits.
Support 1: Children need the freedom of expression that comes in the form of choosing their own clothing.
Support 2: Children tend to do whatever they can to undermine authority figures.
Support 3: Child-molesters do not choose their victims based on their choice in clothing.
Thesis: Because children should not have their freedoms restricted, they should be given the option to dress whatever way they like.

B. Model Essay

Children should have the freedom to dress however they want. First of all, it's one of the few forms of expression children have. Secondly, kids are going to change their clothes away from authority figures when they're made to dress according to their parents' wishes. Thirdly, most of the parental fears about attracting unwanted attention from child molesters is widely overblown. So children ought to be able to express themselves through their clothes.

The first thing we need to remember is that children's lives are so regimented that they have very few outlets for self-expression. When children are given the freedom to choose their own clothes, they can show their tastes and personalities by the kinds of clothes or colors that they wear. Bright colors show that the child is in a good mood or is happy with life. They can display the cartoon characters or sports they like most by wearing their likeness on their shirt. This is a display of who this child is, and every child has a right to an identity and to share that with the world.

We must remember that kids have to deal with stern authority figures, and when they're able to get away from those authority figures, they'll do whatever they can to oppose them. This is why kids will often change their clothes when they are away and change back when they return. This can get tiresome for the children and can upset the parents should they find out. So if that restriction were lifted in the first place, the kids won't feel like they'll have to be sneaky about their clothing and the parents will be able to relax. No one will have to get angry at anybody and everyone will feel better if children could just choose their own clothes.

The real reason that parents often loathe letting children choose their own clothes is that they're afraid that they're going to choose sexually provocative clothes that might attract child molesters. This fear is ridiculous for three reasons. First off, child molesters only go after children because their children; they don't care how they dress. Second of all, the number of child molester cases has dropped off significantly thanks to the numerous laws providing stiff penalties and sex-offender registries that act as deterrents to would be molesters. Third, children don't dress to look sexy. They have no knowledge of sex at this point of their lives, so they won't purposely expose themselves to that form of abuse. So the fears of molestation should be taken with a grain of salt in today's world.

Children have rights just like everybody else and that should always include their wardrobe choices. This is a way for children to express themselves freely. It shouldn't be controlled by parents or authority figures because children will always defy them when it comes to fashion. And we must remember that children don't dress to be sexy. That's why I believe that children should be given the freedom to wear whatever they want.

C. Useful Expressions

1. Secondly, kids are going to change their clothes away from authority figures when they're made to dress according to their parents' wishes.

_____

2. The first thing we need to remember is that children's lives are so regimented that they have very few outlets for self-expression.

_____

3. They can display the cartoon characters or sports they like most by wearing their likeness on their shirt.

_____

4. This is a display of who this child is, and every child has a right to an identity and to share that with the world.

_____

5. We must remember that kids have to deal with stern authority figures and when they're able to get away from those authority figures, they'll do whatever they can to oppose them.

_____

_____

6. So if that restriction was lifted in the first place, the kids won't feel like they'll have to be sneaky about their clothing and the parents will be able to relax.

_____

_____

7. The real reason that parents often loathe letting children choose their own clothes is that they're afraid that they're going to choose sexually provocative clothes that might attract child molesters.

_____

_____

8. Second of all, the number of child molester cases has dropped off significantly thanks to the numerous laws providing stiff penalties and sex-offender registries that act as deterrents to would-be molesters.

_____

_____

9. So the fears of molestation should be taken with a grain of salt in today's world.

_____

10. It shouldn't be controlled by parents or authority figures because children will always defy them when it comes to fashion.

_____

_____

Q137. Would you save your money at a bank or at your home? Why?

A. Essay Outline

Argument: I would save my money at the bank.
Support 1: My money is safer in the bank than at home.
Support 2: I can earn interest by keeping my money in the bank.
Support 3: If I keep my money in a bank, I can withdraw money from lots of places.
Thesis: Because saving my money at a bank is much more advantageous than keeping my money at home, I prefer to save my money at a bank.

B. Model Essay

I would always choose a bank to keep my money safe over my home. First off, the bank is always more secure than my house. Second of all, I can earn interest by depositing my money into an account. Finally, a bank keeps money digitally these days, as opposed to securing hard currency which is much harder. A bank has so much more technological and security advantages than a home that it's obvious that the bank is a better choice.

The first thing that we must always remember is that a bank will have many layers of security while the average home usually has just one. Banks will have large vaults where they will keep their reserve cash safe and for their safe deposit boxes. They will also have armed guards stationed in their office to thwart any attempt to rob the place. It is also harder to break in from the outside because it has thick walls, heavily secured doors, laser alarms and surveillance cameras. If someone were to try to break in, they'll quickly be caught by the police.

Secondly, an account at the bank entitles me to earn interest on my investment. This is because banks charge interest on loans that they give out from the deposits of their depositors. That interest then gets added to the deposits that I and other bank depositors. So with every dollar I put into the bank, I can expect a percentage added to that every month, and this helps build my savings. Saving money in a bank is always a smart and safe investment.

Finally, we must all remember that leaving large amounts of cash anywhere is incredibly risky. It can easily be stolen and there's no way of recovering it when it is stolen. Banks don't store money as hard cash these days; it's all done digitally. When you put money into the bank, they'll take the cash and use it to pay out other depositors or to make loans, but your information will be stored on their computer banks and that initially becomes the currency you invested into the bank. So your money cannot be taken as easily as if it were left in the form of cash in your house.

So the advantages of saving money in a bank are too great to be ignored. The security of a bank will make it nearly impossible for your funds to ever be stolen. The money you put in a bank can get you interest in that investment and give you more money in the long-run. And banks never leave it in cash form, which can be stolen easily. That's why I choose saving in a bank over saving at home.

C. Useful Expressions

1. Second of all, I can earn interest from depositing my money into an account.

2. A bank has so much more technological and security advantages than a home that it's obvious that the bank is a better choice.

3. The first thing that we must always remember is that a bank will have many layers of security while the average home usually has just one.

4. They will also have armed guards stationed in their office to thwart any attempt to rob the place.

5. If someone were to try to break in, he'd quickly be caught by the police.

6. Secondly, an account at the bank entitles me to earn interest on my investment.

7. So with every dollar I put into the bank, I can expect a percentage added to that every month, and this helps build up my savings.

8. Banks don't store money as hard cash these days, it's all done digitally.

9. When you put money into the bank, they'll take the cash and use it to pay out other depositors or to make loans, but your information will be stored on their computer banks and that initially becomes the currency you invested into the bank.

10. The money you put in a bank can get you interest in that investment and give you more money in the long-run.

Q138. If you could choose your own study hours, how many hours would you study? Why?

A. Essay Outline

Argument: If I could choose my own study hours, I would study for five hours a day
Support 1: If I study more than five hours, I will get distracted.
Support 2: Spending more than five hours studying will just be a waste of time.
Support 3: I need to have time to work my part-time job.
Thesis: Because studying for more than five hours will cause me to be unproductive and it will interfere with other activities, I would choose to study for five hours a day.

B. Model Essay

I would probably set aside five hours for studying each day. That's a good moderate amount that doesn't take too much time away from other things that either need to be done or that can be used for recreation. Anything more than five hours could be seen as simply wasteful because after a certain point our attention span shuts down. And we need to remember that there's more to school life than just studying. So students should only have to dedicate five hours of their time to studying.

Five hours is a good number of hours to set aside, particularly in the middle of the day, for studying. The hours between 1 and 6 P.M. are probably the best to study because at that time, you have the most energy and the most focus. You're not just waking up, you are not hungry, and you're not yet sleepy, so this is when you can get the most done. If you go over that limit or try to start to late, you'll probably burn out, you're mind starts to reject the task at hand. Too early, and your grogginess or hunger could distract you. So that five hour stretch in the afternoon is actually the best time for anyone to study.

Going any longer than five hours could be potentially wasteful because our minds will eventually tire if we try to go on for too long. For me this happens when I start studying at the beginning of the day. I find myself having to break for lunch because I get hungry. But when I start again, I find myself getting tired in the midafternoon, when most students start to think about their free time. By that time, I found that I have wasted a good portion of study time in the morning because I'm still a bit groggy from waking up and from the hunger I feel before lunch, the only time I really learn anything is after lunch and by the time mid-afternoon rolls around, I'm burned out. So that period between one and six ought to be the time I study.

We also need to remember that as students, we have lives outside of studying. Many of us do volunteer work or work part-time jobs to earn money. I work at nights to save up for paying for school, something my parents insist me on doing. The reason I put in at least five hours of study time is so that I can balance out my work schedule with my schooling. This is so that nothing can distract me from receiving high marks and working my way through.

So those are the reasons that five hours in the afternoon should be all one needs for studying. The right five hours can help you focus your energy and attention on the task at hand. Any more than that, and you could burn out or lose focus and that just wastes. And many of us have jobs or other extracurricular activities that require us to stop studying for a bit. That's why five hours in the afternoon is all one needs to study during the day.

C. Useful Expressions

1. Anything more than five hours could be seen as simply wasteful because after a certain point our attention span shuts down.

_____

2. So students should only have to dedicate five hours of their time to studying.

_____

3. So that five hour stretch in the afternoon is actually the best time for anyone to study.

_____

4. Going any longer than five hours could be potentially wasteful because our minds will eventually tire if we try to go on for too long.

_____

5. The only time I really learn anything is after lunch and by the time mid-afternoon rolls around, I'm burned out.

_____

6. The reason I put in at least five hours of study time is so that I can balance out my work schedule with my schooling.

_____

7. This is so that nothing can distract me from receiving high marks and working my way through.

_____

8. The right five hours can help you focus your energy and attention on the task at hand.

_____

9. And many of us have jobs or other extracurricular activities that require us to stop studying for a bit.

_____

Q139. Do you think it's important for children to learn how to swim at an early age? Why or why not?

A. Essay Outline

Argument: I think it's important for children to learn to swim at an early age.
Support 1: It will be easier to learn more advanced swimming techniques if you start swimming early on.
Support 2: Kids should know how to swim to increase their self-confidence.
Support 3: Kids will be more comfortable in the water.
Thesis: Because it will help them later in life, children should learn how to swim at an early age.

B. Model Essay

I think it is absolutely important for children to learn to swim at an early age. Learning to swim early assures that they will have success learning to swim in the future. It gives children confidence in their abilities to do thing on their own if they can do this one thing on their own. Finally, it will help children be comfortable in the water because they'll have early experience being in the water. So if children learn to swim early, they'll be at a great advantage in the future.

First of all, helping children learn to swim early can help them in improving their swimming abilities in the future. If they learn to swim in early childhood, they'll simply learn the basic of moving in water, holding their breath, and buoyancy. Once they get the basics, they can move on to more advanced swimming techniques such as racing strokes or holding one's breath underwater for longer periods of time. But before they can do any of that, they must learn how to tread water, breathe, and move through water. When they can master the basics, they can excel at swimming when they want to move on.

The next thing that makes getting children to swim early is that it will increase their confidence in doing many things on their own. When children are able to swim on their own, they accomplish one of the first difficult tasks they'll come across in their lives. Along with riding a two-wheeler, learning this difficult skill will help them gain confidence in navigating the world themselves. Then they can move on to learning to cook, travel through their hometowns, and walking to school by themselves. Children need to have confidence if they want to become successful adults, and learning to swim early can attribute to that.

The last thing that makes learning to swim a good idea is that it helps children become comfortable in water much earlier. Many people find it difficult to be in water because it can throw off one's sense of direction and gravity. It can certainly throw a person off and cause him to panic. But if a person is comfortable in water, then that person can navigate it without trouble. So getting comfortable in water is an important reason why it's good to learn to swim early.

So it's very important that children learn to swim early because it will help them later in life. It helps them learn more difficult forms of swimming. It gives them confidence in finding their way to navigate their world. And it helps people be less fretful being in the water when they're older. Therefore, it is a good idea to get children to swim at an early age.

C. Useful Expressions

1. Learning to swim early assures that they will have success learning to swim in the future.

2. So if children learn to swim early, they'll be at a great advantage in the future.

3. If they learn to swim in early childhood, they'll simply learn the basics of moving in water, holding their breath, and buoyancy.

4. But before they can do any of that, they must learn how to tread water, breathe, and move through water.

5. When they can master the basics, they can excel at swimming when they want to move on.

6. The next thing that makes getting children to swim early beneficial is that it will increase their confidence in doing many things on their own.

7. Along with riding a two-wheeler, learning this difficult skill will help them gain confidence in navigating the world themselves.

8. Children need to have confidence if they want to become successful adults, and learning to swim early can attribute to that.

9. The last thing that makes learning to swim a good idea is that it helps children become comfortable in water much earlier.

10. It can certainly throw a person off and cause him to panic.

Q140. In some families, the mother does all the cooking. Do you think older children should learn to cook so they can help prepare the family meals sometimes? Why or why not?

A. Essay Outline

Argument: Some of the children should learn to cook for the family at times.
Support 1: Their parents might be unable to cook.
Support 2: They need to learn to be independent.
Support 3: Kids in general want to do things on their own.
Thesis: Because it will help kids grow and be more independent, I think older children should learn how to cook.

B. Model Essay

I think that some of the children should learn to cook for the family at times because the parents might both end up being unable to. It's also good to learn for when the kids can no longer be expected to be cared for by someone else. And it's a good way for kids to show that they can do things on their own. This is something useful they can learn that can help them down the road.

First off, parents may not be able to do the task themselves. They might both work or they might end up getting sick. Either way, the kids are on their own. Now, smaller children may not be the right ones to do the job because they can't reach certain tools or handle large objects that are needed to do the job. But when they reach a certain height and have a certain amount of trust and responsibility, they should be allowed to learn some basic skills and some easy recipes to make. When they get older, they can start learning to make more complex meals and even be able to serve their parents one night. This can be a big help to the family if the kids can be an additional source of meals.

Secondly, kids will need to learn this because one day they'll have no one else to care for them. Parents always expect their kids to leave home as soon as they're able to and they expect them to find and make their own food as part of that departure. The kids will also have to expect this, so the parents should not only teach them, but require them to cook on a night or two. That way, the kids learn to feed themselves. So teaching the kids to make meals while they're still kids makes sense in the scheme of preparing for their futures.

The last thing we need to remember is that kids want to be able to do things by themselves. Today a lot of parents are overprotective to the point that they won't even let kids walk to school by themselves. But when the kids reach about the age of ten, they feel that they are smart enough to do things that their parents help them with constantly. Kids always feel the most proud when they can do things themselves. So making a meal by themselves can be a source of pride for kids who get very little trust because their parents fear the worst.

So those are the reasons kids should learn to cook when they're old enough. The parents may not be able to at times, because of work or health problems. Also, one day, the parents will not be there to take of them, so they better learn now. Finally, it can be a source of pride for kids who have little trust placed in them. That's why kids need to learn to cook.

C. Useful Expressions

1. First of all the parents might both end up being unable to.

_____

2. This is something useful they can learn that can help them down the road.

_____

3. Now, smaller children may not be the right ones to do the job because they can't reach certain tools or handle large objects that are needed to do the job.

_____

4. This can be a big help to the family if the kids can be an additional source of meals.

_____

5. Parents always expect their kids to leave home as soon as they're able to and they expect them to find and make their own food as part of that departure.

_____

6. The kids will also have to expect this, so the parents should not only teach them, but require them to cook on a night or two.

_____

7. So teaching the kids to make meals while they're still kids makes sense in the scheme of preparing for their futures.

_____

8. Today a lot of parents are overprotective to the point that they won't even let kids walk to school by themselves.

_____

9. So making a meal by themselves can be a source of pride for kids who get very little trust because their parents fear the worst.

_____

10. Finally, it can be a source of pride for kids who have little trust placed in them.

_____

> **Q141.** When learning a foreign language, some people think that speaking is important, when others think that writing is more important. Which skill do you think is more important?

A. Essay Outline

Argument: Speaking is the most important skill in foreign language learning.
Support 1: We have to talk to people when are abroad.
Support 2: Fluency is judged through speaking, not writing.
Support 3: Speaking a foreign language well will help us more when trying to get a job.
Thesis: Because speaking is fast and useful, I think that speaking is the most important skills when learning a foreign language.

B. Model Essay

I feel that speaking is a much more important skill to learn than writing in that it's more directly involved in the real world. First off, when traveling, we talk to other people rather than write notes to one another. Secondly, people often judge your fluency by how you speak, not how you write. Thirdly, when searching for a job, you'll have to speak face-to-face to potential employers. So this emphasis on speaking is not unjustified because it's the way people perceive your speech that ultimately decides other people's judgments on your knowledge of the language.

When we travel overseas, to the country with the language we learn, we speak to other people directly. It's rather inconvenient to be writing notes constantly when you're trying to ask questions. It also looks silly to anyone who happens to be nearby when they see this. After all you're standing right next to each other, why do you need to write letters? It's just more natural to see two people speaking in a social situation such as that. So speaking face to face while abroad is a lot more expected than writing short notes to each other.

The next thing to remember is that fluency is judged through speech, not through writing. Grammar and spelling mistakes can easily be overlooked, but speech mistakes are going to be noticed right away. The people you're speaking to may also find your accent hard to understand or find your speech patterns hard to decipher. If a person cannot understand you, they're going to write you off without a second thought. People judge you by your speaking abilities and it's one that last throughout your life, at least in that country.

The last thing that needs to be remembered is that should you look for a job in the language you're learning, the interviewer is testing your speaking ability, not your writing abilities. That's the main point of the interview, how you present yourself and communicate with others. Not having fluency in the interview will hurt your standing with the employer and have someone else possibly take the job. The employer will also want you to speak about your abilities with confidence and a good fluent speech is key in that area. So an interview shows how well you speak could be a make or break factor in getting employed.

So those are why speaking is more important than writing. We always speak face to face because writing while face to face looks odd. Fluency is judged on how fluent and accent-free your speech. That is something not easily explained away. And job interviewers will look for speaking ability as the main factor in communication. So speech is more important than writing.

C. Useful Expressions

1. I feel that speaking is a much more important skill to learn than writing in that it's more directly involved in the real world.

_____

2. So this emphasis on speaking is not unjustified because it's the way people perceive your speech that ultimately decides other people's judgments on your knowledge of the language.

_____

3. It's rather inconvenient to be writing notes constantly when you're trying to ask questions.

_____

4. It's just more natural to see two people speaking in a social situation such as that.

_____

5. So speaking face to face while abroad is a lot more expected than writing short notes to each other.

_____

6. Grammar and spelling mistakes can easily be overlooked, but speech mistakes are going to be noticed right away.

_____

7. If a person cannot understand you, they're going to write you off without a second thought.

_____

8. Not having fluency in the interview will hurt your standing with the employer and have someone else possibly take the job.

_____

9. So an interview shows how well you speak could be a make-or-break factor in getting employed.

_____

10. Fluency is judged on how fluent and accent-free your speech is. And that not easily explained away.

_____

Q142. Which is your favorite ethnic (Italian, Chinese, Korean, Mexican, French, etc.) food?

A. Essay Outline

Argument: My favorite ethnic food is Mexican food.
Support 1: Mexican cuisine uses very simple ingredients.
Support 2: Mexican food always reminds one of home-cooking.
Support 3: Mexican food can be made either mild or spicy.
Thesis: Because it is simple, comforting, and versatile, Mexican food is my favorite ethnic food.

B. Model Essay

I would have to say that my favorite ethnic food is Mexican food. It's a simple food that uses simple ingredients to make beautiful dishes. It's the kind of food that would remind one of home cooking. And the food can be spicy or mild depending on how the person likes his meals. These are the traits of Mexican food that I enjoy so much.

First, Mexican cooking doesn't need a lot of fancy or expensive ingredients to make good food. The ingredients used in Mexican cooking are the kinds of ingredients that people can afford easily or can grow themselves in their own gardens. It uses common spices like pepper and common vegetables like tomatoes and onions. This is because most Mexicans can't afford fancy ingredients and make do with whatever they can get and this is where the imagination comes in, because combining simple ingredients into delicious food requires a lot of creativity. It's this creativity through simplicity that makes me admire Mexican cooks.

Another reason, I like this kind of food is because it reminds me of old-fashioned home cooking. Most chefs in other styles of cooking try to make their dishes look fancy for presentation at expensive restaurants. But Mexican chefs learn their skills at home, not at expensive schools, so they concentrate more on making the dish taste good, as opposed to making it look good. Mexican restaurants are not where one goes for frills, but for full stomachs. This homey approach makes Mexican food much more enjoyable to me.

Lastly, Mexican food can be spiced to an individual's taste for spicy or mild food. Whenever, my friend and I go out to our favorite Mexican restaurant, we always order different levels of spiciness. I really like my food spicy, so I always get it hot. My friend on the other hand cannot tolerate anything too spicy, so he gets his food more mildly flavored. Even though we like different kinds of flavors and spice, we can enjoy Mexican food together because of this flexibility.

Mexican food is the ethnic foods I can always count on to be enjoyable. This is because it is simply made with simple, basic ingredients anyone can buy. The cooks always focus on making the food look and taste like something one can make at home by themselves. And the different levels of spiciness means anyone can enjoy it. That is why Mexican food is my favorite ethnic food.

C. Useful Expressions

1. It's the kind of food that would remind one of home cooking.

2. These are the traits of Mexican food that I enjoy so much.

3. This is where the imagination comes in because combining simple ingredients into delicious food requires a lot of creativity.

4. It's this creativity through simplicity that makes me admire Mexican cooks.

5. Most chefs in other styles of cooking try to make their dishes look fancy for presentation at expensive restaurants.

6. Another reason, I like this kind of food is because it reminds me of old-fashioned home cooking.

7. But Mexican chefs learn their skills at home, not at expensive schools, so they concentrate more on making the dish taste good, as opposed to making it look good.

8. Mexican restaurants are not where one goes for frills, but for full stomachs.

9. My friend, on the other hand, cannot tolerate anything too spicy, so he gets his food more mildly flavored.

10. Mexican food is the ethnic food I can always count on to be enjoyable.

Q143. Do you agree or disagree with the following statement? Laughter and joy are essential aspects for a healthy life. Why or why not? Give specific reasons and details to support your answer.

A. Essay Outline

Argument: I believe that laughter and joy are an indispensable part of a healthy life.
Support 1: By filling your life with laughter and joy, you are not leaving any room for sadness to take control.
Support 2: Laughter and joy are medically proven to better your health.
Support 3: Laughter and joy in your life will bring laughter in joy to the lives of others.
Thesis: Because there are no disadvantages to laughter and joy, I believe one must have them in his life.

B. Model Essay

As the old adage goes, "Laughter is the best medicine." I firmly believe in the healing power of both laughter and joy and their ability to improve your quality of life. So, I agree with the statement that laughter and joy are essential aspects for living a healthy and happy life. First and foremost, having laughter and joy in your life equates to a life free of debilitating unhappiness. Furthermore, both laughter and joy have been proven to better one's physical wellbeing. Finally, having laughter in joy in your life helps to better the lives of those you encounter.

To begin with, if your life is full of laughter and joy, there is no room for sadness. Looking on the bright side of a situation can make any challenge seem significantly less daunting. If you laugh in a situation where all you want to do is cry, you'll reduce the amount of unhappiness in your heart. Being joyful in all circumstances will help you to see the good that is inevitably in every situation. Eventually, you'll be able to effortlessly see the silver lining in every dark cloud. Laughter and joy are the best safeguards against anxiety and depression and a sure way to keep your thoughts positive.

Just as laughter and joy can help your mind stay healthy, so too can they aid in bettering the health of your body. Laughter is an instant stress alleviator. Stress can lead to all kinds of strain on your body, such as insomnia, fatigue, and muscle aches. By engaging in the relaxing activity of laughing, you can decrease the amount of stress in your life and thus live a more pain-free life. Additionally, laughing and living joyfully can actually help to boost your immune system by increasing immune cells and infection-fighting antibodies. As a result, your body will be able to fight off illnesses such as the flu more quickly. So, by simply adding laughter and joy to your life, you can increase your physical wellbeing.

One last benefit of having laughter and joy in your life is that you will be able to bring laughter and joy to the lives of others as well. For example, laughter is contagious. If you begin laughing in a roomful of people, it won't be long before they are all laughing as well. By thinking positively, you'll teach those around you to do the same. People will be drawn to you because of your positive attitude and ability to make them laugh. You'll be able to share the benefits of laughter and joy with those around you simply by having laughter and joy in your own life.

In conclusion, I believe that having laughter and joy in your life is necessary. While the disadvantage of laughter and joy are nonexistent, the benefits that laughter and joy bring are great. By simply laughing and being joyful, you can increase your mental health. Likewise, you can become a healthier person by adding laughter and joy to your life. Furthermore, by being joyful and laughing, you can extend the benefits of laughter and joy to those around you as well. If everyone incorporated more laughter and joy into their lives, the world would be a much more pleasant place to inhabit.

C. Useful Expressions

1. As the old adage goes, "Laughter is the best medicine."

_____

2. First and foremost, having laughter and joy in your life equates to a life free of debilitating unhappiness.

_____

3. Looking on the bright side of a situation can make any challenge seem significantly less daunting.

_____

4. Eventually, you'll be able to effortlessly see the silver lining in every dark cloud.

_____

5. Laughter and joy are the best safeguards against anxiety and depression and a sure way to keep your thoughts positive.

_____

_____

6. Just as laughter and joy can help your mind stay healthy, so too can they aid in bettering the health of your body.

_____

7. Stress can lead to a wealth of strain on your body, such as insomnia, fatigue, and muscle aches.

_____

8. If you begin laughing in a roomful of people, it won't be long before they are all laughing as well.

_____

9. While the disadvantages of laughter and joy are nonexistent, the benefits that laughter and joy bring are great.

_____

10. Furthermore, by being joyful and laughing, you can extend the benefits of laughter and joy to those around you as well.

_____

_____

> **Q144. When you feel sad, what are some of things you do to help yourself feel better?**

A. Essay Outline

Argument: I have some surefire tactics that enable me to feel better when I am feeling low.
Support 1: I like to take a long walk when I'm feeling down.
Support 2: It's good to contact friends and family when you're feeling sad.
Support 3: Turning to literature also seems to help all of my problems disappear.
Thesis: Because they help to alleviate my sadness in the fastest manner possible, I always take these three steps when sadness strikes.

.

B. Model Essay

Whenever I am feeling sad there are a few things I may do to help myself feel better as soon as possible. First, I would go for a walk and think about my feelings. Then the next step would be to contact close friends or family members to seek support. Then, I would try to find some good books to read in order to learn how to deal with my feelings in a positive manner.

First, whenever I am feeling sad I would try to go for a walk somewhere. One of my favorite places I like to go is the woods, because it is isolated and there are not many people there. The woods provide a good atmosphere for a person to think clearly about their feelings, and even cry if they need to without being around a lot of people. Plus, the scenery can also help one to clear their mind and elevate their mood.

Second, when I feel ready to talk with others about my problems I will try to seek out close friends or family members to consult with about my problem. Trying to repress feelings or not talk about them could make the problem worse. My friends and family may have been through a similar situation before, and may be able to offer positive solutions to my problem. At best, they can be a good support network and allow me to just talk.

Finally, after reflecting on my feelings and talking with others, I would usually find some good self-help books to find advice on how to move on past the sadness. Some of the best books that have helped me were books that discussed NLP. NLP helps because it helps people to focus on the meanings we give to problems. By changing the interpretations of the problems, I can overcome sadness and feel better quicker. As well, I also enjoy reading inspiring stories of people who have had to deal with certain problems in their lives and how they overcame them. This could also provide a plan of action for me to overcome my problems.

Many people have their own methods of dealing with sadness. For me, I find the best way to help myself feel better is to go on a walk alone and gather my thoughts. As well, talking with and getting support from friends and family is important as well. Books are also important too because of the professional advice or inspiring stories of people who have dealt with and overcome major life problems.

C. Useful Expressions

1. Whenever I am feeling sad I have a few go-to techniques I may do to help myself feel better as soon as

possible.

---

2. Then next step would be to contact close friends or family members, my support network, to seek comfort and guidance.

---

3. First, whenever I am feeling sad I would try to go for a walk somewhere to clear my head.

---

4. Also, sometimes one needs to be alone with his thoughts.

---

5. Trying to repress feelings and keep them under wraps could make the problem worse.

---

6. At best, they can lend me an ear and allow me to just talk.

---

7. Finally, after some soul searching and talking with others, I would usually find some good self-help books to find advice on how to move on past the sadness.

---

8. This could also provide a plan of action for me to overcome my problems.

---

9. Many people have their own methods of dealing with their demons.

---

10. For me, I find the best way to help myself feel better is to go on a walk alone and gather my thoughts.

Q145. Do you think it's a good idea to loan money to friends? Why or why not

A. Essay Outline

Argument: I believe that loaning money to friends could actually be quite beneficial for a relationship.

Support 1: You picked that individual to be your friend because he proved himself to be worthy of your friendship.

Support 2: Loaning money can be virtually risk-free by simply setting up a written contract regarding the loan.

Support 3: It is important to consider how you would feel if the roles were reversed and you were the one needing money.

Thesis: Because loaning money to a friend will help strengthen your friendship, I believe loaning money to a friend is a good idea.

B. Model Essay

Loaning money to anyone, regardless of his relationship to you, is always a risky move. This is especially true when it comes to loaning money to your friends. What may start out as a kind gesture could easily backfire, resulting in the loss of money and a good friend. However, I believe loaning money to a friend is a good idea, as long as you trust your friend, both you and your friend understand the terms of the loan, and are able to put yourself in your friend's position.

To begin with, your friend is your friend for a reason. There is a certain level of mutual trust that two people share that allows them to become good friends. Your friend is the one with whom you spend most of your time, share your secrets, and discuss any problems either of you is having. You know him and you still like him enough to remain his friend. Therefore, if your friend asks for money, you should be able to understand his situation well enough to justify lending him the money.

However, prior to lending him the money, you and your friend should make sure that you both understand the terms of the loan. Your friend should be able to tell you how he plans on spending the money and when he will be able to pay you back. Furthermore, you need to understand that you may never get that money back. You should only lend your friend the amount that you are comfortable with losing.

Most importantly, you should put yourself in your friend's position. What if the roles were reversed? Wouldn't you want your friend to loan you the money? If you were in a difficult situation and needed help from a friend, you would expect your friend to trust you enough to help you out. So, you should loan your friend money if he needs help.

Although many believe that loaning money to a friend will end up ruining the relationship, it doesn't have to end disastrously. Everyone needs some help sometimes, and we should be able to count on our friends to help us out. For that reason, I believe you should lend money to friends. If you truly trust your friend, understand the details of the loan, and are able to empathize with his situation, loaning your friend money will help to strengthen your friendship.

C. Useful Expressions

1. Loaning money to anyone, regardless of his relationship to you, is always a risky move.

_____

2. What may start out as a kind gesture could easily backfire, resulting in the loss of money and a good friend.

_____

3. There is a certain level of mutual trust that two people share, a certain it-factor that allows them to become good friends.

_____

4. Your friend is the one with whom you spend most of your time, share your secrets, and discuss any problems either of you is having.

_____

_____

5. However, prior to lending him the money, you and your friend should make sure that you both understand the conditions of the loan.

_____

_____

6. You should only lend your friend the amount that you are comfortable with losing.

_____

7. Most importantly, you should put yourself in your friend's position.

_____

8. If you were in a difficult situation and needed help from a friend, you would expect your friend to trust you enough to help you out.

_____

9. Everyone needs help sometimes, and we should be able to count on our friends to help us out.

_____

10. If you truly trust your friend, understand the details of the loan, and are able to empathize with his situation, loaning your friend money will help to strengthen your friendship.

_____

_____

Q146. Is it important to have expensive but beautiful things, such as fancy cars and designer label clothes?

A. Essay Outline

Argument: It is definitely not important to surround oneself with luxurious items.

Support 1: By spending money on luxury items, we are leaving ourselves with less money for the more important things in life.

Support 2: Looks can be deceiving, so higher prices do not necessarily equate to better quality.

Support 3: If we waste money on a large amount of luxury items, we give people a negative impression of us.

Thesis: Due to the numerous disadvantages associated with luxury items, I think it's best to not to have an excess amount of expensive items.

B. Model Essay

There are many ways to spend our money. Some of those ways are on expensive but beautiful things, such as fancy cars and designer label clothes. However, it is not important, to me, to have these items due to all the negatives that surround these luxurious items; they take away from the real important things in life, they aren't necessarily quality items, and they send a bad message to those around us.

First of all, having expensive things takes money away from the more important things. In life, we have basic needs to meet. Some examples of these needs are food, shelter, and companionship. When we start spending money on expensive cars, it takes away from the money we could be investing on improving our fundamentals in life. I could better use the money spent on a car towards a good college education for my children, or I could use it towards a family vacation. So, having luxury items doesn't lead to happiness because other things in our life are lacking.

Secondly, just because something is beautiful and expensive, it doesn't mean that that item is a quality item. Let's take designer clothes for example. We go out and buy hundreds and hundreds of dollars worth of clothing that we assume is a good quality because of the name that is sewn on to it. But, within a few months, that clothing wears away just as quickly, if not quicker, then the clothing bought at a less expensive department store. In the end, having expensive clothing doesn't guarantee a quality item.

Finally, having all of these luxury items sends the wrong message to those around us. When we buy high-dollar value items, it says that we are a rich person and that we waste our money on frivolous things. Don't we want to raise our children to know that looks are not what is important in life? We should be teaching them that it is what is inside a person that counts. I am not denying that a person who looks rich will have more friends than a person who looks poor. On the contrary, what type of message is that? We should instead put our focus on improving our mind and body, versus improving our clothing line and garage stock.

Since having expensive but beautiful things has so many downsides, I think that luxury items are not worth buying. We need to stop the thinking that a brand name has more importance than the quality of something. We also should strive to save our money for more important things and not waste it on an item that will lose its value over time.

C. Useful Expressions

1. Finally, it sends the wrong message to those around us.

_____

2. First of all, having expensive things takes money away from the more important things.

_____

3. When we start spending money on expensive cars, it takes away from the money we could be investing on improving the fundamentals in life.

_____

4. We go out and buy tons of dollars worth of clothing that we assume is a good quality because of the name that is sewn onto it.

_____

5. But, within a few months, that clothing wears away just as quickly, if not more quickly, than the clothing bought at a less expensive department store.

_____
_____

6. When we buy high-dollar items, it says that we are a rich person and that we waste our money on frivolous things.

_____

7. We should be teaching them that it is what is inside a person that counts.

_____
_____

8. We should instead put our focus on improving our mind and body versus improving our clothing line and garage stock.

_____
_____

9. Since having expensive but beautiful things has so many downsides, I think luxury items are not worth buying.

_____

10. We also should strive to save our money for more important things and not waste it on an item that will lose its value over time.

_____
_____

Q147. Exercise is a useful means of alleviating stress, and many doctors suggest that people should exercise every day to stay healthy and fit. What is your favorite type of exercise?

A. Essay Outline

Argument: My favorite way to stay in a shape and keep my body healthy is playing soccer.

Support 1: Soccer requires various physical skills.

Support 2: Through playing soccer, one can develop his social skills.

Support 3: Soccer is easy because it can be played anywhere.

Thesis: Due to the entertainment and health values associated with soccer, it is my favorite type of exercise.

B. Model Essay

In today's technology-based society, people are spending more and more time indoors working and studying. Because of this, it is more important than ever to make sure that we are engaging in some kind of physical exercise in order to keep our bodies healthy and strong. My favorite way to stay in shape is playing soccer. Playing soccer is a great way to utilize many different physical skills. In addition, soccer helps one to develop his social skills. Finally, soccer is an easy sport to play anywhere.

First of all, one of the reasons soccer is an excellent sport to play is because it requires one to use several different physical skills. Soccer allows one to build up his endurance because he will need to run up and down the field several times throughout the game, at times quickly sprinting in order to score a goal or stop his opponent from doing the same. In addition, one must practice his footwork. Many of the great soccer players, such as Landon Donovan, Cristiano Ronaldo, and Leonardo Messi, are able to use their feet to manipulate the soccer ball and confuse their opponents. Also, one must develop his coordination in order to pass and shoot with accuracy.

Along with being physically demanding, soccer is also a great way to develop your social skills. Soccer is a team sport, so one must learn how to appropriately socialize with both his teammates and his opponents. Both winning and losing need to be handled gracefully. No one likes a conceited winner or a sore loser. Also, one has to develop his communication skills to notify his teammates of what he is planning on doing or where he plans on positioning himself on the field. Soccer encourages fair play as well, as unsportsmanlike behavior could result in a yellow or red card, potentially causing one to be expelled from the game if he is acting inappropriately.

Finally, one of the best parts about soccer is that it can be played almost anywhere. While one can play soccer in a formal setting using all of the proper gear and referees, many people all over the world simply play pickup games of soccer. All they need is something that can be used as a soccer ball, objects with which to mark the goals, and a few willing players. A game of soccer is an entertaining way to spend a Saturday afternoon with your friends. Anyone can play because it does not require any special or advanced skills.

Due to the different physical demands of soccer, its ability to develop social skills and the accessibility of the sport, soccer is my favorite way to stay in shape both physically and mentally. I am not alone in my opinion, as soccer has been, is, and will remain one of the world's most popular sports. However, regardless of whether one enjoys playing soccer or not, he needs to find some kind of physical activity that he enjoys doing. Exercise must remain an important part of our lifestyles in order for us to live fulfilling lives.

C. Useful Expressions

1. Because of this, it is more important than ever to make sure that we are engaging in some kind of physical exercise in order to keep our bodies healthy and strong.

_____

2. Soccer allows one to build up his endurance because he will need to run up and down the field several times throughout the game, at times quickly sprinting in order to score a goal or stop his opponent from doing the same.

_____

_____

3. Many of the great soccer players, such as Landon Donovan, Cristiano Ronaldo, and Leonardo Messi, are able to use their feet to manipulate the soccer ball and confuse their opponents.

_____

4. Both winning and losing need to be handled gracefully.

_____

5. No one likes a conceited winner or a sore loser.

_____

6. Soccer encourages fair play as well, as unsportsmanlike behavior could result in a yellow or red card, potentially causing one to be expelled from the game if he is acting inappropriately.

_____

7. While one can play soccer in a formal setting using all of the proper gear and referees, many people all over the world simply play pickup games of soccer.

_____

_____

8. A game of soccer is an entertaining way to pass a Saturday afternoon with your friends.

_____

9. Due to the different physical demands of soccer, its ability to develop social skills and the accessibility of the sport, soccer is my favorite way to stay in shape both physically and mentally.

_____

_____

10. I am not alone in my opinion, as soccer has been, is, and will remain one of the world's most popular sports.

_____

_____

Q148. When you choose a friend, which quality is more important in that person, honesty or physical appearance? Give reasons for your choice.

A. Essay Outline

Argument: Honesty is undoubtedly the more important quality to look for in a friend.
Support 1: A friend's main role should be secret keeper, not super model.
Support 2: A dishonest friend would be a negative influence on me.
Support 3: One's physical appearance is not necessarily an accurate indicator of someone's personality.
Thesis: Because my life would be markedly more pleasant if I had an honest friend versus an attractive one, I would definitely choose to befriend an honest person.

B. Model Essay

Though one can alter her physical appearance with the aid of cosmetics or surgeries, honesty is a quality that is not as easily accessible. Therefore, when choosing my friends, I seek people who value honesty as much as I do. Honesty is a much more important characteristic to have in a friend than physical appearance, for I can trust an honest person. Furthermore, I do not want to be around people who might encourage me to be dishonest. Lastly, honesty is a much better judge of someone's personality than her looks are.

Honesty is much more important than physical appearance because a friend's primary function is to be my secret keeper and problem solver. When I have a problem that I need help resolving, I like to be able to ask advice from my friends. However, I want to know that I can discuss private things with my friend and that she won't tell anyone else. Also, I want my friend to be able to give me her honest opinion. I don't want her to lie to me or try to cover the truth. That would only hurt me and make me upset.

In addition, I like being an honest person that people can trust. I don't want to be around someone that might encourage me to lie. I believe friends should have a positive influence on you and help you to better yourself. If I am around someone who repeatedly lies or stretches the truth, I might pick up her habits. Then, I would become someone that others cannot trust.

Another reason I would choose honesty over physical appearance is because physical appearance is not always a good reflection of how someone is on the inside. Personality is much more important than how someone looks because your friend's looks cannot help you to solve a problem or make you feel better when you're feeling bad. However, an honest person will have a good personality because she will respect your feelings enough to tell you the truth, even when telling the truth may be difficult. Unlike a good personality, good looks do not last.

Overall, my social life would be much more pleasant if I had an honest friend rather than a physically attractive one. An honest friend would be able to help me solve my problems and keep my secrets. Additionally, if I were friends with a dishonest person, I might pick up her habits and become someone that others cannot trust. Finally, honesty will outlast good looks and is a better indicator of someone with a good personality. Because a pleasant physical appearance is easier to obtain than honesty, I would rather have a friend who is honest. The phrase that suggests, "Honesty is the best policy," is especially true when it comes to keeping and maintaining lasting friendships.

C. Useful Expressions

1. Though one can alter her physical appearance with the aid of cosmetics or surgeries, honesty is a quality that is not as easily accessible.

_____

_____

2. Lastly, honesty is a much better gauge of someone's personality than her looks are.

_____

3. Honesty is much more important than physical appearance because a friend's primary function is to be my secret keeper and problem solver.

_____

_____

4. I don't want her to lie to me or try to cover the truth to save my feelings.

_____

5. I don't want to be around someone that might pressure me into lying as well.

_____

6. If I am around someone who repeatedly lies or stretches the truth, I might pick up her habits.

_____

7. Another reason I would choose honesty over physical appearance is because physical appearance is not always a good reflection of how someone is on the inside.

_____

_____

8. However, an honest person will have a good personality because she will respect your feelings enough to tell you the truth, even when telling the truth may be difficult.

_____

_____

9. Unlike a good personality, good looks do not last.

_____

10. Additionally, if I were friends with a dishonest person, I might pick up her habits and become someone that others cannot trust.

_____

_____

Q149. If there was a fire or some other type of disaster in your house, what would you take with you? Why?

A. Essay Outline

Argument: If a disaster were to strike my home, I would make sure to take my family's photo albums with me.

Support 1: My photo albums tell the story of my family.

Support 2: There are life-defining moments captured in those photos that inspire me.

Support 3: Photos from my childhood are irreplaceable.

Thesis: Because my history would be lost if my photo albums were destroyed, I would make sure to save those.

B. Model Essay

Disasters are a terrible part of life, especially when one is not prepared for them to strike. A bad fire or flood could destroy a house and everything inside of it. If there was some kind of disaster in my house, I would try my hardest to save the photo albums my family has collected over the years. One of the main reasons I would want to save the photo albums is because they contain pictures that chronicle my family's history. Additionally, those photos albums captured parts of my life that made me who I am today. Most importantly, the photo albums are one of the very few things in my home that could never be replaced if they were damaged.

First of all, my family has collected several photo albums over the years. We even have albums from when my parents were younger, telling the story of how they grew up back when the world was recovering from the destruction of World War II. Those photo albums contain my family's history. They show how we grew up, what our lives were like, and what the latest fashions of the time were. I love going through the albums with my parents because they are able to weave all of the individual pictures into one continuous story about our lives. Therefore, if we were to lose the photo albums, we would lose part of our family's story.

Furthermore, the photo albums contain pictures of moments that have helped to define my life and made me the person I am today. My family didn't just capture the happy moments, but the sad moments as well. Flipping through the pages of the photo albums remind me of moments that really changed me for the better. For example, pictures of my time with family members that are no longer living help me to remember all of the valuable life lessons they taught me. Also, the photo my mother took of me after I won my first art competition reminds me how much I hated art class because I thought I was a terrible artist. Winning the competition reminded me not to ever stop believing in my own abilities.

The most important reason I would try to salvage my family's photo albums from a disaster is because those photos cannot be replaced. I can't go back in time and become a little kid again. I cannot bring back people that have passed away. I cannot recreate those memories captured in the photos that shaped my life both negatively and positively. Computers, televisions, clothing—those are all things that can be repurchased and replaced. Photos cannot. I would hate to lose all of those wonderful memories.

Recovering from a disaster is not an easy task, especially if one loses most or all of his personal belongs in the disaster. However, I think I would be okay as long as I had my family and the photo albums. Those photo albums would be invaluable to me in the process of recovering from a disaster, as they would remind me of who I am. Photo albums chronicle my family's history, capture the life changing moments in my life, and can never be replaced. I would save my family's photo albums from any disaster that might affect my home.

C. Useful Expressions

1. A bad fire or flood could destroy a house and everything inside of it.

_____

2. Additionally, those photos albums capture parts of my life that shaped me into the person I am today.

_____

3. So, all things considered, I would save my family's photo albums.

_____

4. We even have albums from when my parents were younger, telling the story of how they grew up back when the world was recovering from the destruction of World War II.

_____

_____

5. I love going through the albums with my parents because they are able to weave all of the individual pictures into one continuous story about our lives.

_____

_____

6. Flipping through the pages of the photo albums remind me of moments that really changed me for the better.

_____

_____

7. Also, the photo my mother took of me after I won my first art competition reminds me how much I hated art class because I thought I was a terrible artist.

_____

_____

8. I cannot bring back people that have passed away.

_____

9. Recovering from a disaster is not an easy task, especially if one loses most or all of his personal belongings in the disaster.

_____

10. Photo albums chronicle my family's history, capture the life changing moments in my life, and can never be replaced.

_____

Q150. Who is your best friend? Why is he/she important to you?

A. Essay Outline

Argument: Though I have met many amazing friends, Peter Lynch remains my best friend.
Support 1: Because Peter knows me better than anyone, he always gives me sound advice.
Support 2: It's easy to pick up right where we left off, even if we haven't spoken to each other in ages.
Support 3: Peter and I have experienced some pretty dark moments together.
Thesis: Peter will always have my back no matter what, so he will always be my very best friend.

B. Model Essay

I have many friends both here in South Korea and in America, but my best friend is Peter F. Lynch. He and I have been best friends since our junior year at Allentown Central Catholic High School. We had two classes together, where we had numerous projects to do together. These projects started our friendship that has now lasted for 12 years. We formed our friendship from a common love for a book and it has only grown from there.

First, Peter knows me the best and can always give me the best advice. We have known each over for 12 years and because of this, we have learned about each other very well. I often go to him to ask advice about dating, or what I should do next in life. He always gives me advice perfectly suited for me. It is never what he wants me to do, but rather what he knows I should do. To me, this is a very important feature in a best friend. Somebody who knows what is best for you, not for them.

Next, Peter and I have gone two years without talking; but when we saw each other again, it was like that two year gap never existed. After we graduated high school, we went our separate ways but found each other again in college. We caught up with each other and discussed the past and future with each other. Most friendships will fade or drift apart if they have that length of time between them. However, our friendship only became stronger because we realized how important we were in each other's lives.

Finally, Peter and I have been through some of our most difficult and darkest times together. These times challenged our thoughts of others and our plans for the future. Despite these tough times, we worked through them together and can now look back on them and chuckle about the things we got ourselves into. One example was when he was dealing with the death of some soldiers on a Chinook in August of 2011. It was the most difficult time for both of us because he was dealing with a lot of guilt and I was dealing with the fact I almost lost my best friend. He was to have been on the helicopter that crashed, but he gave up his seat to another soldier, who died. He felt guilty because that person had a fiancé and a child but we worked through it together and we have only become stronger because of these difficult feelings.

Because of my friendship with Peter, we have been able to grow as adults together. I am very lucky to have him in my life and I would have been devastated if I had lost him in August of 2011. A best friend should always be there for you, no matter what difficulties may come your way. To me, a best friend is rare and not something that comes along that often.

C. Useful Expressions

1. From those projects blossomed a friendship that has now lasted for 12 years.

2. We formed our friendship over a common love for a book and it has only grown from there.

3. First, Peter knows me inside out and can always give me the best advice.

4. He always gives me advice suited perfectly to me.

5. Somebody who knows what is best for you, not for him, is the best kind of friend.

6. We are able to pick up quickly where we left off.

7. We caught up with each other and discussed the past and future with each other.

8. Most friendships will fade or friends will drift apart if they have that length of time between them.

9. Despite these tough times, we worked through them together and can now look back on them and chuckle about the things we got ourselves into.

10. A best friend should always be there for you, no matter what difficulties may come your way.

Q151. If you could be famous for something, what would you want to be famous for? Why?

A. Essay Outline

Argument: I want to be famous for curing cancer.
Support 1: The world would be a better place if cancer were cured.
Support 2: I wouldn't have to perform in front of people, like many other celebrities.
Support 3: No one would forget that I cured cancer.
Thesis: Since many people could benefit from me curing cancer and I would always be remembered, I would like to be famous for having found a cure for cancer.

B. Model Essay

If I could be famous for something, I would want to be well-known for discovering the cure for all cancers. By doing this, it will make the world a better place. Also, I would not be famous for something that I would need to perform or do in front of a larger arena of people. Lastly, I would be known for an important thing, not for just a hit song that is played on the radio once.

First, if I could be famous for discovering the cure for cancer, the world would be a better place. So many people are dying from cancer every year. We have gotten better at diagnosing the early signs of this disease but we are still losing too many people. If there is a cure, then we could focus our money and resources on finding more cures for other diseases and to fix other problems we have on Earth. Also, people would not have to be as worried about possibly getting cancer. When I had my scare with cancer, it was so terrifying thinking what could happen to me and my family. So this to me would be a great thing to be famous for because it is personal to me.

Next, I don't like singing or performing in front of extremely large arenas of people, so finding a cure for cancer would be a great 'behind-the-scenes' fame to have. I wouldn't have to get up and sing and dance for anybody. Maybe, I would have to do a speech but speaking is much easier than performing. My speeches would be written and rehearsed and I would have props to help me discuss the way to cure cancer. These speeches would help educate many other doctors who can then use this information to cure their own patients, until all patients are cured around the world.

Finally, my fame would be for something that is important and that has an impact on the world. It won't be like a song that will fade over the years. Because of this cure, people will be happier, resources can be used elsewhere, and I will be making a difference in people's lives. A singer, athlete, or musician might be well-known for a year or two, but after that, their fame will be worth nothing.

Since there are many benefits that could come from my fame, I would want to be famous for being the person who cured all cancer in the world. This is a type of fame that not only is important to me, but also to others. It could change the way the world is and I could feel proud of being the person who started it all.

C. Useful Expressions

1. If I could be famous for something, I would want to be well-known for discovering the cure for all cancers.

2. Lastly, I would be known for an important thing, not for just a hit song that is played on the radio once.

3. So, I would like to get my 15 minutes of fame, or even more, from discovering the cure for cancer.

4. We have gotten better at diagnosing the early signs of this disease, but we are still losing too many people.

5. When I had my cancer scare, it was so terrifying thinking what could happen to me and my family.

6. Next, I don't like singing or performing in front of extremely large arenas of people, so finding a cure for cancer would be a great 'behind-the-scenes' fame to have.

7. My speeches would be written and well-rehearsed.

8. Finally, my fame would be for something that is important and makes an impact on the world.

9. It won't be like a song that will fade over the years.

10. Since there are many benefits that could come from my fame, I would want to be famous for being the person who cured all cancers in the world.

Q152. Do you think teenagers should be allowed to drive? Give specific reasons and details for your answer.

A. Essay Outline

Argument: I don't think teenagers should be allowed to drive.
Support 1: Many teenagers get into traffic accidents when they drive.
Support 2: Because of their changing bodies, some teenagers drive carelessly such as through drag racing.
Support 3: Teenagers are just too immature to understand the responsibilities of driving.
Thesis: Since teenagers are just too underdeveloped and reckless to drive, they should not be allowed to until they are much older.

B. Model Essay

In my honest opinion, I do not believe that teenagers should be allowed to drive. There are too many problems that occur when teenagers get behind the wheel. There are too many traffic accidents involving teens. Also, most teenagers are not responsible enough to handle the financial responsibility of driving.

First of all, most traffic accidents involve teen drivers. There is a saying that the first one hundred days a teen has their license are the deadliest." Many times when teens are driving, they will drive with too many people in the car. This is a distraction for the driver. Another distraction for teens behind the wheel are cell phones. Teen drivers are notorious for texting or talking on their cell phones while driving.

Also, some teens feel the need to prove themselves to others. Because of 'raging hormones' that teens experience, many will become involved in risky behavior such as speeding or drag racing. This not only creates a dangerous situation for the teen drivers, but for other drivers and pedestrians as well. This is one of the reasons why insurance companies tend to charge more for younger drivers, as well as owners of certain sports cars.

Finally, most teens are not mature enough to handle the responsibilities of driving, or owning a vehicle, because they tend to equate driving with freedom. However, most teens need to understand that there is more involved with driving. Most teens never think about the costs of driving such as insurance. They will usually have to pay higher fees, which would require them to work a job in addition to studying. This does not sound like the freedom that teens may imagine.

Since teenagers are at a vulnerable age where they do not fully understand the responsibilities of driving, it would probably be wise for them to hold off on driving until they are older. As well, keeping teens from driving would potentially reduce the number of traffic accidents, and make our roads safer. Driving is not a right, but a privilege, and teens need to be mature enough to understand this.

C. Useful Expressions

1. In my honest opinion, I do not believe that teenagers should be allowed to drive.

2. There are too many problems that occur when teenagers get behind the wheel.

3. Also, most teenagers are not responsible enough to handle the financial responsibility of driving.

4. Teen drivers are notorious for texting or talking on their cell phones while driving.

5. Because of 'raging hormones' that teens experience, many will become involved in risky behavior such as speeding or drag racing.

6. This not only creates a dangerous situation for the teen drivers, but for other drivers and pedestrians as well.

7. Finally, most teens are not mature enough to handle the responsibilities of driving, or owning a vehicle, because they tend to equate driving with freedom.

8. Most teens never think about the costs of driving such as insurance.

9. Since teenagers are at a vulnerable age where they do not fully understand the responsibilities of driving, it would probably be wise for them to hold off on driving until they are older.

10. Driving is not a right, but a privilege, and teens need to be mature enough to understand this.

Q153. If you could meet one world leader, who would it be and why? Give specific reasons and details for your answer.

A. Essay Outline

Argument: I would want to meet Mahatma Gandhi.
Support 1: Gandhi had an interesting life as a civil rights leader.
Support 2: I would like to learn about his life philosophy.
Support 3: I want to ask Gandhi how we can change the world today for the better.
Thesis: Because he was a great inspiration to everyone fighting injustice, I want to meet Mahatma Gandhi.

B. Model Essay

There is so much that one could learn from these individuals to help better our world and avoid mistakes committed by some of the leaders of the past. If I were given the opportunity to meet one world leader, I would love to meet Mohandas Karamchand Gandhi, more commonly known as Mahatma Gandhi. Unfortunately, he passed away several years ago. Despite this, I believe there are many valuable lessons I could learn from him. If I were to meet him, I would ask him about the experiences that had the greatest impact on his life. I would make sure to ask him about his personal philosophy. Also, one of the things I would look forward to the most is asking him for his advice and opinion on the current situation of the world today.

One of the very first things I would like to learn about Gandhi is his life experience. Gandhi has been involved in several important movements, such as the Civil Rights Movement, as well as struggles of independence. He was beaten, arrested, and yet revered by many. I would like to know which of those experiences he felt changed him or inspired him the most. I feel that he would have some very interesting stories to tell and that he would be very entertaining to listen to. I could learn about many important details of the events he experienced that might have been left out of the history books.

Another reason I would enjoy meeting Gandhi is because I would like to learn about his personal life philosophy. Everyone has a life philosophy, whether they know it or not. I would like to learn about what drove Gandhi to engage in the types of causes that he did. How would he define a successful or happy life? What was his main goal in life? It would also be intriguing to learn how his life experiences helped shape and alter his personal philosophy. After listening to him, I would be able to evaluate my own goals in life and maybe alter them to encompass what I learned from him.

Most importantly, if I were given the opportunity to meet Gandhi, I would make sure to ask him for his opinion on the world we're living in now. Gandhi has a lot of experience and was so successful that there is a holiday commemorating his work, so he would be a valuable source of information. I would want to know what he thinks is positive about the world and what we need to change. Moreover, I would ask him for his advice on how to change those things about the world that he believes are negative. He and I would exchange thoughts and opinions. I would be sure to take notes so I wouldn't forget anything that he told me.

Meeting any world leader would be beneficial and an amazing experience, but I would prefer to meet Gandhi. I could learn so much from him! Meeting him would allow me to ask him about his life experiences, his personal philosophy, and his opinion on the world we live in today. Because Gandhi is such a patient man, I'm sure he would allow me to ask as many questions as I would like. He would be so inspiring to talk to! By talking to him, I might even have the opportunity to become the next great world leader.

C. Useful Expressions

1. There is so much that one could learn from world leaders to help better our world and avoid mistakes committed by some of the leaders of the past.

_____

2. I would love to meet Mohandas Karamchand Gandhi, more commonly known as Mahatma Gandhi.

_____

3. I would make sure to ask him about his personal philosophy.

_____

4. He was beaten, arrested, and yet revered by many.

_____

5. I would like to learn about what drove Gandhi to engage in the types of causes that he did.

_____

6. It would also be intriguing to learn how his life experiences helped shape and alter his personal philosophy.

_____

7. After listening to him, I would be able to evaluate my own goals in life and maybe alter them to encompass what I learned from him.

_____

8. Gandhi has a lot of experience and was so successful that there is a holiday commemorating his work, so he would be a valuable source of information.

_____

9. He and I would exchange thoughts and opinions.

_____

10. I could learn so much from him! Meeting him would allow me to ask him about his life experiences, his personal philosophy, and his opinion on the state of the world we live in today.

_____

Q154. Which do you think is better, going to college right after high school or after taking a few years off?

A. Essay Outline

Argument: I think people should go to college directly after high school.
Support 1: College life is more enjoyable when fellow students are the same age as you.
Support 2: We might lose the motivation to go to school after being away for a couple of years.
Support 3: College itself is the perfect time for people to find themselves because of the many opportunities available.
Thesis: Because college life is more enjoyable with peers our own age and university provides such great opportunities, I think people should go to college straight after finishing high school.

B. Model Essay

Graduating high school is no longer very impressive, as everyone now has the opportunity to do so. In order to increase your chances of being successful in the world, it is important to obtain a college degree. I believe that one should go to college right after graduating from high school because it is more advantageous to do so. By going to college upon high school graduation, one is able to be around his peers. Furthermore, if one takes time off, he might not be as motivated to go back to college later. Finally, college offers many experiences for one to 'find himself' while still remaining in an academic setting.

First of all, attending college right after one graduates high school ensures that he will be surrounded by his peers at school. Being around people one's own age going through the same adaptation to college life as him will help him be more comfortable in the college setting. College life will be more enjoyable if one is able to hang out around friends his own age. Meeting new friends and forming life long bonds with them is an important part of the college experience. By taking time off, one will enter college when he is older than the rest of the freshman starting out. This might make his experience more difficult because he won't have anyone his own age to relate to.

Another reason it is best to attend college immediately after completing high school is because one might not be motivated to return to school later. However, having a college degree is extremely important in today's society. Having time off from school might become too appealing. If one finds a job, he might end up staying in that job instead of going back to school and getting a degree that would allow him to obtain an even better job. Also, it becomes much harder to learn as one ages. The longer he stays out of school, the greater the risk that he will not go back to get his college degree. He'll be thrown into the real world that he may not be quite ready to enter yet.

Although some people argue that taking a few years off will enable one to 'find himself' or better understand what he really wants in life, I believe that college is the perfect time to do that. College allows one to partake in many different clubs, volunteer organizations, and trips that will help him figure out what he really desires to do with his life. Furthermore, in college, one is able to meet inspiring professors, crazy friends, and mentors all while still intellectually stimulating his mind. The people that he meets in college will help mold him into the person he will be for the rest of his life. College is the perfect opportunity to discover one's true aspirations.

In conclusion, going to college upon graduation from high school is the best option. One of the advantages it offers is that it allows one to be surrounded by his peers. Moreover, one might not actually be motivated to attend college after he has taken time off. Most importantly, college gives one several opportunities to explore himself and figure out where his interests truly lie. College is an amazing experience that will shape your mind and drive you to become successful at whatever it is that you desire to do. It should be experienced as soon as possible.

C. Useful Expressions

1. Graduating high school is no longer very impressive, as everyone now has the opportunity to do so.

2. I believe that one should go to college right after graduating from high school because it is more advantageous to do so.

3. Furthermore, if one takes time off, he might not be as motivated to go back to college later.

4. First of all, attending college right after one graduates high school ensures that he will be surrounded by his peers at school.

5. College life will be more enjoyable if one is able to hang out around friends his own age.

6. This might make his experience more difficult because he won't have anyone his own age to relate to.

7. He'll be thrown into the real world that he may not be quite ready to enter yet.

8. Although some people argue that taking a few years off will enable one to 'find himself' or better understand what he really wants in life, I believe that college is the perfect time to do that.

9. Furthermore, in college, one is able to meet inspiring professors, crazy friends, and mentors all while still intellectually stimulating his mind.

10. College is the perfect opportunity to discover one's true aspirations.

Q155. Which do you think is better—to live on campus or to rent an apartment off campus?

A. Essay Outline

Argument: I believe that it is better to rent an apartment off campus.
Support 1: It is cheaper to rent an apartment off campus than live in the dormitories.
Support 2: College dorms can be too noisy and prevent people from studying.
Support 3: It's good to take a break from all the activities on a college campus.
Thesis: Because off campus apartments are cheaper, college dorms can be too distracting, and it's good to take a break from campus, I think it's better to rent an apartment off-campus.

B. Model Essay

While living in the college dormitories can be a fun and exciting experience, sometimes it can detract from the main purpose of attending college, studying and learning. So, I believe it is better to rent an apartment off campus rather than live in the dorms on campus. One reason renting an apartment off campus is more beneficial is because it can severely cut the cost of attending college. Secondly, college dorms typically do not create an atmosphere conducive to academic success because they are so noisy. Finally, it is good to be able to escape from the commotion of the college campus.

Although obtaining a college degree is a necessity in today's society, the costs of college may feel daunting to some wanting to attend. However, one will be able to dramatically reduce the cost of his college bill by choosing to live off campus. Dormitories typically cost much more per month than the average apartment. It is much cheaper to rent an apartment off campus and use the money saved to pay for the most important college cost, tuition. Furthermore, stores around college dorms tend to have higher prices, as they know that the students in the dorms will prefer to pay extra for the convenience of being able to simply walk to the store. Shops off campus, however, are much cheaper. By renting an apartment off campus, one will not only be able to slash the cost of his housing, but save money on everyday necessities as well.

Another important reason to live off campus is that college dorms are very noisy places. Because most colleges require their incoming students to live on campus for their first year, the dorms are normally filled with underclassmen who are becoming accustomed to the college lifestyle for the first time. Many of the students are quite noisy and, due to their newfound freedom, will stay up much later and be much louder than normal. Additionally, college dorms are small and most require one to live with a roommate. The atmosphere created in the college dorm setting is not favorable for academic success, as it is much harder to focus with so many distractions. Living in an off-campus apartment would help to minimize the distractions and allow one to be more efficient while studying.

Moreover, one needs a break from the college campus. A student will spend most of his day on campus, attending classes, studying in the library, or simply hanging out with his friends between classes. However, he needs some time away from the campus. Students need to stay in touch with the idea that there is life outside of college. It is very easy to become overwhelmed by all of the activity and stress that accompany the college experience. Therefore, I think it is important for a student to be able to escape that. A beneficial way of doing that is living off campus.

Overall, the benefits of living off campus make it the best choice for one's housing arrangement during his college years. Living on campus is much too expensive, and that money could be better spent towards paying for books or tuition. Not only that, but living off campus enables one to study without the incessant distractions one will inevitably face while living in the college dorms. Last, but not least, it is important for one to have an opportunity to escape the daily stress and excitement that he will encounter on campus. In order to get the most of one's college experience, I believe that one should rent an apartment off campus.

C. Useful Expressions

1. While living in the college dormitories can be a fun and exciting experience, sometimes it can detract from the main purpose of attending college, studying and learning.

2. One reason renting an apartment off campus is more beneficial is because it can severely cut the cost of attending college.

3. Although obtaining a college degree is a necessity in today's society, the costs of college may feel daunting to some wanting to attend.

4. Shops off campus, however, are much cheaper.

5. Many of the students are quite noisy and, due to their new-found freedom, will stay up much later and be much louder than normal.

6. The atmosphere created in the college dorm setting is not favorable for academic success, as it is much harder to focus with so many distractions.

7. Students need to stay in touch with the idea that there is life outside of college.

8. Overall, the benefits of living off campus make it the best choice for one's housing arrangement during his college years.

9. Not only that, but living off campus enables one to study without the incessant distractions one will inevitably face while living in the college dorms.

10. In order to get the most out of one's college experience, I believe that one should rent an apartment off campus.

Q156. Some people prefer going to a movie theater instead of watching a movie at home. Which do you prefer? Why?

A. Essay Outline

Argument: I like watching movies at home more than watching movies in a movie theater.
Support 1: There are too many distractions in movie theaters.
Support 2: It costs more to watch movies on the big screen.
Support 3: It's more comfortable to watch movies at home.
Thesis: Because it's cheaper and more comfortable and offers less distractions, I think watching movies at home is the best place to watch movies.

B. Model Essay

I prefer staying at home to watch a movie rather than to watch a movie at a theater. Movies theaters are usually the preferred place for most, but not for me. With the few advantages of the movie theater, there are many more disadvantages: distractions, cost, and comfort.

First, there are many distractions that come along with watching a movie at a theater. Movie theaters are made for large groups of people, about 100 or more. With this large number come many distractions, such as loud chewing, talking, walking in front of the viewers, and cell phones. When I am in the comfort of my own home, I don't have any of these distractions. If I do, they only affect me and nobody else.

Next, the cost is higher to watch a movie at the theater. The initial ticket price might not seem very expensive, but when you add in all the other costs, it becomes a larger price than expected. Take for instance, the cost of gas to get to the theater, the cost of snacks and drinks, and also the cost of parking at some places. As you can see, these all add up to be much more expensive than just a $5 movie on TV.

Finally, it is more comfortable to see a movie at my own home. When I am at a theater, the seats are usually very comfortable but they are also very close to others. I cannot spread my legs out or curl my feet up without being in the way of somebody else. I am one who likes to move a lot during a movie, so being at a theater prevents me from doing this. Also, if I have to go to the bathroom, I can pause the movie, go and start the movie when I come back. I cannot do that at a movie theater. Therefore, it is much more comfortable to me at my own home to view a movie.

As stated above, I prefer the comfort of my own home to view a movie rather than a noisy and distracting movie theater. The movie theater has some comforts and amenities that I can't receive at my home, but my home has more advantages. Not having to deal with many people distracting me during a movie, the price being cheaper, and the ability to pause and start the movie again are the reasons I prefer watching movies at my own home.

C. Useful Expressions

1. Movies theaters are usually the preferred place for most, but not for me.

2. First, there are many distractions that come along with watching a movie at a theater.

3. Finally, watching a movie at home is far more relaxing.

4. First, movie theaters have many people who cause a myriad of distractions.

5. When I am in the comfort of my own home, I don't have any of these distractions.

6. With this large number come many distractions, such as loud chewing, talking, walking in front of the viewers, and cell phones.

7. If I do, they only affect me and nobody else.

8. The initial ticket price might not seem very expensive, but when you add in all the other costs, it becomes a price larger than previously expected.

9. I cannot spread my legs out or curl my feet up without being in the way of somebody else.

10. The movie theater has some comforts and amenities that I can't receive at home, but my home has more advantages.

Q157. What is your favorite way to spend your free time? Explain and include details and examples to support your explanation.

A. Essay Outline

Argument: I spend my free time in three very distinct ways.
Support 1: I read books when I have the time.
Support 2: I have lunch or dinner with my friends from time to time.
Support 3: I also love to go hiking in the woods.
Thesis: Reading books, spending time with friends, and going hiking are my three favorite ways to spend my free time.

B. Model Essay

I work a lot and have very little free time. However, when I do get free time, I enjoy spending it in a variety of ways. First, I enjoy reading books. Second, I visit my friends. Third, I go outdoors and do many different activities in the fresh air.

First, most of my free time is spent reading books. I really like to read books, but I don't have much time to do so. Therefore, I would take advantage of my free time. I enjoy both electronic books and paperback books at a local park or coffee shop. There is something exciting about being able to read a book and imagining you are one of the characters in the story. It is a very exciting thing to do in my free time, even though most others would think it to be rather boring.

Second, I enjoy spending time with my friends. During my lunch and dinner time, I usually spend it eating at a restaurant with one of my many friends. We enjoy going to different types of ethnic food restaurants and learning about new countries through their food. We also like to see movies together and talk about the story and actors afterwards. I am lucky to have good friends to keep me company during my free time at lunch and dinner.

Finally, my most favorite thing I enjoy doing during my free time is hiking or any other outdoor activity. I don't get to do these activities that often because they take up more time than I have, but they are the types of things that I enjoy the most. There are many mountains surrounding the area I live in, along with many trails that follow the rivers. So, my location is fantastic for outdoor activities. Being outdoors keeps me healthy, active and happy.

I have three favorite pastimes. The three ways I enjoy my free time are split between reading, socializing with friends, and doing outdoor activities. These three things keep my happy, healthy, and enjoying my life. I wish I had more free time to do all these things more often.

C. Useful Expressions

1. However, when I do get free time, I enjoy spending it in a variety of ways.

2. Third, I go outdoors and do many different activities in the fresh air.

3. I really like to read books but I don't often have time to do so, so I take advantage of them during my free time.

4. I enjoy cracking open both electronic books and paperback books at a local park or coffee shop.

5. It is a very exciting thing to do in my free time, even though most others would think it to be rather boring.

6. We enjoy going to different types of ethnic food restaurants and learning about new countries through their food.

7. I am lucky to have good friends to keep me company during my free time at lunch and dinner.

8. I don't get to do these activities that often because they take up more time than I have, but they are the types of things that I enjoy the most.

9. There are many mountains surrounding the area I live in, along with many trails that follow the rivers.

10. As you can see, I have three favorite pastimes.

Q158. Some people prefer learning from books, while others prefer learning from experiences. Which one do you prefer?

A. Essay Outline

Argument: I prefer to learn through experience.
Support 1: We remember things better when we learn them through experience.
Support 2: Experiencing something is more fun and exciting.
Support 3: Knowledge gained through experience is more useful when we are trying to get a job.
Thesis: Since it is more memorable, exciting, and useful, I prefer to learn through experience.

B. Model Essay

Many have argued about this topic whether it is better to learn through books or to learn through experience. I prefer learning through experience for three reasons. We will gain more if we have the experience and not just book knowledge.

First, when we experience things ourselves, we can remember them better. As C.S. Lewis said, "Experience: that most brutal of teachers." We learn more when we actually experience something and make the mistakes ourselves. Take for example, making a cake. You can read the recipe all you want, but you need to actually experience it in order to remember it and to do it properly. The more you do it, the more you will remember it and it will become second nature to you.

Second, learning through experience is much easier and more exciting than learning through books. When we learn through books, we are only just memorizing facts, which is very boring. However, when we learn through experience, we are more interested in the materials and we will be able to learn it more easily. For instance, learning to paint can be very boring if all you do is read theories about colors and brush strokes. But, if you are given a paint brush and some paints, you will be able to learn them on your own, with a teacher's guidance from behind. This is much more exciting and fun to do than reading books.

Finally, having knowledge through experience is more useful in the real world. Many jobs require experience over knowledge already, so it is more beneficial to you if you get that experience. Many times, the employer will chose a candidate that has the experience over the knowledge because they won't have to train a new employee. This saves them time and money which makes a better business. Not every job or specialty is going to follow this rule though; some need the knowledge in order to do their job properly, such as doctors and lawyers.

Since having experience over knowledge is more beneficial in the real world and in the long term, I prefer to learn through experience rather than to learn from books. Many jobs require experience in order to do perform their job. Book knowledge is important as a basis, but it is the experience that will carry you through life more successfully.

C. Useful Expressions

1. We will gain more if we have the experience and not just book knowledge.

2. As C.S. Lewis said, "Experience: that most brutal of teachers."

3. You can read the recipe all you want, but you need to actually experience it in order to remember it and to do it properly.

4. The more you do it, the more you will remember it and it will become second nature to you.

5. But, if you are given a paint brush and some paints, you will be able to learn them on your own, with a teacher's guidance from behind.

6. When we learn through books, we are only just memorizing facts, which is very boring.

7. Many jobs require experience over knowledge already, so it is more beneficial to you if you get that experience.

8. This saves time and money which makes a better business.

9. Since having experience is more beneficial in the real world and long term, I prefer to learn through experience rather than to learn from books.

10. Book knowledge is important as a base, but it is experience that will carry you through life more successfully.

Q159. Who do you admire the most? Give specific reasons to explain your answer.

A. Essay Outline

Argument: I admire my mother the most.
Support 1: My mother helped raise three children after she got divorced.
Support 2: She taught me and my sisters how to be strong and independent.
Support 3: She has fought health problems and lost a lot of weight
Thesis: Since my mother is such a strong-headed, encouraging, and positive woman, I admire her the most.

B. Model Essay

I have many people whom I admire a lot. They have all taught me many life lessons. However, if I have to choose one person, I would choose my mother for many reasons.

First, my mother took on three children after the divorce between my parents. She packed us up, put is in a car, and drove three children, herself, a cat, and all of our household belongings from Pennsylvania to Texas. This was a huge feat for her but she navigated it successfully. We lived in Texas for six years; every summer we would fly to Pennsylvania to spend the summers with our dad. My mom worked hard to give us a good life with what little she had.

Second, my mother taught her three daughters to be strong, resilient, and independent women. She did this by teaching us how to shop, cook and clean for ourselves at a very young age. Once a week, we would be given $20, which was a lot of money then, to go shopping a mile away by walking to the local grocery store. We would have a list and some coupons, then we would compare prices and figure out which was the better deal. Also, once a week, each of us would have a day to cook a meal for the family. So, when our mom came home, we would have a meal all ready, prepared, and set on the table. It seems like a dangerous thing for children to do, but I am very fortunate to have a mother who encouraged this type of behavior.

Finally, despite her challenges from health issues that came about after her military service and deployments, she has fought off her weight problems. She has dropped from a size 24 to a size 14 in just a year! I'm so proud of her for continuing to look at life in a positive light and not let all the negatives get her down.

As you can see, my mother has some unusual teachings for children, but because of these teachings, I am the women I am today. If I had been raised differently, I don't think I would be as independent as I am now. I am faced with problems, and through her example, I am come back, even stronger. My mom has taught me many great things, and this is why she is the person whom I admire the most.

C. Useful Expressions

1. This was a huge feat for her and she navigated the route successfully.

2. She packed us up, put us in a car, and drove three children, herself, a cat, and all of our household belongings from Pennsylvania to Texas.

3. My mom worked hard to give us a good life with what little she had.

4. Second, my mother taught her three daughters to be strong, resilient, and independent women.

5. We would have a list and some coupons, then we would compare prices and figure out which was the better deal.

6. It seems like a dangerous thing for children to do, but I am very fortunate to have a mother who encouraged this type of behavior.

7. Finally, despite her challenges from health issues that came about after her military service and deployments, she has fought off weight problems.

8. I'm so proud of her for continuing to look at life in a positive light and not let all the negatives get her down.

9. I am knocked down a lot, and through her example, I am able to get back up and become even stronger.

Q160. Describe an important social or political event in your country. Why do you think it is important?

A. Essay Outline

Argument: Prom is an important social event in my country.
Support 1: Prom makes everyone feel special.
Support 2: Students spend a lot of money on prom to look beautiful.
Support 3: Local businesses make a lot of money on prom too.
Thesis: Because students spend a lot of money on prom and get to feel special, prom is one of the most important social events in my country.

B. Model Essay

Prom is an important social event in the USA that brings about many positives and negatives. Most high schools participate in this coming of age event. It is held mostly for the seniors, but will include juniors as well, in May or June. Prom is meant to be the last big farewell for the graduating class.

First, prom brings about many positive things for the students. It allows the students to be excited about a big party just for them. Also, it teaches the students how to be rejected and how to reject others. This skill might not seem important, but it is when it comes to larger things in life. Another positive aspect of prom is that the students get to feel special for a day. They usually get very beautiful dresses or suits, do their hair in a special up-do, and take special photographs.

On the other hand, there are many negatives that come about because of prom. Students spend too much money focusing on looking beautiful or having the most stylish dress. They also focus a lot on who to choose to bring with them to this dance. It is often a very harsh, stressful, and disappointing time of year for a young high school student. This time of year, there are also many demands on relationships that most students are not ready for.

Finally, this time of year is a big money maker for the local businesses. Also, the schools get to show pride in their students one last time. Flower shops, hotel ballrooms, restaurants, tuxedo rental stores, dress shops, limousine companies, and many more receive a great deal of money to support these functions. It is a great thing for the local economy, but also a taxing thing for the parents to support for just one event.

Prom is an important event in the USA because it teaches the students many positive and negative aspects of life. Also, businesses receive a financial boost during this time of year. So, these are the reasons why prom is an important social event in America for high school students.

C. Useful Expressions

1. Most high schools participate in this coming-of-age event.

_____

2. Prom is meant to be the last big farewell for the graduating class.

_____

3. Also, it teaches the students how to be rejected and how to reject others.

_____

4. They usually get very beautiful dresses or suits, do their hair in a special up-do, and take several photographs.

_____

_____

5. Students spend too much money focusing on looking beautiful or having the most stylish dress.

_____

6. This time of year, there are also many demands on relationships that most students are not ready for.

_____

7. Finally, this time of year is a big money maker for the local businesses.

_____

8. Flower shops, hotel ballrooms, restaurants, tuxedo rental stores, dress shops, limousine companies, and many more receive a great deal of money by supporting this function.

_____

_____

9. It is a great thing for the local economy, but also quite taxing for the parents to support just one event.

_____

10. Also, businesses receive a financial boost during this time of year.

_____

Q161. What are the advantages and disadvantages of moving to a new home?

A. Essay Outline

Argument: There are many advantages and disadvantages to packing up your house and moving to a new location, assuming that it is to a new city, state, or even country.

Support 1: Some advantages of moving to a new town, city or country are making new friends, gaining a more open mind to a different society or culture, and starting over fresh.

Support 2: Some disadvantages of moving to a new town, city or country are the financial burdens obtained, losing friends, and being lost or out of place in the new environment.

Support 3: I wouldn't mind moving to a new place because I have already done so numerous times.

Thesis: Since it can bring about both ups and downs, moving to a new home in another place can be both exciting and terrifying at the same time.

B. Model Essay

Sometimes we are forced to move and other times we choose to move. Some reasons might be that our parents found a better job, or maybe the school district is a better one for our education. Or maybe, we lost money and can afford to live in a new place, or came into more money and can live in a more luxurious house. Whatever the reasons may be, there are many advantages and disadvantages to packing up your house and moving to a new location, assuming that it is to a new city, state, or even country.

To begin with, I will discuss some advantages of moving to a new town, city or country. One of them is making new friends for both the parents and the children. This can often be a good thing because there is no such thing as having too many friends. Secondly, the family can gain a more open mind to a different society or culture. Maybe they lived in a single-racial society, and then moved to a more multi-racial society. This has numerous benefits for the families' perceptions and acceptance of others' differences. Finally, starting over fresh can be a great way to clear your life of a negative past. Maybe the former town's people were not very friendly because of one mistake you had made many years before. Moving to a new place will completely obliterate this haunted past of yours.

Next, I will explain in more detail some disadvantages of moving to a new town, city or country. Moving puts a major financial burden on the family. The process requires a large number of packing supplies, realtor fees, and vehicle rental fees. Probably the most influential factor of moving for the children is the loss of their longtime childhood friends. Losing a friend to a move can have a major impact on a child's social skills, but it can be easily overcome if done in the proper manner. By making it a positive thing, the students will gain new friends while keeping the old ones too. To conclude with the negatives, being lost or out of place in a new environment can add some unnecessary stress on the family. This holds to be especially true in a new country or even state where having to adapt to a new environment can be difficult due to a language barrier.

In my opinion, I wouldn't mind moving to a new place because I have already done so a copious amount of times. Moving brought an excitement to my life, because my parents put a positive spin onto it, as I previously mentioned. Also, I was able to sort through my old clothes and toys and donate those things that I didn't need to the shelters in my current town. On the other hand, it was a great feeling to do this type of thing every time I moved. It was a little bit scary for me because I would have to start all over again, make new friends, and be the new kid in school, again. However, I didn't mind being the new kid that much because I could learn from my mistakes I made in the last school, and not make them again in this school, such as telling them that I sucked my thumb until 3rd grade.

Since it can bring about both ups and downs, moving to a new home in another place can be both exciting and terrifying at the same time. Being challenged financially and being in a new environment can be quite intimidating. On the other hand, being in a new surrounding can bring about a new perception on different people. I've had the opportunity to move many times, and despite the negatives, I would move again in a heartbeat!

C. Useful Expressions

1. Or maybe, we lost money and can afford to live in a new place.

_____

2. We came into more money and can live in a more luxurious house.

_____

3. This can often be a good thing because there is no such thing as having too many friends.

_____

4. Maybe they lived in a single-racial society, and then moved to a more multi-racial society.

_____

_____

5. Finally, starting over fresh can be a great way to clear your life of a negative past.

_____

6. Moving puts a major financial burden on the family.

_____

7. Losing a friend to a move can have a major impact on a child's social skills,

_____

_____

8. This holds true in a new country or even state where having to adapt to a new environment can be difficult due to a language barrier.

_____

_____

9. In my opinion, I wouldn't mind moving to a new place because I have already done so a copious amount of times.

_____

_____

10. Since it can bring about both ups and downs, moving to a new home in another place can be both exciting and terrifying at the same time.

_____

_____

Q162. You found $20 under your desk at school. What would you do, tell the teacher or keep it?

A. Essay Outline

Argument: I would keep the $20 I found.
Support 1: Someone may have meant to leave it for me.
Support 2: I am poor, but the person who would leave money on the floor must be rich.
Support 3: I can spend the money on important things, like food.
Thesis: Because I could really use the money, I would keep the $20.

B. Model Essay

If I found $20 under my desk at school, I would be more inclined to keep the money. While this may seem wrong, I have a few good reasons why I would keep the money. First, it's possible that someone may have meant to give me the money. Second, the person who dropped the money on the ground clearly does not care enough about the money; if he did, he would not have lost it in the first place. Third, I could spend the money on important things, while the student who lost his money would probably spend it on things he didn't need. For these reasons, I would keep the money.

It is definitely possible that someone may have left me money on purpose. Although I am poor, I am also popular and sometimes lend money to other people. This may have been an attempt to repay me for lunch. Because my desk is locked, this student may not have been able to put the money in my desk and put it on top instead. Then, the wind might have blown and put the money under my desk. This is a definite possibility, and if this were the case, there would be no need to tell a teacher.

Second, if a person actually did lose the money, he was probably rich. Because my family does not make a lot of money, we are fairly poor. While $20 means a lot to me, this person was reckless with his money and lost it. In all likelihood, he probably does not care about the $20; his allowance might be a lot more, maybe $50 or $200. In that case, he could definitely spare $20. Therefore, it would be better to hold on to the money and wait; if someone really cared about the $20, he would ask around and then I would give the money back. That way, I would definitely get the money instead of the teacher.

Lastly, because I am poor, I could really use the money. While some other students might spend the money on less important things like a smart phone or going to the movie theatres, I would spend the money on something really important: food. Sometimes, my family does not have enough money, and so my brother and I go to bed hungry. With this money, we would not have to go bed hungry for at least a week, maybe more.

Because of these reasons, I would keep the money rather than tell the teacher. I know that I would use the money better than other students and the main reason I would keep it is out of necessity. The money would be best spent by me.

C. Useful Expressions

1. I would be more inclined to keep the money.

2. It is possible that someone may have left me money on purpose.

_____

3. If this were the case, there would be no need to tell a teacher.

_____

4. While $20 means a lot to me, this person was reckless with his money and lost it.

_____

5. In all likelihood, he probably does not care about the $20.

_____

6. In that case, he could definitely spare $20.

_____

7. Therefore, it would be better to hold on to the money and wait.

_____

8. Lastly, because I am poor, I could really use the money.

_____

9. My brother and I go to bed hungry.

_____

10. The main reason I would keep the money is out of necessity.

_____

Q163. What is your preferred place to visit on weekends?

A. Essay Outline

Argument: My preferred place to visit on the weekends is the spa.
Support 1: Visiting a spa helps me to relax and reduce stress.
Support 2: I can have fun at the spa with my friends.
Support 3: I look and smell great after visiting the spa for a couple of hours.
Thesis: Because visiting a spa makes for a wonderful trip, it is my preferred place to visit on the weekends.

B. Model Essay

Many people like to visit different big cities on the weekend. For them, a new place can be an exciting change of pace from the average day. However, I like to visit the spa on weekends because it helps me to relax and reduce stress, I can have fun there with my friends, and because I look and smell great at the end.

One of the most relaxing things I can think to do is go to a spa. While many people think that spas are just people sitting in tubs of warm water, there are a lot of other things you can do at a spa, like getting a soft facial. My favorite thing to do at a spa is to get a massage. I always get a full-body massage when I go to a spa, and my muscles and joints feel more limber after I'm done. Plus, soothing, classical music is played, which always makes me feel at peace. Just walking into a spa, I can feel the entire daily stress go away, if only for an afternoon.

Another reason that I got to the spa is that I can go with my friends and we can share a great time together, even if we don't talk to each other. Although there are other quiet activities I can do with my friends, these tend to be things that are difficult to enjoy with other people. Take, for example, going to the library. If I go to the library with others, we usually cannot share what we're reading with each other because the library forbids any talking. At a spa, we can get massages at the same time or swim in the pool together. It makes for a great weekend with my friends.

Last, I always end up looking, smelling, and feeling great after going to a spa. There are always fresh flowers and lavender soap throughout the building. Facials help clear my pores and I also love to get pedicures or manicures, which make my nails look great and the perfect shade of pink. The best part is when a staff member removes all of the dead skin cells on my body. My skin feels so much softer as a result.

In conclusion, visiting a spa makes for a wonderful trip. Not only do you end up relaxing, but it can be a great way to get closer to your friends, not to mention you end up looking and feeling great at the end. That is why going to the spa is my favorite place to visit on weekends.

C. Useful Expressions

1. For them, a new place can be an exciting change of pace from the average day.

2. It helps me to relax and reduce stress.

3. One of the most relaxing things I can think to do is go to a spa.

4. Just walking into a spa, I can feel all of the stresses of daily life go away, if only for an afternoon.

5. Another reason that I got to the spa is that I can go with my friends and we can share a great time together, even if we don't talk to each other.

6. Take, for example, going to the library.

7. It makes for a great weekend with my friends.

8. Facials help clear my pores and I also love to get pedicures or manicures.

9. Not only do you end up relaxing, but also it can be a great way to get closer to your friends.

10. It can be a great way to get closer to your friends, not to mention you end up looking and feeling great at the end.

Q164. Explain in detail your happiest childhood memory and provide reasons as to why it is your happiest.

A. Essay Outline

Argument: My happiest childhood memory was when my mom took me to the amusement park.

Support 1: I got to go on many rides, including the merry-go-around.

Support 2: I got to eat a lot of junk food that day.

Support 3: It was a special time between just me and my mom.

Thesis: Because it was a very special day, my happiest childhood memory was the day my mom took me to the amusement park.

B. Model Essay

I have many childhood memories ranging from the dull and unexciting to sad and depressing to the downright humiliating. However, my happiest memory from when I was a kid was the day my mom took me to the amusement park. On that day, I got to go on many rides, eat as much junk food as I wanted, and spend all day with my mom.

First of all, on that day, I got to go on many different rides. The one I remember most is the merry-go-around. It had many different animals that you could ride on. I got to ride on a big unicorn. It went up and down as the merry-go-around spun and played music. It was definitely my favorite. Another ride that I remember vividly is the bumper cars. My mom and I were in one car. I was still too small to drive, so she drove us all around the arena. We bumped into at least ten other cars! I don't think she liked it very much, but we still had fun together.

I also remember eating a lot of junk food that day. My father was very strict about food; he did not let me have junk food at all and always made me eat my vegetables. My mother was more relaxed, so when he was away, I could eat things like candy, cake, and popcorn. When I went to the amusement park with my mother that day, I got to eat whatever I wanted. I got to eat this thing called cotton candy, which is nothing more than spun sugar dyed blue or pink. I also remember eating a hot dog and drinking some of my mom's soda. It was a definite departure from the usual salad I ate at home.

Last, the day I spent with my mom at the amusement park was special because it was a day I got to spend with my mom. Although I am close with my dad, I am a lot closer with my mom, so I was glad I got to spend time with her alone, just the two of us. We got to talk about a lot of things: school, my love of horses, and maybe getting a new bicycle. My mother is a very kind woman and that it why that day was the happiest day I can remember from my childhood.

In summary, the day I spent with my mom at the amusement park was probably the best day I've ever had. I got to do so many special things compared to my otherwise mundane life. I hope that one day when I have a child, my kid can share a special day with me.

C. Useful Expressions

1. On that day, I got to go on many rides.

2. The one I remember most is the merry-go-around.

_____

3. Another ride that I remember vividly is the bumper cars.

_____

4. I don't think she liked it very much, but we still had fun together.

_____

5. When I went to the amusement park with my mother that day, I got to eat whatever I wanted.

_____

6. I got to eat this thing called cotton candy, which is nothing more than spun sugar dyed blue or pink.

_____

7. It was a definite departure from the usual salad I ate at home.

_____

_____

8. I was glad I got to spend time with her alone, just the two of us.

_____

9. My mother is a very kind woman and that is why that day was the happiest day I can remember from my childhood.

_____

_____

10. I got to do so many special things compared to my otherwise mundane life.

_____

Q165. What is your most valued possession non-reflective of monetary value, but of sentimental value?

A. Essay Outline

Argument: My couples' ring is my most valued possession of sentimental value.
Support 1: My boyfriend sacrificed a lot to get me this ring.
Support 2: The ring signifies the bond we have made together.
Support 3: Every time I look at the ring, it reminds me of my boyfriend.
Thesis: Because my ring means a lot to me and my boyfriend, it is my most valued possession of sentimental value.

B. Model Essay

I have many things that mean a lot to me because they are worth a lot of money. I have a smart phone, nice clothes, and even a pricy, brand new computer. However, my most cherished possession is the ring my boyfriend gave to me, not because it was expensive, but because it represents the union my boyfriend and I have made together.

First of all, my boyfriend sacrificed a lot to get me the ring I'm wearing now. When we decided to get the rings, my boyfriend was not making a lot of money. He was still a student and couldn't afford a lot of lavish presents. He saved up a lot of his money from his part-time job as a busboy to pay for our couple's rings. I was so surprised when he got them because I could not believe he could afford them. It was so nice for him to have done that for me.

Second, the rings we were signify the bonds we have made together. My boyfriend and I have been together for three years now. Though we have our differences, we have decided that we care for one another deeply. Even after we have an argument, we still tell each other, "I love you." Because we are willing to make our relationship work despite some difficulties, I know that our bond is strong. That is why I love the ring he gave me: even when we may not be enjoying the other's company, I can look down and remember that it's worth it.

Last, every time I look at my ring, it reminds me of my boyfriend. Recently, my boyfriend moved to America for his new job. Although I will be moving to America in just a couple of months, the separation is stressful and many times I miss my boyfriend. That is when I remember to look down at my ring; I always know that my boyfriend is there in spirit, even though he may not be there physically. I know somewhere out there he is wearing the same ring as me. My ring helps me get through the difficult times without my boyfriend.

Because my couples ring shows off the special union I've made with my boyfriend, it is the most special thing that I own. My ring helps me get through the difficult portions of our relationship. I hope our relationship will last for as long as our rings do: a lifetime.

C. Useful Expressions

1. However, my most cherished possession is the ring my boyfriend gave to me.

2. My most cherished possession is the ring my boyfriend gave to me not because it was expensive, but because it represents us.

3. It represents the union my boyfriend and I have made together.

4. First of all, my boyfriend sacrificed a lot to get me the ring I'm wearing now.

5. He was still a student and couldn't afford a lot of lavish presents.

6. It was so nice for him to have done that for me.

7. Though we have our differences, we have decided that we care for one another deeply.

8. I always know that my boyfriend is there in spirit.

9. I know somewhere out there he is wearing the same ring as me.

10. My ring helps me get through the difficult times without my boyfriend.

Q166. Talk about a teacher who has inspired you. Explain why this person is an inspiration.

A. Essay Outline

Argument: Mr. Lee influenced me positively.
Support 1: He encouraged me to behave both in and outside of class.
Support 2: He helped improve my writing tremendously.
Support 3: He helped shape my career goals.
Thesis: Because Mr. Lee helped shape who I am today, he is the most inspirational person in my life.

B. Model Essay

There are many teachers who have influenced me in my life, all making me a better person today than I was then. However, none of them can compare to Mr. Lee, my eleventh grade English teacher. Mr. Lee encouraged me to behave in class, improved my writing enormously, and inspired me to become a writer. For these reasons, Mr. Lee is the most influential teacher I've had.

First of all, Mr. Lee taught me to be more respectful towards others. When I was younger, I would often disrupt class. I talked while the teacher was talking, teased and made fun of other students, and sometimes I would take other kids' school supplies. Although this wasn't very nice of me, the other teachers said nothing. Mr. Lee seemed to barely notice at first. Then one day, he told me to come into class early. He told me that he noticed me being mean to other students since the beginning of the year and also told me, in a very kind way, to be nicer to other students. From that point on, I acted on my best behavior and received a citizenship award at the end of the year. Mr. Lee helped me achieve this, and I am very happy he had that conversation with me.

Additionally, Mr. Lee is a great writing teacher. When I first started school, my writing was not very good. I often made grammatical mistakes and I would write in a very informal style for formal essays. However, by the end of the year, I was able to write much better and even got an A on my final, 15-page paper. Mr. Lee was so dedicated to me and I owe him so much for having spent as much time as he did working on my writing.

Last, but not least, Mr. Lee made me want to become a fiction writer. Before I took his class, I was not sure what I was going to do with my life. Although I knew that I wanted to do something intelligent, I wasn't sure what that was going to be, but after I taking Mr. Lee's class, I was certain that I wanted to write novels for a living. Mr. Lee inspired me every day and I loved the books that he chose for class, from Madame Bovary to The Stranger. I know that I now have the skills to become someone great and it is all thanks to Mr. Lee.

It is for the above reasons that I owe a tremendous debt to Mr. Lee. He has inspired and influenced me so much and made me into someone great. I hope that one day I will leave a positive mark on someone younger too.

C. Useful Expressions

1. There are many teachers who have influenced me in my life, all making me a better person today than I was then.

2. However, none of them can compare to Mr. Lee, my eleventh grade English teacher.

3. First of all, Mr. Lee taught me to be more respectful towards others.

4. Although this wasn't very nice of me, the other teachers said nothing.

5. He told me that he noticed me being mean to other students since the beginning of the year.

6. From that point on, I acted on my best behavior.

7. Mr. Lee was so dedicated to me and I owe him so much for having spent as much time as he did working on my writing.

8. Before I took his class, I was not sure what I was going to do with my life.

9. I know that I now have the skills to become someone great.

10. It is for the above reasons that I owe a tremendous debt to Mr. Lee.

Q167. What is your favorite location or establishment to eat at?

A. Essay Outline

Argument: Of all the dining establishments in the United States, my favorite place to eat is my grandparents' house.

Support 1: My grandmother has over 60 years of cooking experience.

Support 2: The atmosphere at my grandparents' home is much nicer than that of any restaurant.

Support 3: At my grandparents' home, I know how clean the cooking environment is.

Thesis: Because eating at my grandparents' home is always a delicious and worry-free experience, I prefer to dine there more than anywhere else.

B. Model Essay

My hometown is known for its vast array of restaurants. People from neighboring cities, travel to my town to eat at one of our delicious restaurants. However, my favorite location to eat isn't any of those restaurants; it's my grandparents' house. I love to dine with my grandparents because my grandmother is an amazing cook. Furthermore, the atmosphere is much more homey and relaxed than one can find at any other restaurant. Finally, at my grandmother's house, I can participate in the preparation of the meals. There's no better place to eat anywhere in the USA than at my grandparents' home.

The most obvious reason I prefer to eat at my grandparents' home is because my grandma has about 60 years of cooking experience. She is a true Southern chef. She uses recipes that have been passed down for generations and has perfected each of them. Eating her meals is always a treat because she likes using lots butter and sugar in her meals. With everyone being so health conscious these days, it's difficult to find a truly unhealthy, yet well-made, dish. My favorite meal that she makes consists of macaroni and cheese, mashed potatoes, and pork chops with chocolate cake for dessert. Just thinking about my grandmother's cooking makes my stomach grumble.

Another reason I like to dine at my grandparents' house is because the atmosphere is so pleasant. Most restaurants I eat at are cold inside. If I forget to bring a sweater with me, then I spend my meal freezing. My grandfather gets cold very easily and my grandmother gets hot easily, so their house is always kept at a pleasantly moderate temperature. Also, my grandmother has incredibly comfortable cushions on the chairs in her dining room. A lot of restaurants have uncomfortable seats, which detracts from the overall dining experience. Furthermore, there's not a bunch of noise, like loud music or people, to distract me from conversing with my family over the meal while dining at my grandparents' home. It's easy to have a conversation without needing to resort to yelling in order to be heard. So, at my grandmother's house, I am very comfortable and I can easily engage in conversation with my friends and family.

The final reason I prefer to eat at my grandparent's house is because my grandmother lets me help prepare the meals. My least favorite part about eating out is waiting for the meal to arrive. When I eat at my grandmother's house, time passes quickly because I am allowed to help her in the kitchen. It's enjoyable to see how the food gets made and know that it comes from a clean kitchen. It's hard to tell how clean the kitchens in restaurants are. My grandmother, on the other hand, always keeps her kitchen spotless, so I don't have to worry about contracting any illnesses while eating at her house.

To sum up, my grandparents' home is my favorite location to eat at. My grandmother's cooking is so delicious that I'm certain she could become a world renown chef if she wanted to. Furthermore, the atmosphere there is warm, quiet, and relaxing. Finally, eating at my grandparents' home eliminates the unpleasant experience of wondering when your food will come out and how clean the location it came out of truly is. The dining experience at my grandparents' home cannot be beat, which is why I would choose to eat there rather than go to any other restaurant in the USA.

C. Useful Expressions

1. My hometown is known for its vast array of restaurants.

_____

2. Furthermore, the atmosphere is much more homey and relaxed than one can find at any other restaurant.

_____

3. There's no better place to eat in the USA than at my grandparents' home.

_____

4. With everyone being so health conscious these days, it's difficult.

_____

5. It's difficult to find a truly unhealthy, yet well-made, dish.

_____

6. Just thinking about my grandmother's cooking makes my stomach grumble.

_____

7. A lot of restaurants have uncomfortable seats, which detract from the overall dining experience.

_____

8. When I eat at my grandmother's house, time passes quickly.

_____

9. My grandmother, on the other hand, always keeps her kitchen spotless.

_____

Q168. Where in your town is a good place to have fun?

A. Essay Outline

Argument: The best place in my town to have fun is the lake.
Support 1: The most obvious reason is that it is the most convenient place to meet my friends.
Support 2: There are lots of activities to partake in down by the lake.
Support 3: In case of bad weather or hunger, there are several restaurants and cafes to go to.
Thesis: The lake is the perfect location to have fun in due to its convenience.

B. Model Essay

Every town has a special place where everyone goes to hang out. Because my hometown is quite big, there are many different popular locations where kids go have fun. However, my favorite location to spend time with my friends is down by the lake. The lake I live by is right next to my high school, so it's the easiest location for all of my friends to get to. Another reason I like hanging out by the lake is because there are many activities to do there. Finally, there are a lot of restaurants and coffee shops close to the lake, so if we get hungry, there's always a place close by to grab food.

The first reason I like hanging out down by the lake is because it's a really convenient place to meet my friends. Our high school is about a ten minute walk away from the lake. My high school soccer team practices at our high school. After practice, my teammates and I like to walk down to the lake and work on our homework together or talk about how our day at school was. There are always friends from my high school there, so whenever I get bored, I like to walk down by the lake. I almost always find someone to chat with.

Another reason the lake is such a great place to have fun is because there is so much to do there! During the summer, the lake is a great place to take a refreshing swim. Also, there are a lot of volleyball nets on the beach, so it's easy to find some kind of volleyball match taking place. My cross country coach even likes to hold practices down by the lake. Running in the sand is very difficult, but very good for developing endurance, so it's a great location to practice. The lake is even a wonderful place to hang out in the winter time! The area by the lake is much warmer than any other place during the winter, so it's a good outdoor location to spend time at. Although we don't go swimming in the winter, there are still other activities, like the playing on the playground or simply skipping rocks on the water.

Finally, I really like the lake because there are a lot of coffee shops and restaurants close by. Because my friends and I are always exerting a lot of energy at the lake, whether it be from physical activity or a really intense study session, it's great to have a location close by where we can grab food or coffee to replenish our energy. Most of the restaurants offer take-out, so we can have picnics by the lake. Also, the weather in my hometown is always changing. One minute it's sunny, and the next there's a thunderstorm, especially during the summer. With the shelter of restaurants and coffee shops close by, the weather isn't much of a concern when we make plans to hang out at the lake.

In conclusion, I think the lake is by far the best place to have fun in my town. The lake is in such a great location! Since it's close to the high school, it's easy to find people hanging out there. Also, the lake offers a plethora of fun and healthy activities. It's great to spend time out in the fresh air rather than being cooped up indoors. Last but not least, with so many restaurants and coffee shops nearby, it's easy to quickly grab some food and continue on with our activities. Though my town has many exciting places, I think the best place for my friends and I to have fun is down by the lake.

C. Useful Expressions

1. However, my favorite location to spend time with my friends is down by the lake.

_____

2. If we get hungry, there's always a place close by to grab food.

_____

3. It's a really convenient place to meet my friends.

_____

4. Whenever I get bored, I like to walk down by the lake.

_____

5. I almost always find someone to chat with.

_____

6. During the summer, the lake is a great place to take a refreshing swim.

_____

7. Running in the sand is very difficult, but very good for developing endurance.

_____

8. There are still other activities, like the playing on the playground or simply skipping rocks on the water.

_____

9. My friends and I are always exerting a lot of energy at the lake.

_____

10. One minute it's sunny, and the next there's a thunderstorm, especially during the summer.

_____

Q169. Talk about an embarrassing experience in your life and describe why it was embarrassing.

A. Essay Outline

Argument: My most embarrassing moment was definitely when I made a fool of myself on television.
Support 1: The experience entailed a tumble down the stairs in a crowded department store.
Support 2: The whole scene was captured on tape.
Support 3: I hurt both my body and my pride at the same time.
Thesis: Because of the vast amount of pain and embarrassment that came along with falling down the stairs, that was my most embarrassing experience to date.

B. Model Essay

Although embarrassing moments are fun to look back on and laugh about, they are mortifying to experience. I like to forget about my embarrassing moments. Unfortunately, there is one that I cannot forget. My most embarrassing moment was when I feel down the stairs at a crowded mall and knocked over the mannequin at the bottom of the stairs. This moment is so embarrassing to me for two reasons. The first is that it was captured on tape. The second reason it was so mortifying was because I ending up hurting myself quite badly. I will never be able to forget this embarrassing moment.

To begin with, I should explain how I ended up tumbling down a flight of stairs and making a fool of myself. The story begins on the day after Thanksgiving, popularly known as "Black Friday." On this day, many of the stores have huge sales to kick off the Christmas season. Despite the crowds of people, it is the best to find amazing Christmas presents for equally amazing prices. It was early in the morning when my mom and I headed to the department store. The shoelaces on one of my shoes had become untied. However, as I was in a crowd of people, I didn't want to stop to bend over to retie it. When I got to the staircase, I ended up stepping on the untied shoelace and falling down the stairs. To make matters worse, there was a mannequin at the bottom of the stairs that I collided with. I can still feel the pain of smacking into the mannequin.

While the actual tumble down the stairs was embarrassing enough, it also happened to get captured on tape. A local news crew was at the store that day, filming all of the Black Friday madness. My fall down the stairs was captured by the camera man, though I didn't know it at the time. Later that night, as I was watching the evening news with my parents, I was excited to see that the crew had been filming at the same department store that I had been at with my mom. I intently watched the segment to try to catch a glimpse of my mom or me. That's when I saw it—a girl in a red jacket colliding with a mannequin. Although it was in the background, it was definitely noticeable. To my horror, later that night I received phone calls from three of my friends, asking me if that had in fact been me on the tape. My friends still make fun of me to this day about the incident.

The accident was made additionally mortifying due to the fact that I hurt more than my pride when I fell down the stairs. I somehow twisted my ankle. Also, when I hit the mannequin, her heavily adorned arm fell right onto my face, giving me a nice black eye. I even started crying, though it was more from embarrassment than it was from actual pain. Some employees at the store took pity on me and gave me a coupon for 50% off at a local ice cream shop in the mall even though I had destroyed their mannequin, so at least something good came from the tears. Furthermore, fortunately for me, because we received a few days off to celebrate Thanksgiving, my black eye had pretty much faded by the time school started up again. It was still embarrassing explaining to people how I hurt my ankle, though.

In conclusion, I think it is safe to say that I will never be able to forget my most embarrassing moment. Every time the holiday season rolls around, I remember that fateful day when I broke a mannequin and my pride. I can close my eyes and see the horrific scene unfold as if it had happened yesterday. The situation wouldn't have been as bad had it not been caught on film and if I had not hurt myself so badly in the process of falling down the stairs. Still, from every bad moment comes a valuable lesson. To this day, you will never catch me with my shoelaces untied.

C. Useful Expressions

1. Embarrassing moments are fun to look back on.

_____

2. The first is that it was captured on tape.

_____

3. To begin with, I should explain how I ended up tumbling down a flight of stairs.

_____

4. I ended up making a fool of myself.

_____

5. Despite the crowds of people, it is the best way to find amazing Christmas presents for equally amazing prices.

_____

_____

6. However, as I was in a crowd of people, I didn't want to stop to bend over to retie it.

_____

7. I can still feel the pain of smacking into the mannequin.

_____

8. I intently watched the segment to try to catch a glimpse of my mom or me.

_____

9. My friends still make fun of me to this day about the incident.

_____

10. In conclusion, I think it is safe to say that I will never be able to forget my most embarrassing moment.

_____

Q170. What is your favorite subject in school?

A. Essay Outline

Argument: Of all the subjects in school, Spanish was my absolute favorite.
Support 1: My first Spanish teacher sparked my interest in the language due to his excellent teaching.
Support 2: I was pretty good at Spanish, which made me like it even more.
Support 3: Spanish is an extremely useful language to know in the United States.
Thesis: Spanish was and still remains my favorite subject because it has benefited me more than any other subject.

B. Model Essay

Although school may sometimes seem very boring, every student inevitably has one subject that makes him look forward to going to school. For me, that subject was Spanish. One reason that I really enjoyed my Spanish classes so much was because the first Spanish teacher I ever had made the language so exciting. Another reason was because I excelled in all of my Spanish courses. The last reason why I thoroughly enjoyed Spanish was because it was easy to see the relevance of learning the language. Spanish was a subject for which I developed a passion due to those three reasons.

I first fell in love with the Spanish language when I took my very first Spanish class in middle school. All students were required to take a semester of Spanish and a semester of French in order to better decide which language to study in high school. My Spanish teacher was a jolly old Mexican man, Mr. Garcia, who was obviously excited to teach us about his native language. I've never had more fun learning about basic grammar than I did with Mr. Garcia. He also taught us about the customs and traditions from his hometown in Mexico and brought in delicious homemade food that his wife had prepared for us. He introduced us to popular Latin music as well as exquisite films by Latin directors. To put it simply, he made the Hispanic culture seem absolutely fascinating. I was enamored with the subject by the time my first semester of Spanish class ended. Mr. Garcia is the reason that I decided to continue on with my studies of the Spanish language.

Though my love for Spanish was ignited by Mr. Garcia's class, it was further fueled by the fact that I was quite good at Spanish. I always studied hard in school in order to maintain a high GPA and learn as much as possible, but Spanish was one of those few subjects that just came naturally to me. The grammar rules seemed quite simple and actually made sense, which isn't always the case with the English language. In my high school, I received many awards for excellence in my Spanish classes. However, the most rewarding moment of my Spanish career was when I was a junior in high school. My brother was a senior that year, but we ended up in the Spanish class. My brother seemed to excel in every subject, so I was extremely proud of myself when I finished the school year with a grade in Spanish that was ten points higher than his! My love for Spanish grew a little stronger that year.

Lastly, the main reason I enjoyed Spanish class so much was because it was very easy to see the importance of learning the language. The United States of America, where I'm from, is becoming increasingly more dominated by the Spanish language due to the influx of immigration from Hispanic countries. Most of the signs in stores are in two languages, English and Spanish. Every time I walk into a grocery or clothing store, I saw Spanish. Furthermore, I worked at a restaurant while in high school in order to save money for college. Most of the cooks that worked in the kitchen were Hispanic. By studying Spanish hard, I was able to eavesdrop on their conversations as well as practice my Spanish with them.

They were always thrilled to help me learn new words or improve my pronunciation. Because I was surrounded by Spanish most of the time, studying Spanish was instantly gratifying.

To sum up, Spanish was undoubtedly my favorite subject in school. Mr. Garcia sparked my interest in Spanish many years ago through his highly entertaining and informative Spanish class. That interest was only made more intense due to the fact that I was able to get excellent grades in my Spanish classes without much effort, which was a nice boost to my ego. Last but not least, the benefits of learning Spanish were so obvious that it actually seemed detrimental to not take full advantage of learning the language while in class. I would advise anyone to take a class or two in Spanish. It is such a beautiful language that will offer a myriad of benefits from anyone who takes the time to learn it.

C. Useful Expressions

1. Every student inevitably has one subject that makes him look forward to going to school.

_____

2. One reason that I really enjoyed my Spanish classes so much was because the first Spanish teacher I ever had made the language so exciting.

_____

3. I've never had more fun learning about basic grammar than I did with Mr. Garcia.

_____

4. He also taught us about the customs and traditions from his hometown in Mexico.

_____

5. To put it simply, he made the Hispanic culture seem absolutely fascinating.

_____

6. However, the most rewarding moment of my Spanish career was when I was a junior in high school.

_____

7. I was extremely proud of myself when I finished the school year with a grade in Spanish that was ten points higher than his!

_____

8. The United States of America, where I'm from, is becoming increasingly more dominated by the Spanish language due to the influx of immigration from Hispanic countries.

_____

9. That interest was only made more intense due to the fact that I was able to get excellent grades in my Spanish classes.

_____

10. Last but not least, the benefits of learning Spanish were so obvious that it actually seemed detrimental to not take full advantage of learning the language.

_____

Q171. Discuss an interesting tourist attraction that you have visited.

A. Essay Outline

Argument: The Great Barrier Reef was probably the most interesting tourist attraction I have ever visited.
Support 1: I got to experience the Great Barrier Reef with a group of my closest friends.
Support 2: The beauty of the Great Barrier Reef was exquisite.
Support 3: Thanks to global warming, the Great Barrier Reef won't be around much longer.
Thesis: Because I was able to experience the Reef with my friends and witness the beauty that won't be available much longer, the Great Barrier Reef was the most interesting tourist attraction that I have ever been to.

B. Model Essay

Throughout my life, I have been given many amazing traveling experiences for which I am very grateful. I have seen things like the Great Wall of China, the Statue of Liberty, and the Eiffel Tower. However, of all the interesting tourist attractions I have visited, I would have to say that the Great Barrier Reef tops them all. One of the reasons the experience was so amazing was because I got to experience it with a group of my best friends. Another reason it was so interesting was because the Great Barrier Reef is one of the prettiest sights I have ever seen in my entire life. Lastly, I am very fortunate to have gotten the chance to see it before it eventually is destroyed by global warming. For all of these reasons, the Great Barrier Reef is one tourist attraction that I will never forget.

First of all, I got the opportunity to visit the Great Barrier Reef while I was studying abroad in Australia. My junior year of college, I studied in Sydney, Australia. While there, I met three of the best friends I have ever had. During one of our university's breaks, my friends and I took a trip to Brisbane in Queensland. While there, we saw an advertisement for a scuba diving expedition in the Great Barrier Reef. I wasn't very adventurous, but all three of my friends were and they dragged me along. I'm so glad they made me come with! I was a little nervous about being completely submerged underwater with only a tank of oxygen between me and death. However, my friends kept me relaxed and made me laugh through the whole experience. We made sure to take a lot of pictures to document the event. I still have several hanging in my room at home.

Furthermore, the Great Barrier Reef was stunningly beautiful. Once I got over the novelty of breathing through a tube, I paid more attention to my surroundings. The reef contained shades of colors that I didn't even know existed. There were several brightly colored flowers and plants growing on the reef. I saw schools of fish flitting through the water, attempting to avoid the gaggle of humans that was invading their territory. I even saw a tortoise that looked like the one in "Finding Nemo!" The scenery was exquisite. No photograph of the reef will ever quite do its beauty justice. I consider myself lucky to have seen this breathtaking sight with my own eyes.

Lastly, I am happy that I had to a chance to the Great Barrier Reef before global warming takes its toll on the site. The burning of fossil fuels is heating up our planet. This increase in temperature is killing the oceanic organisms that provide the reef with its source of food. This is killing the reef and dulling its beautiful colors. Experts predict that if global warming continues to carry on at the same rate, the Great Barrier Reef could be gone within the next 100 years! For this reason, I am very happy I will be one of the lucky few who got to see the reef in all of its glory. It's very sad that someday the site will be gone!

To conclude, though I have seen many wonderful attractions, the Great Barrier Reef will remain my favorite tourist attraction. First of all, the Great Barrier Reef reminds me of all the memories I created with my best friends while on our crazy scuba diving excursion. Additionally, the beauty of the Great Barrier Reef will always remain unparalleled and I am lucky I got to see such exquisite beauty. Finally, the Great Barrier Reef is an endangered site due to global warming, so I'm glad I got to see it before much of its destruction set in. I would highly recommend to everyone that they see the Great Barrier Reef if they ever have the opportunity to. It's an adventure one will not easily forget!

C. Useful Expressions

1. However, of all the interesting tourist attractions I have visited, I would have to say that the Great Barrier Reef tops them all.

_____

2. While there, we saw an advertisement for a scuba diving expedition in the Great Barrier Reef.

_____

3. I wasn't very adventurous, but all three of my friends were and they dragged me along.

_____

4. We made sure to take a lot of pictures to document the event.

_____

5. Once I got over the novelty of breathing through a tube, I paid more attention to my surroundings.

_____

6. No photograph of the reef will ever quite do its beauty justice.

_____

7. I consider myself lucky to have seen this breathtaking sight with my own eyes.

_____

8. Experts predict that if global warming continues to carry on at the same rate, the Great Barrier Reef could be gone within the next 100 years!

_____

9. The Great Barrier Reef will remain my favorite tourist attraction.

_____

10. First of all, the Great Barrier Reef reminds me of all the memories I created with my best friends while on our crazy scuba diving excursion.

_____

Q172. Discuss a time in your life when you felt successful due to a goal or obstacle being overcome.

A. Essay Outline

Argument: I felt most successful when I raised my calculus grade from a D to a B+.
Support 1: I worked very hard to create and stick to a study plan.
Support 2: I made a conscious effort to ask for help more often.
Support 3: Though it was difficult, I tried to change my point of view of math.
Thesis: Because I made several changes to my routine and stuck to it, I felt most successful when I raised my calculus grade.

B. Model Essay

If there's one thing in life I truly disliked, it was math. I had always struggled in every math class I took. It was the bane of my academic career. Though I hated the subject so much, I was normally able to manage to get a decent grade my math classes. However, my senior year of high school, that was not the case. By the end of my first quarter of AP Calculus, I had a D! At that point, I knew I had to make some changes in studying strategy to pull off at least a B by the end of the year. In order to accomplish this goal, I set up a strict study plan for myself. Additionally, I made a stronger effort to ask others for help when I didn't understand a concept. Finally, I tried to mend my broken relationship with the subject of math. Through these three steps, I was successful in raising my grade as well as my self-confidence.

To start with, I decided make a study plan. I mapped out what I planned to study every night, created flash cards to help me memorize formulas, and found YouTube videos that would act as my tutor since I could not afford one. My schedule proved to be quite difficult for me to follow, because, as a high school student, I was very busy. I had school all day, soccer practice at night, and soccer games or work on the weekends, not to mention my regular homework assignments and tests. Due to my busy schedule, I had to make a lot of sacrifices to stick to my schedule. Though it was hard for me, I turned down many invitations to go to the movies, out to dinner, or over to my friends' houses to hang out. I actually surprised myself about how dedicated I had become to my goal.

In addition to making my own schedule, I decided to ask for help more often when I was struggling to understand something. I never really liked going to see my teachers to ask for help. Oftentimes, I was so confused in math class that I didn't even know what questions to ask! I also hated feeling stupid when my teacher asked me questions that I didn't know the answers to. However, my math grade was more important to me than my pride at that point. I started to wake up early in the mornings to go in before school for extra math help, as going after school was not an option for me. This actually benefited me in more ways than one. First of all, my homework and test grades slowly started to increase. More importantly, I was able to develop a good relationship with my math teacher. She saw that I was trying hard to improve my grade and went out of her way to help me succeed. I felt accomplished simply due to the fact that I created a better relationship with my math teacher.

The last step I took to help myself perform better in my calculus class was to take a different approach to the way I viewed math. As I stated earlier, I had always hated math. That hatred of math hampered my performance in the subject. Instead of viewing math as something I could successfully take on, I viewed it as an evil and incomprehensible subject. I decided to start viewing math more positively. Each problem became like a difficult, yet rewarding, game to me. It was fun pushing myself to see how many problems I could successfully solve. Furthermore, I started being less critical of myself when I failed. After all, I was in an AP Calculus class! It was supposed to be hard! I believe this new mindset was the key reason my math scores improved so much.

As a final point, I should mention that I did in fact raise my math grade! While I would like to say that I ended up with an A in my math class, I did in fact only get a B. However, I was extremely proud of myself for raising my grade so much in such a short amount of time. Through my study plan and strict dedication to it, I learned how to budget my time more efficiently and work for an end goal, not instant gratification. Furthermore, I got over my fear of asking for help and even managed to create a better relationship with my teacher. Lastly, I completely changed the way that I viewed difficult situations by making an effort to change the way I viewed math. To this day I still have my report card from my senior year in high school. I tape it up where I am studying to remind me what hard work, determination, and a little help from others can achieve.

C. Useful Expressions

1. I had always struggled in every math class I took.

_____

2. It was the bane of my academic career.

_____

3. In order to accomplish this goal, I set up a strict study plan for myself.

_____

4. My schedule proved to be quite difficult for me to follow.

_____

5. Though it was hard for me, I turned down many invitations to go to the movies, out to dinner, or over to my friends' houses to hang out.

_____

6. Oftentimes, I was so confused in math class that I didn't even know what questions to ask!

_____

7. The last step I took to help myself perform better in my calculus class was to take a different approach to the way I viewed math.

_____

8. That hatred of math hampered my performance in the subject.

_____

9. I believe this new mindset was the key reason my math scores improved so much.

_____

10. I tape it up where I am studying to remind me what hard work, determination, and a little help from others can achieve.

_____

> **Q173. When hiring a new employee, should the employer hire a person based on their knowledge or on their experience?**

A. Essay Outline

Argument: An employer should hire an employee based on personal relationships when able to do so.

Support 1: If you know someone personally, you will have a better idea of his ability to complete the work assigned to him.

Support 2: By hiring based on personal experience, you will know that you are hiring someone who will get along with your current employees.

Support 3: It can be tricky to hire a genuinely good person if you are not hiring based on personal relationships.

Thesis: Because of the adverse effects that could result from hiring someone based on his experience alone, I think it is best to hire an individual based on personal relationships.

B. Model Essay

Hiring new employees can be a risky undertaking. Employees are the face of a company, so it is important to hire only the best of the best. Nowadays, it is difficult to find someone who is intelligent, hardworking, and personable. So, I believe that it is better for an employer to hire someone based on his personal relationship with that individual rather than simply experience alone. By hiring based on personal relationships, one can ensure that he truly is hiring someone who is capable of handling the work, that he will be able to get along with that employee, and that the employee is honest. Thus, hiring based on personal relationships is the safest route to take when hiring new employees.

First, by hiring someone based on a personal relationship, you know that the employee will be capable of effectively completing the work assigned to him. For example, my uncle owns a paper distribution company. He likes to tell stories about some of his employees to me. He once told me a story once about a man he hired. While my uncle normally hires people that he has some kind of personal relationship with, one time he hired someone that had just moved into town. Although the man's resume indicated that he was more than qualified for the job, his actual performance proved that he was not. My uncle said that the man was easily confused by all of the technology in the office and broke the copier not once, but twice, before he finally learned how to make a copy. However, if you have a personal relationship with someone, you tend to know about his abilities. If you know the strengths and weaknesses of someone well before you hire him, you can save yourself the expense of hiring someone not suited for the job.

In continuation, if you hire someone that you know through some kind of personal relationship, you have a better idea of his personality, and if you and your current employees will be able to work with him. When I was a junior in college, I worked at a law office. We once got a new employee that was studying law at the local law school. He was extremely smart, but also extremely difficult to work with. To put it bluntly, he was a know-it-all. It was very difficult to have a conversation with him in which he wasn't trying to teach you something. He once tried to correct my boss, a prominent lawyer in the office, on a legal issue. Not only was the employee incorrect, but he also offended my boss. While it was great that he shared his opinions so freely with us, he did not go about it in a tactful way. Nobody in the office liked him very much and my boss politely asked him to resign after only two weeks. If my boss had hired someone he heard about through a personal relationship, he could have saved himself and the new employee from disappointment.

Finally, it is very tricky to hire someone who is always looking out for the best interests of the company. As the old saying goes, "Never judge a book by its cover." By hiring someone based on his experience alone, you are essentially judging a book by its cover. This can be especially damaging in a business situation. If you don't have a personal relationship with someone, you can never be truly sure of his true colors. Though he may seem pleasant and friendly to the customers, he could be a thief who steals office supplies. Furthermore, he may be the type that will try to sabotage others in order to further his own success within the company. If you have a personal relationship with someone, you know a lot more about him and can make a safer judgment on his true character.

To sum up, in the long run, I think it is better to hire individuals based on personal relationships rather than on experience alone. By hiring someone that you know, you can avoid hiring an employee who isn't prepared to handle all of the tasks that the job entails. Additionally, only through knowing someone well can you figure out if you and your employees will be able to get along with him at work. Most importantly, if you don't know a person well before hiring him, you might end up hiring someone who will try to advance himself at the expense of the company. While it is important to note that it is not always feasible to hire an employee based on a personal relationship, I think that it is best to do so when you are able to.

C. Useful Expressions

1. Hiring new employees can be a risky undertaking.

_____

2. It is important to hire only the best of the best.

_____

3. By hiring based on personal relationships, one can ensure that he truly is hiring someone who is capable of handling the work.

_____

_____

4. Although the man's resume indicated that he was more than qualified for the job, his actual performance proved that he was not.

_____

_____

5. To put it bluntly, he was a know-it-all.

_____

6. While it was great that he shared his opinions so freely with us, he did not go about it in a tactful way.

_____

7. Finally, it is very tricky to hire someone who is always looking out for the best interests of the company.

_____

8. By hiring someone based on his experience alone, you are essentially judging a book by its cover.

_____

9. It is important to note that it is not always feasible to hire an employee based on a personal relationship.

_____

Q174. There is such a thing as being too independent. Do you agree or disagree?

A. Essay Outline

Argument: I believe that too much independence can be detrimental to your well-being.

Support 1: If you are too independent, you will miss out on the experience of helping other people.

Support 2: You will be unable to achieve all of your goals without the help of others.

Support 3: In today's society, networking is of the utmost importance, so you cannot simply isolate yourself from others.

Thesis: Because being too independent can cause one to lose many important opportunities in life, I believe that there is such a thing as being too independent.

B. Model Essay

My country, the United States of America, has long been known for its individualism. Unlike many other countries, which focus on the nation as a whole, the United States is much more attuned to the needs of the individual. Though I am an American, I believe that there is such a thing as being too independent. First of all, being too independent can cause one to lose sight of what is truly important in life. Furthermore, being too independent might cause you harm when you do need help. Lastly, by isolating yourself from others, you will lose valuable social skills. So, while independence can be a good thing, too much will be detrimental to you and your well-being.

To begin with, by becoming super independent, you are hindering your ability to help out those in need. One of the most important things to ensure a good life is to help others whenever they need it. The United States learned an important lesson in helping others when it isolated itself from the world in the 1920s and 1930s. My country basically ignored the plight of the rest of the world while it focused on bettering itself. As a result, World War II almost ended unfavorably. When the war first broke out, the United States tried to stay out of it, although its friends, Great Britain and France, were suffering. Eventually, France fell under the control of Hitler and the Germans. Fortunately, the United States eventually stepped up to the plate and began to help out its friend, Britain. Had the United States not decided to help out Britain at the last minute, the British might have fallen to Hitler along with the French. Therefore, it can be dangerous if someone simply ignores the troubles of others in order to maintain his independence.

To continue, if you are too independent and do not seek out the help of others, it could end badly for you. There will come a time in everyone's life when they simply cannot achieve their goals without the aid of others. This happened to me my senior year of high school. I wasn't very good at math, and my AP Calculus class was killing me. I basically didn't understand anything, but I was too proud to ask for help. At the end of the first quarter of the year, I had a D in the class. With college just around the corner, I couldn't risk lowering my GPA with a D in my math class. So, I quit being so independent and simply asked for help. I ended up going in before school to receive help from my math teacher. With his guidance, I was slowly able to bring my grade up and I am happy to say that I finished with a B in that class. Being too independent almost caused me to ruin my good academic record.

Lastly, today's society is very much a networking society. One cannot simply make himself a hermit and be successful. Building connections and relationships is of the utmost importance. By isolating yourself from others, you are losing valuable skills. As the old saying goes, if you don't use it, you lose it. This was especially important for me. As a very shy individual, being a "people person" didn't come naturally to me. I was very awkward and had a terrible time talking to others. It wasn't until I started working with others that I was able to develop my social skills. I did this by seeking out relationships with others. For example, instead of studying for an important test alone, I would call up a few of my classmates and study with them. This helped me to build friendships and social skills. Thus, if you want to succeed in today's world, you must be careful not to become too independent.

To conclude, I firmly believe that there is such a thing as becoming too independent, and its consequences are not pretty. By striving to be overly independent, you are losing out on valuable opportunities to help others succeed in life. Not only that, but you are also inflicting harm upon yourself. Additionally, without practice seeking guidance from others, you are losing your fundamental people skills. As a result, practicing a completely independent lifestyle will cause you nothing but harm.

C. Useful Expressions

1. My country, the United States of America, has long been known for its individualism.

_____

2. Unlike many other countries, which focus on the nation as a whole, the United States is much more attuned to the needs of the individual.

_____

3. First of all, being too independent can cause one to lose sight of what is truly important in life, helping others.

_____

4. So, while independence can be a good thing, too much will be detrimental to you and your well-being.

_____

5. Fortunately, the United States eventually stepped up to the plate and began to help out its friend, Britain.

_____

6. I wasn't very good at math, and my AP Calculus class was killing me.

_____

7. With college just around the corner, I couldn't risk lowering my GPA with a D in my math class.

_____

8. Lastly, today's society is very much a networking society.

_____

9. Building connections and relationships is of the utmost importance.

_____

10. As a very shy individual, being a "people person" didn't come naturally to me.

_____

Q175. Should the mistakes a person makes in the past affect a person's future? Why or why not?

A. Essay Outline

Argument: Mistakes in the past should have an effect on a person's future.
Support 1: Mistakes are not an effective learning tool if they don't shape your future.
Support 2: It is safest for everyone involved if grave mistakes in the past affect your future.
Support 3: Everything that transpires in one's life does so for a reason.
Thesis: Because mistakes help to mold one's life into the best life for them, mistakes one makes in the past should affect his future.

B. Model Essay

Mistakes are an inevitable part of life. Everyone will make many mistakes, whether big or small, throughout their lifetime. Those mistakes will, and should, affect their future. If the mistakes you make don't affect your future, then making those mistakes served no purpose to you. Furthermore, by letting the mistakes one made in the past affect his future, others are ensuring that that individual will not repeat the same mistake. Finally, I firmly believe that everything happens for a reason. The mistakes you made will only help you to figure out what future plan is best for you. So, I think it is for the best that past mistakes affect your future.

First of all, if the mistake you made in your past doesn't affect your future, that means you have not learned from your mistake. Most of the time, the only valuable thing that comes from a mistake is the lesson that you learn from it. Learning a lesson helps you to change your old habits. For example, one time I made the mistake of lying to my mother about where I was going after school. She always wanted me to study after school, but one day I wanted to go over to my friend's house. I told her I was going to the library instead. When she found out, I was grounded and never able to go anywhere after school by myself for a long time. From this I learned to never lie to my mother. That mistake still affects my life today. Every time I think it would be easier to lie to my mom, I remember the consequences of doing so. In that way, I think it is beneficial for your past mistakes to affect your future.

In addition, it is safer for everyone if the grave mistakes one makes in the past negatively affect his future. This is especially the case when one is hiring someone for a job. If, as a teenager, a man got into a fight with his friend and ended up killing his friend, he should probably not be hired for a position that entails working closely with people later on in life. Even though the man made the mistake in the past, who's to say that he won't commit the same error in the future? While it would be nice to believe that the man has changed from his murderous ways, I don't believe it is worth the risk to hire him for a people-oriented position. If a mistake that one commits is heinous enough, he deserves to have it negatively affect his future. That might help to deter others from making the same mistakes that he did.

Finally, everything happens for a reason. The mistakes you made in the past will help to shape your future into one that is perfect for you. This idea is evident through the movie "The Lion King." When Simba's father dies, he makes the mistake of running away from his problems and hides out in the jungle with his friends. He leaves his mother and evil uncle to run the kingdom alone while he enjoys a life of ease. Fortunately for the animals of Pride Land, Simba's home, he is forced to go back and face the problems he had run away from. Though it was not the best decision from Simba to run away from his problems, the lessons he learned while in the jungle helped prepare him to be the king he was born to be. Had he not run away, he probably would have submitted to the will of his uncle or even been killed. His father's death and his cowardice happened for a reason, and that reason benefited everyone in Pride Land. Though this may seem like a silly example, the movie contains a powerful lesson about the necessity of mistakes.

So, because mistakes cannot be avoided, I think it is best for mistakes to affect one's future. If they don't affect your future, then the only purpose the mistakes served was to make you feel some kind of pain. Also, society is a safer place if the grave mistake that one made in the past follows him into the future. Lastly, everything that transpires in life, including a mistake, helps to mold your future into one that will make you the happiest. Mistakes should no longer be synonymous with failure, because, in a variety of ways, they truly help to make our lives more pleasant.

C. Useful Expressions

1. Mistakes are an inevitable part of life.

_____

2. Everyone will make many mistakes, whether big or small, throughout their lifetime.

_____

3. Learning a lesson helps you to change your old habits.

_____

4. When she found out, I was grounded and never able to go anywhere after school by myself for a long time.

_____

_____

5. In that way, I think it is beneficial for your past mistakes to affect your future.

_____

6. I don't believe it is worth the risk to hire him for a people-oriented position.

_____

7. The mistakes you made in the past will help to shape your future into one that is perfect for you.

_____

8. When Simba's father dies, he makes the mistake of running away from his problems and hides out in the jungle with his friends.

_____

_____

9. Had he not run away, he probably would have submitted to the will of his uncle or even been killed.

_____

_____

10. Mistakes should no longer be synonymous with failure, because, in a variety of ways, they truly help to make our lives more pleasant.

_____

_____

Q176. Describe a tactic that helps you to study better.

A. Essay Outline

Argument: Taking breaks throughout my studying time my foolproof study tactic.
Support 1: By taking small breaks, I can better focus on my studies.
Support 2: Science has proven that taking breaks while studying helps one to retain more information.
Support 3: The small break acts as an incentive to help me push through my studies.
Thesis: Because I can more efficiently study, my favorite study technique is to take small breaks.

B. Model Essay

My junior year of high school was quite challenging. I took a number of AP classes in order to prepare myself for college and the upcoming SAT. In addition to my school work, I was also involved in after school activities as well as a part-time job. So, whenever I studied, I had to make the most of the time. Luckily, I was able to perfect my studying techniques during that busy year. I found that the best studying tactic was to take brief breaks intermittently throughout my study sessions. The reasons for this are threefold. First of all, by taking small breaks, I was able to eliminate any potential distractions. Additionally, it helped me to better retain the information that I was studying. Finally, it increased my studying stamina. I owe much of my academic success in high school to this studying tactic.

First, taking small breaks helps me avoid the distractions that cause my mind to wander during my study time. For every hour or so of studying, I reward myself with a ten to fifteen minute break. During this time, I address any potential distractions before they surface. For example, I tend to eat a lot. When I get hungry, my mind seems to focus on one thing and one thing only: food. So, I take my break time to grab a snack. Another distraction that tends to plague my study time is my cell phone. I like to chat with my friends. If I chatted with my friends every time it crossed my mind while studying, I would never get anything done! A ten minute break is a good amount of time to check my Facebook or reply to a few text messages from my friends. By addressing all of these distractions during my break-time, I am ensuring myself a more fruitful study session.

Another more important reason for taking breaks while studying is because it helps me to retain the information better. There's actually science supporting this! This technique is known as the Zeigarnik Effect. The Zeigarnik Effect states that if you interrupt your studying with a short break before you have finished studying what it was you were studying, you will actually be able to remember the information better. Though this idea is still debated, I can attest to the validity of it, especially when I am attempting to memorize facts or formulas. However, a key part of the success of this tactic comes from the fact that you should not actually finish what you are studying before you take your break. So, if you are midway through memorizing a particularly difficult concept and it's time for your break, do not delay the break to finish memorizing! This technique was a lifesaver for me when I was bogged down with formulas from my AP Physics class.

The last benefit of giving myself short breaks is that it gives me something to look forward to. It's much easier to push through your studies if there is a definite light at the end of the tunnel. Many times when I am studying, I just want to give up and finish studying later. However, I simply have to remind myself that soon I will have a break and will be able grab a chocolate bar or some other kind of reward. That is generally enough motivation for me to keep carrying on with my studies. Because I was so busy in high school, I didn't necessarily have the luxury of giving up on my studies for the day and picking them up later. If I did that, I doubt I would have passed any of my classes. This tactic ensured that my studying willpower remained strong.

To sum up, this studying tactic saved me from performing poorly in my classes my junior year of high school and pretty much every year since then! Taking short breaks enabled me to study effectively and still have time left to partake in my other activities. The amount of time it took me to successfully study was much lower because my study time was virtually distraction-free. In addition, taking short breaks enables my brain to remember information better! Furthermore, taking short breaks provided me with an incentive to keep on studying even when I was ready to throw my books out the window. I would recommend this studying technique to any serious student, as it has served me well over the entirety of my academic career.

C. Useful Expressions

1. In addition to my school work, I was also involved in after school activities as well as a part-time job.

_____

2. So, whenever I studied, I had to make the most of the time.

_____

3. Luckily, I was able to perfect my studying techniques during that busy year.

_____

4. Additionally, it helped me to better retain the information that I was studying.

_____

5. By addressing all of these distractions during my break-time, I am ensuring myself a more fruitful study session.

_____

6. Though this idea is still debated, I can attest to the validity of it.

_____

7. This technique was a lifesaver for me when I was bogged down with formulas from my AP Physics class.

_____

8. The last benefit of giving myself short breaks is that it gives me something to look forward to.

_____

9. That is generally enough motivation for me to keep carrying on with my studies.

_____

Q177. Is 18 an appropriate age to make a decision about the future of a country, state, or city? Why or why not?

A. Essay Outline

Argument: Without a doubt, 18 is an appropriate age to make decisions concerning one's country, state, or city.

Support 1: In the United States, one is considered an adult in the eyes of the law once he reaches the age of 18.

Support 2: By allowing one vote at the age of 18, we are giving him the opportunity to become more politically minded at a young age.

Support 3: The younger generation has a variety of information at their disposal, so they are more than capable of making sound decisions.

Thesis: Those who have reached the age of 18 are more than ready to tackle the issues of their generation; therefore, I believe that 18 is a good age for one to start making political decisions.

.

B. Model Essay

In the United States of America, the legal voting age is 18 years. At this age, a teenager has the ability to vote on policies that will shape not only his life, but the lives of everyone in the world. Though some Americans have expressed interest in raising the voting age, citing that these important decisions should not be left in the hands of a teenager, I disagree. I believe that those who are 18 years old are ready to take on the responsibility of voting. First of all, at 18 years of age, a person is legally considered an adult. Every adult should have the right to vote. Secondly, by allowing 18 year olds to engage in the democratic process of voting, we are helping them to become more politically minded at a younger age. Finally, due to the advancements in technology, those who are 18 have enough knowledge to make informed decisions. For all of these reasons, I maintain that when one is 18, he is more than capable of making decisions that will shape the future of his country.

To start off, in the United States, 18 is the age when an individual is considered an adult by the government. Being an adult in the eyes of the law is quite different than simply being a juvenile. Punishments for illegal activities become much more severe. Additionally, at 18, an individual can join the army without receiving permission from his parents to do so. So, when a citizen turns 18, the politics of the country start affecting him in a completely different way. As such, he should have the ability to help determine which political decisions he will be affected by. It is unfair to subject one to a harsher lifestyle and not allow him any choice in in the matter. Therefore, as adults, those who are 18 must be given the right to vote.

Furthermore, by allowing a teenager to vote, we are helping to ensure that he will become more politically minded at a younger age. For example, I didn't care at all about the politics of my country when I couldn't vote. In my opinion, I couldn't do anything about the politics of the time, so why should I care? While this isn't the best attitude to take on, I am sure others under the age of 18 agree with me. It wasn't until I turned 18 years of age that I started actively trying to understand who ran my government and the way in which it was governed. By allowing 18 year olds to vote, we are getting them engaged in the world of politics much sooner. So, if we want a more politically minded youth, we should allow those who are 18 to vote.

Finally, teenagers today are much smarter than we give them credit for. Today's society is much more technologically advanced than it has been in the past. Teenagers have access to all kinds of information through the internet and their smart phones. Furthermore, with the world becoming more globalized, students have to learn even more in order to be a competitive force in the future. So, teenagers have enough knowledge to make informed decisions. We simply need to trust them. By the time an individual is 18, he is definitely capable of voting on people and policies that will shape his world.

To conclude, it is obvious that those who are 18 should be allowed to make important decisions that will affect their nation. By the time one is 18, he is legally considered an adult. As such, he should take on an adult responsibility. Additionally, allowing them to vote will force them to become more involved in the decisions that shape their world at a younger age. Furthermore, teenagers today are quite intelligent due to the vast amount of information they have at their fingertips. They are more than capable of making good decisions. Due to these three factors, I think 18 is indeed an appropriate age to make important political decisions. Anyone who is 18 or older needs to make sure that he takes full advantage of this democratic duty!

C. Useful Expressions

1. At this age, a teenager has the ability to vote on policies that will shape not only his life, but the lives of everyone in the world.

_____

2. I believe that those who are 18 years old are ready to take on the responsibility of voting.

_____

3. We are helping them to become more politically minded at a younger age.

_____

4. Finally, due to the advancements in technology, those who are 18 have enough knowledge to make informed decisions.

_____

5. It is unfair to subject one to a harsher lifestyle and not allow him any choice in in the matter.

_____

6. By allowing 18 year olds to vote, we are getting them engaged in the world of politics much sooner.

_____

7. Finally, teenagers today are much smarter than we give them credit for.

_____

8. Today's society is much more technologically advanced than it has been in the past.

_____

9. To conclude, it is obvious that those who are 18 should be allowed to make important decisions that will affect their nation.

_____

10. Anyone who is 18 or older needs to make sure that he takes full advantage of this democratic duty.

_____

178. Libraries, bookstores, coffee shops, parks, and other locations are where people study. Where is your favorite place to study and why?

A. Essay Outline

Argument: The best place for me to study is Starbucks Coffee Shop.
Support 1: Starbucks has a menu filled with delicious baked goods and coffee that will keep me from getting distracted by hunger.
Support 2: Starbucks has the perfect atmosphere to make my study time efficient.
Support 3: I always run into people that I know at Starbucks.
Thesis: Because Starbucks provides the perfect balance of distractions and solitude, my favorite place to study is Starbucks.

B. Model Essay

Studying is a necessary, but not always fun, task. Whenever I have any major tests or projects to study for, I always head to the coffee shop closest to where I live, Starbucks. Starbucks is my favorite place to study because they have an assortment of beverages and snacks for me to purchase if I get hungry. Furthermore, the ambiance at Starbucks is quite soothing, which helps my mind absorb the information I am studying. Finally, because Starbucks is close to my home, I normally run into one or two people to chat with while studying there.

To begin with, Starbucks has a delicious and expansive variety of coffees, as well as baked goods. Although they can be a bit pricey, I like to treat myself when I am studying for major tests or working on important projects. The coffee helps to keep my mind alert and stimulated while I am tackling long essays or memorizing complicated formulas. Also, whenever hunger strikes, I am within a ten foot radius of tasty snacks. When I am hungry, I tend to be unable to focus on my studies and focus instead on what I would like to eat. So, if I have quick access to filling food, I will be able to concentrate on my studies for a longer period of time. It's beneficial to study at a location that has both coffee to keep you alert and food to dull your hunger pains, knocking out two major distractions that will inevitably occur while studying.

In addition to sustenance, Starbucks has an atmosphere that is quite conducive to effective studying. One of my favorite things about studying at Starbucks is the calm music they play. Most of the songs they play at Starbucks I have never heard before, so I won't get distracted singing or humming along to the music. I also enjoy the lighting in Starbucks. I like that Starbucks doesn't use harsh florescent lighting. That type of lighting tends to give me a headache and make me feel like I am in a hospital. The lighting at Starbucks is much softer, which makes it easier on my eyes when I am reading a textbook. Lastly, the tables are the perfect height and very spacious. Tables that are too high or too low hurt my back as I am leaned over them studying. Also, there is plenty of room to lay out my food, drinks, and books. The atmosphere at Starbucks is perfect for keeping my mind focused on studying.

The final reason I love to study at Starbucks is because I normally run into people I know there. The Starbucks that I study at is very close to my college campus and a popular place for people to study. My friends and professors tend to frequent Starbucks, especially around exam period. Talking to them provides me with the perfect study break. Even if I don't see any friends, the employees are great to talk to because they're so friendly. Because I come go to Starbucks so often, they know me by name and sometimes give me free coffee! Chatting with friends or professors is a great way to give my mind a brief respite from studying. This is especially helpful when I am stumped over a difficult concept or I cannot think of what to write next in an essay.

So, while studying a Starbucks is not great for my wallet, studying there is beneficial in many other ways. I thoroughly enjoy the coffee and snacks at Starbucks that keep my mind alert and my stomach content. Also, the relaxing atmosphere helps my brain to absorb and retain information more efficiently. Finally, I love running into friends and professors at Starbucks because it provides me with a necessary study break as well as giving me social interaction. In my opinion, the studying experience at Starbucks cannot be beat. I would highly recommend to anyone that he study at Starbucks if he is looking for a distraction-free zone.

C. Useful Expressions

1. Studying is a necessary, but not always fun, task.

_____

2. Whenever I have any major tests or projects to study for, I always head to the coffee shop closest to where I live, Starbucks.

_____

_____

3. Furthermore, the ambiance at Starbucks is quite soothing, which helps my mind absorb the information I am studying.

_____

4. Also, whenever hunger strikes, I am within a ten foot radius of tasty snacks.

_____

5. So, if I have quick access to filling food, I will be able to concentrate on my studies for a longer period of time.

_____

6. In addition to sustenance, Starbucks has an atmosphere that is quite conducive to effective studying.

_____

7. The Starbucks that I study at is very close to my college campus and a popular place for people to study.

_____

8. Chatting with friends or professors is a great way to give my mind a brief respite from studying.

_____

9. This is especially helpful when I am stumped over a difficult concept or I cannot think of what to write next in an essay.

_____

10. So, while studying a Starbucks is not great for my wallet, studying there is beneficial in many other ways.

_____

Q179. Explain about the one food you can't live without.

A. Essay Outline

Argument: Though I love all kinds of food, eggs are one food that I could legitimately not live without.
Support 1: There are multiple ways to prepare eggs into delicious meals.
Support 2: The uses of eggs extend far beyond simply eating them.
Support 3: Eggs have a variety of health benefits.
Thesis: Due to the fact that eggs have a wide range of healthy uses, I would be traumatized if I could never have any more eggs.

B. Model Essay

I am a food aficionado. For me, one of the principal pleasures in life comes from eating a hearty meal. As such, I have many favorite foods. However, there is one staple food item that life would be much worse with—eggs. I absolutely love eggs. The most obvious reason is because they are delicious on their own or mixed in with other dishes. Another reason I love eggs is because they are a multifaceted food. They can be used for all sorts of different activities! The last reason is that eggs are a healthful food. For all of these reasons, I would undoubtedly list eggs on the top of my favorite foods list.

To begin with, eggs are delectable. My favorite way to eat eggs is scrambled with a little bit of American cheese mixed in. Other ways to cook eggs include frying, boiling, and poaching, just to name a few. Any breakfast is not complete with a few eggs cooked to taste. Furthermore, eggs are a fundamental ingredient in a variety of other tasty dishes. For example, the recipe for my favorite dessert, chocolate cake, calls for two eggs. Eggs can be added to pastas, casseroles, desserts, vegetable dishes, potatoes...the list goes on and on! Life would be a lot less tasty without the incredible egg.

In addition to the multiple ways to cook eggs, they can be used in quite a few non-eating related activities as well. The most obvious example of this is around Easter time. At Easter, many American children partake in the dyeing of Easter eggs. Once they are dyed and dried, they can be used in Easter egg hunts. Another fun way to use eggs is to have races with them. This is a popular game at birthday parties. Children try to balance an egg on a spoon while racing to the finish line. Another use, though I do not at all condone this one, is to express displeasure at something. Sometimes, rambunctious teenagers throw eggs at buildings, like schools, when they are upset. This action is illegal and has consequences, so I would recommend that one simply exercise his freedom of speech in order to express displeasure rather than resort to wasting perfectly good food. So, when you're feeling bored, you can find a few hours worth of entertainment in your refrigerator!

Finally, eggs are not only delicious and great for a vast array of activities, but they are healthy as well! They are a wonderful source of protein, as well as an abundance of vitamins, like vitamins A and B. Recently, eggs have caught a lot of flak for being high in fat. However, what many don't realize is that fats are an essential part of one's diet, as long as healthy fat is consumed in moderation. Eggs are one of those types of healthy fat. In fact, the vitamins in food are actually better absorbed if they are consumed with fat. So, eggs are extremely healthy. Eggs can also be used topically to better one's health. Many face masks use egg whites to help shrink facial pores. The protein in eggs is also good for the hair and would be very beneficial if included in hair treatments. I contribute much of my good health to the consumption of this super-food.

In conclusion, eggs are definitely one food that I could not live without. Without eggs, my favorite breakfast foods and desserts would not exist! Also, the Easter and birthday activities in households across America would be a little less entertaining if the egg were not around. Lastly, my hair would lose its shine and my body would be worse for the wear without this amazing food as a staple part of my diet. So, to be honest, I really don't care which one came first, the chicken or the egg. All I care about is the fact that the egg is in my life.

C. Useful Expressions

1. I am a food aficionado.

2. Another reason I love eggs is because they are a multifaceted food. They can be used for all sorts of different activities!

3. Furthermore, eggs are a fundamental ingredient in a variety of other tasty dishes.

4. Eggs can be added to pastas, casseroles, desserts, vegetable dishes, potatoes...the list goes on and on!

5. At Easter, many American children partake in the dyeing of Easter eggs.

6. Another use, though I do not at all condone this one, is to express displeasure at something.

7. I would recommend that one simply exercise his freedom of speech in order to express displeasure rather than resort to wasting perfectly good food.

8. Eggs can also be used topically to better one's health.

9. So, to be honest, I really don't care which one came first, the chicken or the egg.

10. All I care about is the fact that the egg is in my life.

Q180. What place has given you fond memories?

A. Essay Outline

Argument: I have created the fondest memories in Daegu, South Korea.
Support 1: Everyone in South Korea was super friendly to me, despite the fact that I was an awkward young girl.
Support 2: I was introduced to and fell in love with K-Pop during my stay in South Korea.
Support 3: The food in Daegu was delicious!
Argument: Because Daegu introduced me to a wonderful new culture, I made the best memories while living there.

B. Model Essay

Because my father is in the army, I have traveled to many places all over the world. I never really had a single place to call home. However, I have made many amazing memories because I was able to experience so many different places. The place in which I created the fondest memories was probably Daegu, South Korea. The first reason I loved spending time in Daegu was because everyone there was so friendly! Another was because I fell in love with the popular music there, K-Pop. Finally, South Korean food is delicious! For these reasons, I created the fondest memories in Daegu.

First of all, my family and I moved to Daegu, South Korea when I was 13 years old. My early teens were some of the most awkward years of my life. I always seemed to be saying or doing the wrong thing. However, even when I was clumsy and stumbling over my words, Koreans were always patient and kind to me. There is one guy in particular that I took a liking to. Every time I passed by his restaurant, he was always standing at the door with a friendly smile and wave. Also, he was very cute! Another person that was always friendly to me was an elderly woman and her loving dog. Whenever the dog spotted me, she would run up and beg to be petted. The elderly woman tried to engage in conversation with me about her dog. Although we never made much progress due to the language barrier, I enjoyed socializing with her. Because of the friendly nature of the people in Daegu, I felt right at home, even as a blonde hair, blue-eyed foreigner.

To continue, I fell in love with the music in Daegu. As K-Pop is the most popular style of music there, I heard it everywhere. I soon fell in love with it. K-Pop groups are like Justin Beiber multiplied by five and with better dance moves, so what's not to love? My favorites are Big Bang and 2NE1. The most impressive part of K-Pop is not the actual singing, but the dance moves. They are so creative! American pop stars could learn a lesson or two from K-Pop stars. I loved K-Pop so much that I collected a ton of posters and plastered them all over the walls of my room. K-Pop is so much better than J-Pop, C-Pop, or really any type of pop. So, whenever I think of South Korea, I fondly remember the dreamy voices of GD and Top.

Lastly, I adore South Korean cuisine. Prior to arriving in South Korea, I was a little worried that I wouldn't like the food very much. I heard much of it was seafood-based, and I wasn't the biggest fan of seafood. The very first dish I had in Korea was of course Kimchi. I loved it! Though it was a little bit too spicy for me to handle, the flavor was absolutely perfect. Over time I gradually built up my spice tolerance and I could eat even the spiciest of Kimchis. Another food I really liked was samgyeopsal, or Korean barbeque. My family and I liked to go out on the weekends and order that. It was fun to eat, talk, and simply spend time together as a family. Also, I must admit that I was the best cook at the table! I cooked the meat perfectly. The Korean fast food burgers in South Korea, from Lotteria, were tasty as well. I loved the sauce that was on the Lotz burger. To this day, I still get cravings for South Korean dishes.

To sum up, I miss South Korea! I was able to create so many wonderful memories in Daegu! I truly miss the kindness of the strangers there. I still daydream about the cute Korean guy at the restaurant. Furthermore, I discovered a delightful genre of music while in Korea, K-Pop. Also, I often crave the delectable dishes of South Korea. It's very difficult to find a good South Korean meal in the United States. Someday, when I have enough money to purchase a plane ticket, I will return to Daegu. If you haven't been there yet, I suggest that you go! I guarantee that you will love it as much as I did.

C. Useful Expressions

1. Another was because I fell in love with the popular music there, K-Pop.

2. However, even when I was clumsy and stumbling over my words, Koreans were always patient and kind to me.

3. Every time I passed by his restaurant, he was always standing at the door with a friendly smile and wave.

4. Although we never made much progress due to the language barrier, I enjoyed socializing with her.

5. K-Pop groups are like Justin Beiber multiplied by five and with better dance moves, so what's not to love?

6. American pop stars could learn a lesson or two from K-Pop stars.

7. I heard much of it was seafood-based, and I wasn't the biggest fan of seafood.

8. To this day, I still get cravings for South Korean dishes.

9. I was able to create so many wonderful memories in Daegu!

10. Also, I often crave the delectable dishes of South Korea.

Q181. Describe a person with historical significance in your country. Explain the reason for his or her importance.

A. Essay Outline

Argument: Barack Obama is the person with the most historical significance in my country.
Support 1: With his election to office in 2008, Obama made political history.
Support 2: He served as an inspiration to children worldwide.
Support 3: He has instigated groundbreaking policies that transformed the political system in the United States.
Thesis: Due to his political and personal feats, Barack Obama is the person with the most historical significance in my country.

B. Model Essay

I was born and raised in the United States of America. Throughout my lifetime, there have been many individuals who have influenced my country in various ways. However, I think the most historically important person in my country is former US Senator and newly reelected president Barack Obama. Though President Obama has received mixed reviews, there is no doubt that he has made quite the impression and will leave a lasting mark on the history of the United States of America. The most obvious reason that Obama is historically significant is because he was the first ever African-American elected to the most prominent position in the United States. Furthermore, I believe Barack Obama is so influential because exemplifies the motif of the underdog that will forever change the way children dream. Finally, Barack Obama is actively working to revamp the image of the United States that will majorly impact the country. Whether or not one agrees with President Obama's politics is irrelevant because all can agree that Barack Obama has left an indelible mark on American society as we know it.

First of all, Barack Obama set a new record with his 2008 election that all Americans should be proud of. Barack Obama beat out Senator John McCain to claim the title of President and, more importantly, the title of the first African-American president in the United States. This accomplishment could not come soon enough. Slavery has long marred American history and is regarded as an embarrassment to many Americans. Though Obama's election does not erase the heinous crime from America's record, it does show the progress my country has made in attempting to rehabilitate itself from its crimes of the past. Though we are not the first country to elect a black president, nor will we be the last, the election of Obama does still prove to be quite significant in the United States.

In addition to being the first African-American president, Obama perfectly demonstrates how an underdog can rise to the top with hard work and determination. As is well-known in the USA, Barack Obama did not come from an affluent family. He was raised primarily by his mother, who took a strong interest in Obama's education. His father died at an early age and was therefore not involved in Obama's life. Though his mother worked in order to make ends meet, she woke Obama up at four in the morning in order to review his school lessons with him before she left for work. His mother's efforts paid off, as well as his own, when he graduated from Harvard Law School with honors. As we all know, he then went on to become the Senator of Illinois and, most importantly, President of the United States of America. Through Barack Obama's life, one can see that anything is possible as long as he is willing to devote himself to his dreams. Hard work can produce some unlikely heroes, as was the case with Barack Obama. This has changed the way children in America dream. His example will remain an important influence on America's youth.

However, Barack Obama's significance did not come to a halt after his election to office. He has caused a stir in American politics with ideas that are strikingly different than the president that preceded him, George W. Bush. One of Obama's most controversial acts has been the Affordable Health Care Act. Although still in the works, this plan would completely alter how health care in the United States is run. The health care system in the US has long been problematic and Barack Obama is taking active steps to solve the problem. Obama has also implemented changes in the US with regards to foreign policy. Though former President Bush may have started the war in Iraq, Barack Obama intends to finish it, along with the war against terrorism. These decisions will have a profound impact on US Foreign Policy either for the better or for the worse. Regardless, these are changes that greatly influenced the United States.

In conclusion, Barack Obama is a man who has both showcased the changes the American population has made as well as made quite a few changes of his own. The election of Obama as President of the United States has helped to alter the racial dynamic within the United States. Secondly, Obama has demonstrated to everyone that hard will does in fact pay off. To conclude, as president, Obama has shown that he is willing to take risks and change those parts of American politics with which he disagrees. The election of Barack Obama to the office of President will go down in American history as one the most important events our country has experienced.

C. Useful Expressions

1. Though President Obama has received mixed reviews, there is no doubt that he has made quite the impression and will leave a lasting mark on the history of the United States of America.

_____

2. The most obvious reason that Obama is historically significant is because he was the first ever African-American elected to the most prominent position in the United States.

_____

3. Furthermore, I believe Barack Obama is so influential because he exemplifies the motif of the underdog that will forever change the way children dream.

_____

4. This accomplishment could not come soon enough.

_____

5. Though his mother worked in order to make ends meet, she woke Obama up at four in the morning in order to review his school lessons with him before she left for work.

_____

6. Through Barack Obama's life, one can see that anything is possible as long as he is willing to devote himself to his dreams.

_____

7. He has caused a stir in American politics with ideas that are strikingly different than the president that preceded him, George W. Bush.

_____

Q182. What types of places, tropical, desert, rainforest, etc., would you like to go t o spend a vacation?

A. Essay Outline

Argument: My ideal vacation spot would be the Amazon Rainforest.

Support 1: The Amazonian culture is one that I don't know too much about.

Support 2: As an environmental studies major, the richness of the biodiversity there is extremely appealing to me.

Support 3: Due to deforestation and other environmental concerns, the Amazon Rainforest will not be around much longer in the majestic state it is today.

Thesis: Due to the amount of knowledge I could obtain from the Amazon Rainforest, as well as simply the opportunity to see it in its splendor, I would love to take a vacation to the Amazon Rainforest.

B. Model Essay

During my school vacations, I normally don't do anything terribly exciting. In fact, I rarely even get myself out of bed before noon. However, if I had the opportunity to go anywhere for my vacation, I would love to go to the Amazon Rainforest. First of all, I adore experiencing new cultures, so I would like to check out the culture of the people of the Amazon. Additionally, I am currently studying environmental science in college, and the Amazon has a plethora of biodiversity that I could study. Also, due to the incredible environmental stress that it is currently undergoing, the Amazon Rainforest isn't going to be around much longer. Therefore, my ideal vacation spot would be the Amazon Rainforest.

Starting off, the people of the Amazon have a culture that I do not know very much about. I once played a computer game about an Amazonian adventure, and it included parts in which I could interact with the Amazonian people. The clothes they wore and the way in which these people lived sparked my interest. Because a computer game is definitely not reality, I would like to go to the actual Amazon and see for myself what it's like. Maybe they could teach me different herbal cures for illnesses, like how to relieve a runny nose or how to make my mosquito bites stop itching. Also, I would love to purchase some of the crafts that they make. I once bought a purse from a website that sold Amazonian crafts. I bet I could get a much better price on objects if I eliminated the middle man and went straight to the source of the products. Because it would be so beneficial to meet the people of the Amazon, I would totally go to the Amazon Rainforest if I am given a chance to.

Another reason it would be cool to go to the Amazon Rainforest is because I could experience all of the biodiversity there. I currently live in a big city that I like to call the "concrete jungle." I would love a chance to go to a real jungle and see the life that thrives there. I learned a lot about the Amazon Rainforest from my computer game, including the fact that almost three million species of insects live there! While I'm not a big fan of bugs, there is also quite a bit of diversity in the plants there. As an environmental science major, that is extremely interesting to me. I would love to make a photo journal of all the different plants I encounter and perform some in depth research on those plants that currently don't habitat the United States. As I am approaching my final year in college, my senior thesis is coming up. A vacation in the rainforest would give me a myriad of information for a thesis paper. Due to my love of nature, the Amazon Rainforest would give me plenty of entertainment.

Lastly, and most importantly, the Amazon Rainforest is facing the very real danger of deforestation. I learned a lot about this in one of my geology classes. The Amazon Rainforest contains a wealth of resources, and people have figured this out. Trees are continually being cut down in order to make room for agriculture. Apparently, the rainforest has very productive soil. Another reason the Amazon is being deforested is because the people who live there want room for their cattle. While I understand people need to make a living, their actions are destroying the biodiversity of the beautiful rainforest. Though there are measures being taken to protect the rainforest, I worry that they won't be enough. Consequently, I want to travel to the rainforest and investigate it before the whole forest is destroyed.

Although there are many wonderful places in the world that I could travel to, I would undoubtedly go to the Amazon Rainforest if I had the opportunity to. The Amazonian people probably have tons of secret cures that I could benefit from, as well as beautiful crafts that I could purchase. Also, by traveling to the Amazon Rainforest, I could research the native plants and secure an awesome topic for my senior thesis. Finally, at the rate that the rainforest is being deforested, I don't have much longer to experience the beauty and biodiversity it. To conclude, the Amazon Rainforest would be my ideal vacation spot. Save the rainforest!

C. Useful Expressions

1. First of all, I adore experiencing new cultures, so I would like to check out the culture of the people of the Amazon.

_____

2. Additionally, I am currently studying environmental science in college, and the Amazon has a plethora of biodiversity that I could study.

_____

3. Starting off, the people of the Amazon have a culture that I do not know very much about.
_____

4. The clothes they wore and the way in which these people lived sparked my interest.

_____

5. I bet I could get a much better price on objects if I eliminated the middle man and went straight to the source of the products.

_____

6. I would love to make a photo journal of all the different plants I encounter and perform some in depth research on those plants that currently don't habitat the United States.

_____

7. A vacation in the rainforest would give me a myriad of information for a thesis paper.

_____

8. Lastly, and most importantly, the Amazon Rainforest is facing the very real danger of deforestation.

_____

9. The Amazon Rainforest contains a wealth of resources, and people have figured this out.

_____

10. Though there are measures being taken to protect the rainforest, I worry that they won't be enough.

_____

Q183. Describe an activity that you and your family enjoy doing together.

A. Essay Outline

Argument: I enjoy playing board games with my family.
Support 1: It is fun for all ages.
Support 2: We can play a board game quickly.
Support 3: It doesn't matter who wins or who loses.
Thesis: Because playing board games is fun for every member of my family, I like playing board games with
   them.

B. Model Essay

A lot of people like to do things with their family. Some families like to go on vacation; others prefer to ski together. However, my favorite thing to do with my family is play board games. Because board games are easy, quick, and just plain fun, playing them is one of my favorite activities to do with my family.

To start with, playing board games is fun for everyone. Some games are really not good for everyone because they are boring. For example, my parents never want to play Starcraft; it just doesn't interest them. Plus, my little sister can't play Starcraft because she is too little. However, my parents, my sister, and I can all play board games like checkers, chess, and mahjong together. They are very easy to play and because they don't require my computer, my parents will feel a lot safer. My sister is especially good at checkers; she loves to play dominoes all the time. I just wish that we had more time to play together.

Second, board games are very quick. My parents are especially busy. My mom works full time and still has to take care of the house, me and my sister. My dad works full time and has an extra job. My sister always has piano classes and has to spend a lot of time in English academy so her grades can improve, and I am always studying for the high school exit exam. In short, my family is very busy, but one of the greatest things about board games is that they don't take a lot of time or set up. You can play a game of checkers in about fifteen minutes altogether. It's a lot easier than finding time to go on vacation to Paris! Playing board games is also great when I don't want to spend that much time with my parents. Sometimes, I just want to be alone, but my parents want to spend time with me. It's a good compromise because we can spend just a little bit of time together.

Third, it doesn't matter who wins or who loses whenever we play a game. A lot of other games are really competitive because they require some kind of skill. For example, many sports like tennis and soccer determine who is faster or who can kick a ball harder. However, one of the things I love about board games is that there is usually no skill involved; so many board games, like Sorry or Monopoly are almost completely based on chance or what number you get when you roll dice. For me, it's a lot less stressful to play with my family members when it's not really a competition. Instead, everything is just for fun, and that is the beauty of board games.

In summary, I think my favorite thing to do with my parents and my sister is play board games. Because board games take very little time, appeal to everyone, and are just for fun, playing them is an ideal way to spend a weekday night. I hope all families get the opportunity to play board games together, even if it is just for a small period of time.

C. Useful Expressions

1. To start with, playing board games is fun for everyone.

---

2. It just doesn't interest them.

---

3. They are very easy to play and because they don't require my computer, my parents will feel a lot safer.

---

4. My sister always has piano classes and has to spend a lot of time in English academy so her grades can improve, and I am always studying for the high school exit exam.

---

5. It's a lot easier than finding time to go on vacation to Paris!

---

6. It's a good compromise because we can spend just a little bit of time together.

---

7. Third, it doesn't matter who wins or who loses whenever we play a game.

---

8. In summary, I think my favorite thing to do with my parents and my sister is play board games.

---

9. I hope all families get the opportunity to play board games together, even if it is just for a small period of time.

---

10. In summary, I think my favorite thing to do with my parents and my sister is play board games.

Q184. Who is the wisest person you know? What makes him or her so wise?

A. Essay Outline

Argument: The wisest person I know is my mother.
Support 1: She always gives me the best advice when I am sad.
Support 2: She is a great professor at a prestigious university.
Support 3: My mother is very understanding and always tries to understand people, rather than judge them.
Thesis: Because she is always understanding, gives me the best advice, and does her job really well, my mother is the wisest person I know.

B. Model Essay

A lot of people don't have anyone in their lives who is even vaguely smart. However, I live with someone whom I consider one of the wisest people in the world. My mother is that person. Not only does she always give me the best advice and is always understanding whenever I make a mistake, she is a world-renown researcher with a lot of experience.

First off, my mother always gives me the best advice. A lot of times, I get really sad because of bad things that happen to me at school. Sometimes, I get into fights with some of my friends or I get made fun of for wearing a purple scarf with a blue sweater. However, I always go to my mom and she always makes me feel better. She always knows just what to say and what I should do. The last time I went to my mom was when I got into a fight with my best friend, Tiffany. Tiffany told me that I was ugly, but my mom reassured me and told me that I was beautiful. She also encouraged me to tell Tiffany how I felt. At first, I didn't want to; I just wanted to spread bad rumors about her. Instead, I approached Tiffany the next day and told her how I felt. Tiffany immediately apologized and we are still friends today. It's all thanks to my mom.

Second, my mom is one of the best researchers in the social sciences. My mom is a professional linguist and studies languages for a living. She has done a lot of great things for society in general. She studies Native American languages and has helped a lot of Native American groups with her work. For example, my mom helped the Mohawk people when the Mohawk tribe almost lost its language. When my mom went to the tribe, there were only a couple of hundred people who could speak the Mohawk language. However, with the help of my mom and some money from the federal government, she was able to help keep Mohawk alive. My mom developed an immersion schools for the Mohawk children to learn their heritage language. Now, thousands of people speak Mohawk and every time she goes on the reservation, everyone thanks her. In fact, her project was such a success that she has been given numerous awards for her work.

Lastly, my mother is one of the most understanding human beings alive. She will never judge somebody no matter who they are or where they come from. One time a little boy knocked on our door and was crying. He was dirty and it didn't look like his parents made a lot of money. He didn't know where he was. My mother could have gotten angry at him because he should not have gotten lost; however, instead of yelling at him, my mom simply took him inside our home and made him some hot cocoa. It made him so happy. Eventually, we were able to figure out where he was and my mom drove him back to his home. His parents were so happy to see him and it's only because my mom was able to see past the boy's appearance that he was able to get help.

In conclusion, I think my mom is one of the wisest people I know. She never judges people, she is a great researcher that is respected among her colleagues and she always helps me whenever I am in trouble. I hope everyone has somebody in their life as wise as my mom.

C. Useful Expressions

1. A lot of people don't have anyone in their lives who is even vaguely smart.

_____

2. She is a world-renown researcher with a lot of experience.

_____

3. Sometimes, I get into fights with some of my friends or I get made fun of for wearing a purple scarf with a blue sweater.

_____

4. She always knows just what to say and what I should do.

_____

5. At first, I didn't want to; I just wanted to spread bad rumors about her.

_____

6. However, with the help of my mom and some money from the federal government, she was able to help keep Mohawk alive.

_____

7. In fact, her project was such a success that she has been given numerous awards for her work.

_____

8. She will never judge somebody no matter who they are or where they come from.

_____

9. His parents were so happy to see him and it's only because my mom was able to see past the boy's appearance that he was able to get help.

_____

10. She never judges people, she is a great researcher that is respected among her colleagues and she always helps me whenever I am in trouble.

_____

_____

> **Q185. What are more effective rewards, intrinsic rewards, such as praise, or extrins ic rewards, such as money?**

A. Essay Outline

Argument: I for one believe that we should use intrinsic and extrinsic rewards complimentary of each other when it comes to using the most effective method of rewards.

Support 1: To begin with, intrinsic rewards last longer and they give you a sense of self-accomplishment.

Support 2: Next, extrinsic rewards are effective in the short-term, but in the long-term, they lose their luster.

Support 3: Using these internally motivated rewards with a sprinkling of gift-cards, candy, or monetary valued gifts adds a great competition in work and school environments.

Thesis: Since using intrinsic rewards or extrinsic rewards exclusively on their own has some major drawbacks, I have reached a conclusion that they should be used in a complimentary manner to be the most effective.

B. Model Essay

There is a heated debate about how we should reward our employees, students, and children. One side of the debate is through intrinsic rewards, such as praise. The other side of the debate is through extrinsic rewards, such as money. I for one believe that we should use intrinsic and extrinsic rewards complimentary of each other when it comes to using the most effective method of rewards. Both intrinsic and extrinsic rewards have some drawbacks, but they also offer some great incentives; intrinsic rewards last longer, and give a sense of self-accomplishment, extrinsic rewards offer a great short-term incentive, but this eventually decreases.

To begin with, intrinsic rewards last longer and they give you a sense of self-accomplishment. When someone does a stellar job at work, or in the classroom, their employer, or teacher, might give them praise in front of the whole company, office or classroom. This type of praise gives a person an intrinsic motivation to do well, thereby being an intrinsic reward. This then creates a more effective work or classroom environment because the employees or students are doing excellent work on their own without the use of outside factors motivating them.

Next, extrinsic rewards are effective in the short-term, but in the long-term, they lose their luster. If a person is given the same level of reward over a long period of time, such as a monetary bonus, their motivation eventually decreases because it is no longer a challenge to them or it has become an expected behavior. Therefore, the employer, or teacher, has to create an even larger reward to achieve the same level of motivation as before. This is not effective because the employee or student might do the task well, but they won't do it at the same level of intensity as they had initially done it. Also, extrinsic rewards are not sustainable, so once they are withdrawn, then the motivation is gone as well.

From the information above, it might seem that intrinsic rewards are the most effective and extrinsic rewards are not, but as I stated earlier, there should be a balance of the two. While extrinsic motivation hurts intrinsic motivation, because it takes away the internal desire to do one's own work, it still brings about the desired results. Intrinsic rewards should be given the majority of time; they include praise in front of others, hearing from other students or customers how well one did, or being put in charge as a mentor for other new students or employees. Using these internally motivated rewards with a sprinkling of gift-cards, candy, or monetary valued gifts adds a great competition in the work and school environments.

Since using intrinsic rewards or extrinsic rewards exclusively on their own has some major drawbacks, I have reached a conclusion that they should be used in a complimentary manner to be the most effective. Using intrinsic rewards on their own will lead a person to be under-recognized for their work ethics which will lead to a lack of motivation to continue achieving the same superior work as previously done. On the other hand, using extrinsic rewards exclusively will lead one to expect a reward for everything they do. With everything in life, there is a balance, and intrinsic and extrinsic rewards are no different.

C. Useful Expressions

1. There is a heated debate about how we should reward our employees, students, and children.

_____

2. Both intrinsic and extrinsic rewards have some drawbacks, but they also offer some great incentives.

_____

3. When someone does a stellar job at work, or in the classroom, their employer, or teacher, might give them praise in front of the whole company, office or classroom.

_____

4. This then creates a more effective work, or classroom, environment because the employees or students are doing excellent work on their own without the use of outside factors motivating them.

_____

_____

5. Next, extrinsic rewards are effective in the short-term, but in the long-term, they lose their luster.

_____

_____

6. If a person is given the same level of reward over a long period of time, such as a monetary bonus, their motivation eventually decreases.

_____

_____

7. Also, extrinsic rewards are not sustainable, so once they are withdrawn, then the motivation is gone as well.

_____

_____

8. But as I stated earlier, there should be a balance of the two.

_____

9. Intrinsic rewards should be given the majority of the time.

_____

10. Using these internally motivated rewards with a sprinkling of gifts-cards, candy, or monetary valued gifts adds a great competition in the work and school environments.

_____

_____

Q186. What custom or tradition is unique to your country?

A. Essay Outline

Argument: Three of traditions and customs from Poland are the saying of 'thank-you' when purchasing items, the breaking of bread during Christmas, and Name Day.

Support 1: First of all, the Polish people will say 'Dziekuje' ('thank-you') only after receiving their change.

Support 2: Second of all, the Polish people break 'bread' with their families during their Christmas Eve meal.

Support 3: Last, but not least, the Polish people, and other Slovak countries, celebrate Name Days, or 'Imieniny'.

Thesis: As you can see, Poland has a few very unique traditions and customs that are unique to them.

B. Model Essay

Being a Polish person, our culture has many different customs and traditions that are unique to Poland. The Polish people are very proud of their culture, and they are also a very tradition based society. Many families who have immigrated to America still continue some of the basic traditions that were practiced in their home country. Three of these traditions and customs I will discuss more elaborately are the saying of 'thank-you' when purchasing items, the breaking of bread during Christmas, and Name Day.

First of all, the Polish people will say 'Dziekuje' ('thank-you') only after receiving their change. What I mean by this is that when you are in Poland, you should wait to say 'thank-you' until after you have been given your change back. If you do not, you are telling the cashier that they can 'keep the change.' Often times, people visiting Poland will feel that the items are very expensive, until they learn that they are giving the store clerk permission to keep the money that would have been given back. So, wait to say 'Dziekuje' ('thank-you') until after you've received your money back.

Second of all, the Polish people break 'bread' with their families during their Christmas Eve meal. Unlike most Western countries, Poland holds onto the religious roots of this holiday, rather than the materialistic ideas. The Christmas Eve celebration starts with the breaking of the Oplatek, which is a thin wafer-like piece of 'bread' that is stamped with a religious picture on it. In my family, the eldest in the family (my grandfather) takes the big Oplatek and breaks it into large pieces that he then hands down to each of his four children (my aunt, uncles, and father). Then, these family members break their pieces into smaller sizes and pass them out to their children (my cousins, siblings, and myself). Once the last piece is passed down to the youngest, we say a prayer and eat the flavorless piece of thin bread. This is very similar to the idea of Communion in Catholicism, which many Polish people are a part of.

Last, but not least, the Polish people, and other Slovak countries, celebrate Name Days, or 'Imieniny'. This day is more important than one's birthday, and it also comes from a religious origin, like the breaking of the Oplatek. As stated earlier, Poland consists of many Roman Catholics and Christians, and with these religions are the associations of Saints. Polish people often name their children after a Saint that is closest to the date that they are born. Then their Saint's day that they were named after becomes their 'new' birthday. On Name's Day, families and friends gather together to say, 'wszystkiego najlepszego!', which means 'All the best!', to the celebrant. They will also enjoy a variety of food, drinking, and dancing. It's very similar to one's birthday, but both men and women will receive chocolate and flowers, which are usually given in odd numbers.

As you can see, Poland has a few very unique traditions and customs that are unique to them. If you ever by chance meet a Polish person, wish them 'sto lat!' on their Name's Day, meaning 'a hundred years', instead of 'Happy Birthday." I respect my Polish heritage and will pass my culture on to my own children because it is important to know one's own heritage.

C. Useful Expressions

1. The Polish people are very proud of their culture, and they are also a very tradition based society.

_____

2. If you do not, you are telling the cashier that they can 'keep the change.'

_____

3. Often times, people visiting Poland will feel that the items are very expensive.

_____

4. Second of all, the Polish people break bread with their families during their Christmas Eve meal.

_____

5. Unlike most Western countries, Poland holds onto the religious roots of this holiday, rather than the materialistic ideas.

_____

6. In my family, the eldest in the family (my grandfather) takes the big Oplatek and breaks it into large pieces.

_____

7. Once the last piece is passed down to the youngest, we say a prayer and eat the flavorless piece of thin bread.

_____

8. This day is more important than one's birthday, and it also comes from a religious origin, like the breaking of the Oplatek.

_____

9. They will also enjoy a variety of food, drinking, and dancing.

_____

10. I respect my Polish heritage and will pass my culture on to my own children because it is important to know one's own heritage.

_____

_____

Q187. Which person do you depend on for advice when dealing with a problem?

A. Essay Outline

Argument: I depend on two categories of people for advice when dealing with a problem; my parents and my boyfriend.

Support 1: First and foremost, I turn to my parents for assistance with finances and career guidance.

Support 2: Secondly, my boyfriend gives me the best advice that fits the person I am today, unlike my parents who view me as the child I once was.

Support 3: Sometimes, I find it difficult to choose between my parents' advice and my boyfriend's advice.

Thesis: Since not every problem has a clear piece of advice, I turn to my parents and my boyfriend for different pieces of advice on how to solve my trouble spots in life.

B. Model Essay

Throughout our lives, we will be faced with many challenges and obstacles to overcome. Many times, we can get through these issues on our own. However, there are times when we need a helping hand because we can't manage on our own. I depend on two categories of people for advice when dealing with a problem: my parents and my boyfriend. Both my parents and my boyfriend offer me advice, but one is better than the other when dealing with certain snags that might come up.

The first and most important category of people I lean on for assistance is my parents. My mother, father, step-father, and step-mother all offer me a different perspective to my various problems that might arise. When it comes to financial advice, I always go to my mother and her husband because they are the most experienced in dealing with monetary issues. They have done very well financially and have always given me great advice for what to do with my money. For problems concerning my career, I ask my father and his wife because they offer me the most honest advice without letting their personal feelings come into play. It was actually my step-mother who opened my eyes to a career in teaching. She showed me the business and gave me the freedom and guidance to fine tune my skills.

The other person I go to for advice is my boyfriend. Although we have only been dating for a short time, I am able to be completely honest with him. He then in return is one-hundred percent honest with me. His advice is very helpful because he doesn't know my whole, entire life story, like my parents do. Therefore, he can give me the best advice that fits the person I am today, unlike my parents who view me as the child I once was. Recently, I had a difficult decision to make about running in a marathon or not. He gave me the perfect advice, because he knows that I have an injured knee and sees me struggle with it only a daily basis. So, he told me not to push myself and to just enjoy it and have fun. My parents would have told me to do my best, no matter what the cost was to my body because they have such high-expectation levels of me that I want to achieve. Therefore, when it comes to issues dealing with my life here in Korea, I turn to my boyfriend.

Sometimes, I find it difficult to choose between my parents' advice and my boyfriend's advice. On one side, my parents have known me my whole life, and they know my past mistakes and triumphs. However, as I stated earlier, they still view me as a child, and expect me to always take their advice. On the other hand, my boyfriend knows who I am now, but he doesn't know all of the other decisions I've had to struggle with in my life previously, like my parents do. One example of this battle of choosing between the two sides of advice was when I was deciding to stay in Korea for another year. Obviously, my parents want me to come back to America, and my boyfriend wanted me to stay in Korea. It was a very difficult situation to be put in, but in the end, I chose to stay in Korea. Even though I went against my parents' advice, they are still supportive of my decision and are now starting to view me as the adult that I have become.

Since not every problem has a clear piece of advice, I turn to my parents and my boyfriend for different pieces of advice on how to solve my trouble spots in life. By having the support from five different people, I am able to get well-rounded and well-informed advice from many different minds. Having these people in my life to assist me in times of need has gotten me through some of my toughest decisions in life.

C. Useful Expressions

1. Throughout our lives, we will be faced with many challenges and obstacles to overcome.

_____

2. Many times, we can get through these issues on our own.

_____

3. However, there are times when we need a helping hand because we can't manage on our own.

_____

4. One is better than the other when dealing with certain snags that might come up.

_____

5. When it comes to financial advice, I always go to my mother and her husband, because they are the most experienced in dealing with monetary issues.

_____

6. It was actually my step-mother who opened my eyes to a career in teaching.

_____

7. She showed me the business and gave me the freedom and guidance to fine tune my skills.

_____

8. My parents would have told me to do my best, no matter what the cost was to my body because they have such high-expectation levels of me that I want to achieve.

_____

9. On one side, my parents have known me my whole life, and they know my past mistakes and triumphs.

_____

10. Even though I went against my parents' advice, they are still supportive of my decision and are now starting to view me as the adult that I have become.

_____
_____

> ## Q188. Name a place that you have visited in your country that you would recommend to others to visit.

A. Essay Outline

Argument: If I had to recommend one of the places that I have visited for somebody else to visit, I would tell them to venture to New York City.

Support 1: To start, New York City is probably one of the most popular tourism spots in America.

Support 2: Next, visitors from other more mono-cultural societies can experience true cultural diversity in New York City.

Support 3: It is also important to realize that there is a great deal of history in the New York City limits.

Thesis: Since there are a wide variety of activities that one can participate in, learn about, and observe, New York City is my number one choice to suggest a traveler should visit in America.

B. Model Essay

There are hundreds, if not thousands of places to visit within the American borders. I have been to many of these places, but not all of them yet. If I had to recommend one of the places that I have visited for somebody else to visit, I would tell them to venture to New York City. Although this city is a very popular tourism spot, there are a few unique places that not everybody knows of. Also, it offers a diverse location for people to see all types of people. Furthermore, it has a plethora of history to learn about.

To start, New York City is probably one of the most popular tourism spots in America. Everybody knows of the Statue of Liberty, Rockefeller Center, and the Brooklyn Bridge, but there are a few less known, unique places that people can journey. One of these places is the Madame Tussauds Museum. This is an unusual place where you can pose with many different celebrities. Of course they are not real though; they are identical wax replicas. I love bragging about my photo with Tom Cruise to all of my friends. They actually think I was with them, so I think this would be a great photo opportunity for a visitor to have. Then they can show their friends and family something different than the typical Statue of Liberty photo. Other places people can explore that are off the main path include Ripley's Believe It or Not, the Sports Museum of America, and the United Nations. I encourage all tourists to explore outside of the usual and see something unusual.

Next, visitors from other more mono-cultural societies can experience true cultural diversity in New York City. New York is full of all types of nationalities, races, and religions, predominantly due to its large immigration population. In New York, no single country or region of origin dominates, unlike in Los Angeles and Miami where there is a dominate country represented. Among the cultures that are within the New York City limits, Dominican Republic, China, Jamaica, Russia, Italy, Poland, and India are represented the most. As you can see from this, it is a great place to visit to be reminded why America is a place of freedom and equality. Skin color, gender, nationality, and religion are blended together in this amazing city. So visitors will be able to watch a multitude of parades and festivities showcasing one of the many cultures found in New York City.

It is also important to realize that there is a great deal of history in the New York City limits. This is mainly due to the fact that Ellis Island was the gateway for millions of immigrants for a span of thirty plus years. Even though Ellis Island is actually in New Jersey, it is easily accessible from a ferry in New York City. Because of this great diversity in immigration, many history museums were erected to portray the struggles overcome and the battles won by the ambitious travelers from across the oceans. The Museum of Natural History is a fantastic place of history that is often portrayed in movies. So, while you learn about the Earth's history, you can also see some famous locations that were in the movies, such as "A Night at the Museum" with Ben Stiller.

Since there are a wide variety of activities that one can participate in, learn about, and observe, New York City is my number one choice to suggest a traveler should visit in America. In the Big Apple, you can explore many places that are well-known, as well some that are more unknown. It also offers a unique perspective to the mixing pot of various cultures. Finally, a large amount of history is contained within many museums.

C. Useful Expressions

1. If I had to recommend one of the places that I have visited for somebody else to visit, I would tell them to venture to New York City.

2. Furthermore, it has a plethora of history to learn about.

3. This is an unusual place where you can pose with many different celebrities.

4. They actually think I was with them, so I think this would be a great photo opportunity for a visitor to have.

5. Other places people can explore that are off the main path include Ripley's Believe It or Not, the Sports Museum of America, and the United Nations.

6. Next, visitors from other more mono-cultural societies can experience true cultural diversity in New York City.

7. As you can see from this, it is a great place to visit to be reminded why America is a place of freedom and equality.

8. Many history museums were erected to portray the struggles overcome and the battles won by the ambitious travelers from across the oceans.

> **Q189. Of all the types of weather, rainy, sunny, snowy, etc., which is your favorite type of weather?**

A. Essay Outline

Argument: Of all the weather types though, my favorite weather is a warm, partly cloudy day with a cool breeze blowing.

Support 1: To begin with, when the weather is warm and partly cloudy with a cool breeze, it offers many options for outdoor activities.

Support 2: Next, I love being outdoors, and cloud watching is one of my favorite leisurely outdoor activities.

Support 3: Finally, a day that contains a warm air and a cool breeze is the optimal weather day for me to wear my favorite style of clothing.

Thesis: As you can see, I have three distinct reasons why a warm, partly cloudy day with a cool breeze blowing is my favorite weather type: outdoor sports, cloud watching, and perfect clothing.

B. Model Essay

I have a preference to what type of weather I like, just like everybody else. There are some weather types that I absolutely despise; some of these being any amount of snow, very cold weather, and arctic-like winds. Of all the weather types though, my favorite weather is a warm, partly cloudy day with a cool breeze blowing. I have three reasons for this being my ideal weather type: outside activities, cloud shapes, and clothing options.

To begin with, when the weather is warm and partly cloudy with a cool breeze, it offers many options for outdoor activities. I am a huge outdoors person, so anytime I can be outside I take advantage of it. A few of my favorite outdoor activities are hiking a mountain, taking long walks around downtown, and going on a long bike ride along the river. The weather is perfect for these activities because if you work up a sweat, the cool breeze will lower your body temperature and take away the wetness on your skin. I know that when I am bike riding, I can tend to get a little overheated, but this type of weather prevents that from happening.

Next, as I mentioned previously, I love being outdoors, and cloud watching is one of my favorite leisurely outdoor activities. As a child, I would often go hiking up a local mountain with my parents. When we would get to the top of the mountain, we would take out a big blanket, lay it out on the ground, and then lay down to look up at the passing clouds. We would go back and forth telling each other what shapes the clouds would make. If it was a big fat oval with a long rectangle coming from one end, we would say, "Elephant!" It is a great way to expand a child's imagination, so I love this type of weather because I can expose others to keeping their imagination running wild.

Finally, a day that contains a warm air and a cool breeze is the optimal weather day for me to wear my favorite style of clothing. In a warm environment that has a cool breeze blowing, I can wear a few thin layers that can be put on or taken off as the air temperature fluctuates. I love wearing flowing skirts paired with a tank top and a thin long-sleeve jacket over it. It is true that we wear layers in snow and other weather types. However they are not comfortable layers. I find them to be excessively bulky. Moreover, my core gets overheated and I start to perspire, but my appendages are as cold as ice and I can't warm them up enough.

As you can see, I have three distinct reasons why a warm, partly cloudy day with a cool breeze blowing is my favorite weather type. I am able to join in many outdoor activities without being too hot or too cold. Also, I can partake in the affair of cloud watching, where I am able to keep my imagination flowing. Finally, this weather suits my favorite clothing style of flowing skirts, tank tops, and thin long-sleeve jackets. I don't see how people can ever choose snow, rain, or very hot weather as their favorites when my favorite type of weather offers so many positives.

C. Useful Expressions

1. I have a preference to what type of weather I like, just like everybody else.

_____

2. To begin with, when the weather is warm and partly cloudy with a cool breeze, it offers many options for outdoor activities.

_____

3. I am a huge outdoors person, so anytime I can be outside I take advantage of it.

_____

4. The weather is perfect for these activities because if you work up a sweat, the cool breeze will lower your body temperature and take away the wetness on your skin.

_____
_____

5. I know that when I am bike riding, I can tend to get a little overheated, but this type of weather prevents that from happening.

_____

6. When we would get to the top of the mountain, we would take out a big blanket, lay it out on the ground, and then lay down to look up at the passing clouds.

_____
_____

7. We would go back and forth telling each other what shapes the clouds would make.

_____

8. It is a great way to expand a child's imagination, so I love this type of weather because I can expose others to keeping their imagination running wild.

_____

9. In a warm environment that has a cool breeze blowing, I can wear a few thin layers that can be put on or taken off as the air temperature fluctuates.

_____

10. I don't see how people can ever choose snow, rain, or very hot weather as their favorites when my favorite type of weather offers so many positives.

_____
_____

Q190. If you're given a month of leisure to do whatever you'd like to do, what would you do in that month?

A. Essay Outline

Argument: If I were given a whole month of freedom, I'd do three things: travel the world, learn to cook better, and focus on learning Korean more intensively.

Support 1: First, traveling around the world is one of my dreams.

Support 2: Secondly, I would want to spend some time learning to cook more for types of foods.

Support 3: Finally, the most important thing for me to do during a one month hiatus is to focus on studying Korean more intensively.

Thesis: Traveling, learning to cook, and studying the Korean language would be my top three ways to spend this new free time.

B. Model Essay

I have found it to be true that as I have gotten older, I have had less time to do my own leisure activities. So, if I were given a whole month of freedom, I'd do three things. The first thing I'd like to do is to travel the world. The second is to learn to cook better, and the third is to focus on learning Korean more intensively.

First, traveling around the world is one of my dreams. If I were given a whole thirty days of free-time, I'd spend at least two weeks of it traveling to various countries that are on my bucket list. I've always wanted to go to Greece, Rome, Africa, Ireland, and Poland. I know that in two weeks, I can't hit every country on that list, but I definitely can get to half of them. In these countries, I'd go to the see the major tourist spots, but also the more unknown locations. I think it would be an amazing opportunity to take time off away from my busy life and go and relax in a few other countries for a few weeks.

Secondly, I would want to spend some time learning to cook more types of foods. I love to cook, but my options are very limited due to the fact that I don't know what a lot of the different products at the markets here in Korea are. If I was able to spend about four days taking a comprehensive cooking and shopping course, I'd be set for life with a plethora of new recipes to prepare. Once I know what the ingredients are and what spices or seasonings go well with each other, then I can expand beyond the simple style of cooking that I have adapted while living in a foreign country.

Finally, the most important thing for me to do during a one month hiatus is to focus on studying Korean more intensively. Being in a foreign country is exciting, but it is also challenging if you can't communicate effectively. So, I would spend the majority of the month with my nose in my Korean language text books. While I am flying to the foreign countries, I can study, and while I'm at the market shopping for my cooking class, I'm learning even more words. With the remaining weeks, I would spend my waking hours memorizing more vocabulary words, and being around only Korean speakers. During this time, I will listen attentively to their words and try to understand what they are saying.

In conclusion, I would be so overjoyed if I could have a month off to do whatever I wanted to do. Traveling, learning to cook, and studying the Korean language would be my top three ways to spend this new free time. In doing so, I would be increasing my level of happiness and ease while being in a foreign language's land.

C. Useful Expressions

1. I have found it to be true that as I have gotten older, I have had less time to do my own leisure activities.

_____

2. First, traveling around the world is one of my dreams.

_____

3. In these countries, I'd go to the see the major tourist spots, but also the more unknown locations.

_____

4. I think it would be an amazing opportunity to take time off away from my busy life and go and relax in a few other countries for a few weeks.

_____

_____

5. I love to cook, but my options are very limited due to the fact that I don't know what a lot of the different products at the markets here in Korea are.

_____

_____

6. If I was able to spend about four days taking a comprehensive cooking and shopping course, I'd be set for life with a plethora of new recipes to prepare.

_____

_____

7. Once I know what the ingredients are and what spices or seasonings go well with each other, then I can expand beyond the simple style of cooking that I have adapted while living in a foreign country.

_____

8. Being in a foreign country is exciting, but it is also challenging if you can't communicate effectively.

_____

9. During this time, I will listen attentively to their words and try to understand what they are saying.

_____

10. In doing so, I would be increasing my level of happiness and ease while being in a foreign language's land.

_____

_____

> ## Q191. What is your most memorable moment that you have experienced in school ?

A. Essay Outline

Argument: My most memorable moment that I have experienced at school was the attacks on the World Trade Center, Pentagon and the crashing of the plane in Pennsylvania.

Support 1: It frightened me and saddened me very much because so many people were hurt.

Support 2: I was called into the office to be told about my mother being safe, even though I had no idea why.

Support 3: I was in my English writing class, so I wrote in a journal that day to help vent the feelings that had.

Thesis: Because it caused me so much confusion and heartbreak, 9/11 was my most memorable moment in school.

B. Model Essay

The most memorable moment that I have experienced in school is when America was attacked by terrorists on September 11, 2001. Four separate planes were deliberately crashed into three buildings and one field. Two of these planes were crashed into two of the World Trade Centers in New York City and the other was crashed into the Pentagon in Washington, D.C. The third plane was believed to have been heading to another major building, but it instead was crashed into a field in Shanksville, Pennsylvania. I was in my senior year at Allentown Central Catholic, which is less than two hours away from NYC, and many of our students had friends or family members who worked in NYC. So we were all filled with a mix of emotions. This day changed my life and the lives of many other Americans.

As I stated previously, my fellow students, teachers and I were all filled with a mix of different emotions. We had been in a prayer service because I attended a Catholic school where we had a religious service once a month. During this prayer service, the first plane crashed into one of the World Trade Center buildings. We came upstairs and turned on our classroom TVs, and just as we did that, the second plane crashed. Within two hours, both the buildings had collapsed. All teachers were then instructed to turn off the TVs, and to try and focus on class work the best we could. I was so worried about my friends who had family members in the city. We had no idea that there were two more planes that would cause more damage to even more people's lives.

A short while after we turned our TV's off, I was called to the office. I had known that students who were affected by this unforgettable day were being called to be comforted or to tell them bad news. I was shocked because I did not personally know anybody in NYC. I got to the office, and they began to tell me that my mom was ok. I was surprised by them telling me this, because she works at the Pentagon. Why would they be telling my about my mom, who works miles away from NYC? Then, the principal told me that the Pentagon had been hit too. I broke down in tears, because I was so relieved to know that my mom was not harmed. She had fortunately been on business in Ohio for the day and was not in the Pentagon. But many of the people I had worked with all summer long at the Pentagon were there. My mind immediately went to worrying if they were injured or not. I didn't know what part had been hit and it made me more fearful, because my mom's office and all the people I knew were in the outer ring. Therefore, there was a larger possibility that they might have been harmed too. Fortunately, the portion of the five-sided building the plane hit was the newly renovated section and had had minimal personnel working in it.

After the visit to the principal's office, I gathered my composure and went back to class. I sat down and wrote in my English journal, since I was still in English class. We did not change classes because it was easier to keep track of what students were where, if we all just stayed in our original classrooms. So, I spent an hour writing in my journal about the day's events. I asked questions to myself and to the people who did this horrible thing. We had speculations that they were all related and had an idea of who might've done it, but we had nothing confirmed yet. To this day, I still have this journal, and I look back on it when I need a reminder of how precious life is. Also, it helps remind me how I should live life without being surrounded by negatives because life is just too short. We never know when something will change it.

September 11, 2001 changed my life, as well as many other people making it unshakable from our memories. It has been the most memorable day to me, even after 11 years. I haven't read my journal in over 3 years, but I still remember all the details and the feelings that rushed through me that day. I hope that the future children of the world will never have to have a high school experience like the one I had. It still makes me upset when I see something about it on TV.

C. Useful Expressions

1. So we were all filled with a mix of emotions.

_____

2. This day changed my life and the lives of many other Americans.

_____

3. We came upstairs and turned on our classroom TVs, and just as we did that, the second plane crashed.

_____

4. A short while after we turned our TV's off, I was called to the office.

_____

5. I had known that students who were affected by this unforgettable day were being called to be comforted or to tell them bad news.

_____

6. I broke down in tears because I was so relieved to know that my mom was not harmed.

_____

7. She had fortunately been on business in Ohio for the day and was not in the Pentagon.

_____

8. My mind immediately went to worrying if they were injured or not.

_____

9. After the visit to the principal's office, I gathered my composure and went back to class.

_____

> ## Q192. Compare the advantages of positive rewards against the advantages of negative punishments.

A. Essay Outline

Argument: When it comes to children and adults, positive rewards and negative punishments have beneficial aspects to both of them.

Support 1: Positive rewards build upon a person's good deeds.

Support 2: Negative punishments make the negative behavior noticeable to the doer.

Support 3: I fall in the camp of using a mixture of both positive rewards and negative punishments.

Thesis: Between the these two options, we should have a good balance, be consistent with them, and not overuse them, or else they will lose their effect.

B. Model Essay

When it comes to children and adults, positive rewards and negative punishments have beneficial aspects to both of them. While positive rewards build upon a person's good deeds, the negative punishments point out one's wrong doing. So what exactly are the advantages to both sides of the debate? They range from making somebody feel good about themselves, to making one understand what is not acceptable behavior.

As I mentioned above, positive rewards build upon a person's good deeds. When we do something that is noteworthy, it feels good to be recognized for it. So by giving a positive reward, we are encouraging a desirable behavior. Take for instance this example from a workplace. When all of the workers are doing well, but one is doing exceptionally well, that one worker will be rewarded with a bonus check. This will encourage all of the other workers to do that same behavior to receive a bonus check as well. By rewarding the good actions, we are promoting what our expectations are that we want somebody to achieve.

On the other hand, the negative punishments also produce an advantage. The largest advantage is that the negative behavior is made noticeable to the doer. Take for example this scenario from a child's perspective. A child always does their homework on time and they get straight A's. For every A they receive, they get a dollar. But one day, this child comes home late after school and lies about it. By punishing the child for coming home late, they will see that this is not allowed, and they will correct it. If there is a young child who is always being reward for their good behavior, how will they know that their bad behavior is unacceptable? We must correct the child in order to eliminate these undesirable behaviors from continuing.

As for my opinion, I fall in the camp of using a mixture of both positive rewards and negative punishments. As we continue through life, and we only see people receiving positive rewards, then how will we ever know what we are doing wrong? Children need a balance between the two. This is because if we always reward the sought after actions, then they will become accustomed to it, and the rewards will lose their effectiveness; and vice versa.

Both adults and children respond to positive rewards and negative punishments. However, there are times where a negative punishment is needed, or a positive reward is needed. Positive rewards allow a person to be recognized for doing well. While on the contrary, the negative punishments show the person that they are doing something that is not allowed. Between the two of these options, we should have a good balance, be consistent with them, and not overuse them, or else they will lose their effect.

C. Useful Expressions

1. When it comes to children and adults, positive rewards and negative punishments have beneficial aspects to both of them.

_____

_____

2. While positive rewards build upon a person's good deeds, the negative punishments point out one's wrong doing.

_____

_____

3. As I mentioned above, positive rewards build upon a person's good deeds.

_____

4. When all of the workers are doing well, but one is doing exceptionally well, that one worker will be rewarded with a bonus check.

_____

_____

5. Take for example this scenario from a child's perspective.

_____

6. We must correct the child in order to eliminate these undesirable behaviors from continuing.

_____

7. Children need a balance between the two theories.

_____

8. This is because if we always reward the sought after actions, then they will become accustomed to it.

_____

9. Both adults and children respond to positive rewards and negative punishments.

_____

10. Between the two of these options, we should have a good balance, be consistent with them, and not overuse them, or else they will lose their effect.

_____

_____

> **Q193. If a close friend was in need of an organ, such as a kidney, and you were a viable option, would you give them the organ needed?**

A. Essay Outline

Argument: If I were posed with this difficult proposal, I would without hesitation give my friend the needed organ.
Support 1: Life is precious.
Support 2: I can give the organ that I don't need..
Support 3: To conclude, I would feel a huge sense of guilt if my friend would die because I didn't help them.
Thesis: If I were a viable option to donate an organ that my friend was in dire need of, I would without a doubt donate that organ because my friend really needs it.

B. Model Essay

In life, we are given many difficult obstacles to face. One of these obstacles is helping others when it will put you in harm's way. An example of this is the situation of giving one of your organs to save a friend's life. If I were posed with this difficult proposal, I would without hesitation give my friend the needed organ because life is precious, I don't need the organ, and I would live with guilt if I didn't do so.

It is important to remember that life is the most precious thing we have in this world. Nobody knows for sure what will happen after we pass from this world, so we must be sure to live a happy life while we are here on Earth. By giving my viable organ to my friend, I am able to prolong their life, and who knows what great things they will do in their life! For this reason, I want to give them the chance to do these great things. Maybe they will be the person who finds the cure for all cancers, or maybe they will be the next President. The options are limitless!

A point that is often overlooked is that I most likely don't need the organ that they need, or else the doctors would not grant me permission to donate it. Some examples of these organs are the liver and the kidney. Even though I know that the surgery will be dangerous, the recovery will be difficult, and the possibility of me becoming sick will be increased, none of these adversities deter me from wanting to assist my friend in need. Since I am always one who helps others without any care to what I sacrifice in doing so, I want to give them something that my body is in no need of.

To conclude, I would feel a huge sense of guilt if my friend would die because I didn't help them. I tend to take on others peoples problems a lot, and I feel guilt very easily for not assisting somebody else. So, I know that by not helping them, I would have a very difficult time dealing with the fact that I was selfish and let them die. There was a time in high school that a friend needed my help with something, and I didn't help them. It has been ten years since then, and I still feel the same sense of guilt, like I should have helped them. That was a simple request with no major effects from my selfishness, so I could only imagine the guilt I would be overwhelmed by if I didn't give the needed organ to my friend.

In summary, if I were a viable option to donate an organ that my friend was in dire need of, I would without a doubt lay down on the operating table and give them what they needed to survive. A true friend is hard to come by in this world, and I would never want to lose them, especially if I had something I could do to keep them around. Donating an organ is a terrifying experience, but I would see past all of the negatives that could happen to me, by looking at all the positive aspects that will come about, like saving a friend's life.

C. Useful Expressions

1. In life, we are given many difficult obstacles to face.

2. One of these obstacles is helping others when it will put you in harm's way.

3. If I were posed with this difficult proposal, I would without hesitation give my friend the needed organ.

4. I would live with guilt if I didn't do so.

5. Nobody knows for sure what will happen after we pass from this world, so we must be sure to live a happy life while we are here on Earth.

6. Maybe they will be the person who finds the cure for all cancers, or maybe they will be the next President. The options are limitless!

7. None of these adversities deter me from wanting to assist my friend in need.

8. I tend to take on other people's problems a lot, and I feel guilt very easily for not assisting somebody else.

9. I could only imagine the guilt I would be overwhelmed by if I didn't give the needed organ to my friend.

10. I would without a doubt lay down on the operating table and give them what they needed to survive.

194. What would you like to know if you could learn one thing about the future?

A. Essay Outline

Argument: If I could know something about the future, I would want to know what type of new technologies there will be, such as cars, phones and anything else that we don't currently have.

Support 1: I am always curious about what the future technology is, so it will ease my curiosity.

Support 2: I could be better prepared to use new technology.

Support 3: I could make money in the stock market by investing in the companies that will create this new technology.

Thesis: Since I can ease my wandering mind, feel smarter, and increase my money, I would like to know about future technologies.

B. Model Essay

If I could know something about the future, I would want to know what type of new technologies there will be, such as cars, phones and anything else that we don't currently have. I have always been curious about what our future holds for us. By knowing this, I could gain many advantages in my life now and in the future.

First, I often think about what the future holds. So, my wandering mind is always curious about what things will be different. By knowing this, I will be able to ease my curiosity. I think about the past ten to fifteen years and how different our technology has already become. Will our phones be smaller or bigger? Will we have an implant in our head that is our cell phone? It's very exciting to me to think of the future possibilities.

Next, if I know about the future technology, I will be better prepared to use it. Currently, I have a smart phone and I am not very skilled in its applications. I feel that I am always behind the learning curve. Sometimes, I will learn about a feature that people already known about and have been using for months. It's rather embarrassing to not know how to use my own phone. So, having this knowledge will help me to feel smarter.

Lastly, by knowing about future technologies, I could invest my money and make even more income. If I knew what company would be the creators of the new technology, then I could put my money in those stocks early on. I can buy the stocks at a cheap price, and be guaranteed a good return in the future because I'll know that the companies will succeed.

Since I can ease my wandering mind, feel smarter, and increase my money, I would like to know about future technologies. These advantages will lead me to a better life now and also in the future. Just think of the possibilities in technology in just another five or ten years, it's amazing.

C. Useful Expressions

1. If I could know something about the future, I would want to know what type of new technologies there

will be, such as cars, phones and anything else that we don't currently have.

2. I have always been curious about what our future holds for us.

3. By knowing this, I could gain many advantages in my life now and in the future.

4. So, my wandering mind is always curious about what things will be different.

5. It's very exciting to me to think of the future possibilities.

6. Currently, I have a smart phone and I am not very skilled in its applications.

7. I feel that I am always behind the learning curve.

8. Lastly, by knowing about the future technologies, I could invest my money and make even more income.

9. I can buy the stocks at a cheap price, and be guaranteed a good return in the future because I'll know that the companies will succeed.

10. These advantages will lead me to a better life now and also in the future.

Q195. Describe a peculiar dream of yours.

A. Essay Outline

Argument: I had a very peculiar dream that was about me flying with bird wings.
Support 1: I started growing wings at first.
Support 2: Then, I was able to fly to all different countries.
Support 3: When I landed, my wings turned back into my arms.
Thesis: This very peculiar dream about flying, made me want to travel even more.

B. Model Essay

I have had many different types of dreams throughout my life. Some of them are happy or sad dreams, while others are scary dreams. However, about two months I had a very peculiar dream happen to me. I had a dream about growing wings and flying around the world. It was the strangest dream that I've ever experienced I can say without a doubt.

It all started when I fell asleep after having a stressful day. In my dream, I started to walk along the street outside and my arms started to itch. Bird feathers started to grow from my skin. They eventually turned into a full set of bird wings. Fortunately, there was nobody around me to have seen this very strange sight.

After my wings fully grew, I started to flap them. I felt like a baby bird learning to fly for the first time. I was very shaky at first, but I got the hang of it after a few tries. I started to fly more confidently, and within a few months, I was flying all around the world visiting various countries; Hawaii, Japan, China, Australia, Europe, South Korea, Thailand and more! It was so exciting.

When I landed in each of these different countries, I found that as soon as my feet touched the ground, my bird wings receded back into my body. This was a very good thing, because for all I knew, I was the only person who could do such a marvelous and peculiar thing. If my new wings didn't disappear, I'm sure I would have been looked at very unusually.

It was so strange to be thinking of this while I was sleeping, because I've never had a dream quite like this one. I'm not sure why I had this dream, but it left me wanting to travel to more places. It's funny to me, because I've never been to most of the places that I had traveled to in my dreams. So, I'm curious how the real places relate to my own perceptions of those locations.

C. Useful Expressions

1. It was the strangest dream that I've ever experienced I can say without a doubt.

_____

2. In my dream, I started to walk along the street outside and my arms started to itch.

_____

3. Fortunately, there was nobody around me to have seen this very strange sight.

_____

4. After my wings fully grew, I started to flap them.

_____

5. I was very shaky at first, but I got the hang of it after a few tries.

_____

6. I started to fly more confidently, and within a few months, I was flying all around the world visiting various countries.

_____

_____

7. I found that as soon as my feet touched the ground, my bird wings receded back into my body.

_____

8. This was a very good thing, because for all I knew, I was the only person who could do such a marvelous and peculiar thing.

_____

_____

9. If my new wings didn't disappear, I'm sure I would have been looked at very unusually.

_____

10. So, I'm curious how the real places relate to my own perceptions of those locations.

_____

Q196. Describe what you would miss from your home if you went abroad to study
.

A. Essay Outline

Argument: There are a few things I know I would miss the most from my home if I had to go abroad.
Support 1: The first thing I would miss is my photo album collection.
Support 2: The next thing would be my vast selection of books.
Support 3: The last item I would miss a lot from my home is my movie collection.
Thesis: Even though I would miss all these items a lot, I would enjoy and welcome the new environment's
culture, books, and movies.

B. Model Essay

There are a few things I know I would miss the most from my home if I had to go abroad: my photos, my books, and my movie collection. Since I am going abroad, I can't take many things with me. The airlines only allow you to bring two 50 lb. suitcases on board. There is no way that I could fit all those items in my suitcase to take with me, so I could only a take a few of them.

First, I would take my photos with me, because I have so many good memories that I want to remember while I'm away. My photos are mostly of my funny, sad, and happy memories with my family and friends. When I am sad or feeling down, I like to pull out my photo albums and page through them, remembering the many good times we have had together. It's comforting to have something, such as my photos, that can brighten my mood.

Next, the books are something that keeps me entertained in my down time. I love reading books, and I'm pretty sure that I wouldn't be able to find that many English books in a foreign country. If I could, it's almost guaranteed that they will be pricey. Plus, I already have a lot of books, so I wouldn't want to buy the same book twice. When I'm reading books, they take my mind off of my worries and I enjoy relating to the characters in the story. Escaping to another world in stressful times is very soothing.

Finally, movies are something I enjoy seeing a lot. The selection of English speaking movies abroad would also be slim. I currently live in South Korea, and it is often difficult to see many movies in my own home language. Most of them are Korean speaking movies with very few foreign movies being shown. I know that you can download movies, but I love the experience of going to a theater and seeing the new movies on a big screen.

Even though I would miss all of these items a lot, I would still really enjoy and welcome the new environment's culture, books, and movies. Being away from home can be a sad and lonely thing, but it is also an exciting and adventurous thing. By bringing some of these items with me, it would help me not to miss my home as much.

C. Useful Expressions

1. There are a few things I know I would miss the most from my home if I had to go abroad: my photos, my books, and my movie collection.

_____

_____

2. The airlines only allow you to bring two 50 lb. suitcases on board.

_____

3. First, I would take my photos with me, because I have so many good memories that I want to remember while I'm away.

_____

_____

4. When I am sad or feeling down, I like to pull out my photo albums and page through them,

_____

5. It's comforting to have something, such as my photos, that can brighten your mood.

_____

6. Next, the books are something that keeps me entertained in my down time.

_____

7. If I could, it's almost guaranteed that they will be pricey.

_____

8. When I'm reading books, they take my mind off of my worries and I enjoy relating to the characters in the story.

_____

9. I know that you can download movies, but I love the experience of going to a theater and seeing the new movies on a big screen.

_____

_____

10. Even though I would miss all of these items a lot, I would still really enjoy and welcome the new environment's culture, books, and movies.

_____

_____

Q197. Do you prefer to relax or to do another activity when you are taking a break from studying?

A. Essay Outline

Argument: When given the choice between relaxing and doing another activity on my study breaks, I prefer to do another activity.

Support 1: First, when we relax, we tend to feel lazier.

Support 2: I am able to give my mind a chance to do something else.

Support 3: I am able to make the most out of my day.

Thesis: Despite the fact that most people would want to relax during their break from studying, I prefer to do something else during that time.

B. Model Essay

When given the choice between relaxing and doing another activity on my study breaks, I prefer to do another activity. There are three main reasons for opinion. First, I tend to feel lazier if I relax. Second, by doing an activity, I'm still giving my mind a rest from the study materials. Third, I can make the most out of my day.

To start with, when I relax, I tend to feel lazier. When our bodies are too well rested, it is harder for us to be motivated to go back to work. For example, when I am memorizing vocabulary words, and I take a break by just sitting and relaxing, I find it much harder to want to go back to studying again. I will usually say to myself, "Five more minutes, five more minutes." This continues on until it is too late, and then I have lost all of my studying time by relaxing too much.

The next reason is that by doing other activities, such as playing a sport, running, or reading a book, I am still able to give my mind a rest, but I'm not being lazy. By playing sports or running, our body is able to release a lot of the built up stress. Whenever I am tired, I like to go on a long walk or a quick jog somewhere. It refreshes my mind and re-motivates me to want to study harder.

The final reason is that I am able to make the most out of my day. If the only thing I do on my study break is relax, then I won't be able to accomplish all of my tasks for the day. I usually have many other things to do throughout the day, such as paying bills, buying groceries, etc. So, if I relax, I won't be able to get everything done that is on my checklist. Then, this will cause me to be even more stressed, which will take even more time away from studying.

Despite the fact that most people would want to relax during their break from studying, I prefer to do something else more constructive during that time. This is because I won't feel lazier, I can still rest my brain, and I will be able to accomplish everything I want to for that day. It just seems like a smarter option to me to do other activities rather than to relax and become lazy.

C. Useful Expressions

1. When given the choice between relaxing and doing another activity on my study breaks, I prefer to do another activity.

2. First, I tend to feel lazier if I relax.

3. Second, by doing an activity, I'm still giving my mind a rest from the study materials.

4. For example, when I am memorizing vocabulary words, and I take a break by just sitting and relaxing, I find it much harder to want to go back to studying again.

5. By playing sports or running, our body is able to release a lot of the built up stress.

6. It refreshes my mind and re-motivates me to want to study harder.

7. The final reason is that I am able to make the most out of my day.

8. If the only thing I do on my study break is relax, then I won't be able to accomplish all of my tasks for the day.

9. So, if I relax, I won't be able to get everything done that is on my checklist.

10. Despite the fact that most people would want to relax during their break from studying, I prefer to do something else more constructive during that time.

Q198. Do you prefer learning about movies before you see them or not knowing a nything about them and being surprised?

A. Essay Outline

Argument: I am one who likes to be surprised in a movie, so I would prefer to know nothing about the movie before seeing it.

Support 1: I want to enjoy the movie and not be thinking about it as a predictable story.

Support 2: I am able to become a part of the movie.

Support 3: I can make my own opinions and conclusions about the movie.

Thesis: Because I will have a more enjoyable and surprising movie experience, I would rather not know anything about a movie before I go to see it.

B. Model Essay

I am one who likes to be surprised in a movie, so I would prefer to know nothing about the movie before seeing it. When I go to see an action movie, or a suspense movie, I don't want to know how it ends because I will be thinking too much, I will not be able to connect with the characters, and I won't be able to make my own opinions freely.

The first thing to point out is that the movie will become predictable if we know information about the movie. This is because during the whole movie, I will just be thinking about when the certain events that I know will take place. It almost ruins the movie because all I will be doing is thinking. It makes it very hard to be excited or surprised by something when you are trying to always guess when that event will take place. It's always better to me to be guessing and paying attention to all the clues, so I can guess what will happen next myself.

With this in mind, I am able to become a part of the movie because I can let go of my worries. A movie can take you places and be extremely relatable if you let it. When I am watching a love story, I often put myself in one of the characters shoes. It makes the movie more realistic, which allows me to feel the emotions that are portrayed more.

I can make my own opinions and conclusions about the movie. Take, for example, the movie Batman: Dark Knight Rises. If I knew how the movie was going to end, I wouldn't have been as excited or surprised at the ending's twist. I thought that Bane had been the boy from the Hole the whole time. It just isn't the same experience when you know that Miranda, the seemingly innocent women, is the person trying to blow up the city, not Bane, the obvious villain. It ruins the suspense that the movie director and writers worked hard to create.

Because I will have a more enjoyable and surprising movie experience, I would rather not know anything about a movie before I go to see it. Knowing information about a movie, such as plot, twists, and characters, can actually damage your movie watching experience. I love to be surprised and to always be shocked when I see something happen in a movie that I hadn't expected

C. Useful Expressions

1. I am one who likes to be surprised in a movie

_____

2. I will not be able to connect with the characters.

_____

3. This is because during the whole movie, I will just be thinking about when the certain events that I know will take place.

_____

_____

4. It almost ruins the movie, because all I will be doing is thinking.

_____

5. It's always better to me to be guessing and paying attention to all the clues, so I can guess what will happen next myself.

_____

_____

6. With this in mind, I am able to become a part of the movie because I can let go of my worries.

_____

7. A movie can take you places and be extremely relatable if you let it.

_____

8. When I am watching a love story, I often put myself in one of the character's shoes.

_____

9. It just isn't the same experience when you know that Miranda, the seemingly innocent women, is the person trying to blow up the city, not Bane, the obvious villain.

_____

_____

10. Knowing information about a movie, such as plot, twists, and characters, can actually damage your movie watching experience.

_____

_____

Q199. What must be considered when choosing a job or career?

A. Essay Outline

Argument: There are a few important factors to be considered when choosing a job or a career; desire to do the job, location, and benefits.

Support 1: First, I would consider whether or not it is something I want to do for a long period of time.

Support 2: The second factor is the location.

Support 3: Finally, the benefits you will receive are an important thing to consider.

Thesis: It would be detrimental for your future to take a job if any of these important factors were not met or considered in deciding a career or a job for you.

B. Model Essay

There are a few important factors to be considered when choosing a job or a career. I think about the future a lot, so my factors are based all on my future, not my present. I would consider my desire to do the job for a long period of time, where the job is located, and what benefits I would receive.

First, I would consider whether or not it is something I want to do for a long period of time. When choosing a job, you have to remember that you will probably be doing this job for many years. So you want to evaluate whether it is something you are able and willing to do for an extended period of time. For example, if you don't like children, then you shouldn't choose a job in teaching. On the other hand, if you love children and are patient enough to be around them all day long, then teaching is a good career option for you.

The second deciding factor is the location. If you want to live in Southern USA, then you will have to choose a career that is offered there. Likewise, an ice-water fishing career would not be a good choice if you don't want to be in cold climates. Also, what countries, cities or states will you have to travel to? Are you able to go to these locations freely and without any dietary or other issues? Some jobs require us to travel, so these are also very important factors in choosing the right job for you.

Finally, the benefits you will receive are an important thing to consider. If you are planning on having a family, then your job needs to have the appropriate health insurance benefits to allow your family to be covered. This is especially important if you are pregnant or your wife is. Some companies or careers do not cover pregnancy under their basic healthcare packages. So you have to watch out carefully for these minor details.

It would be detrimental to your future if you took a job where any of these important factors were not met or considered during the decision process. As I stated before, I am always thinking about how things in the present will affect my future. So, it is important to think about my long term happiness based on my job's location and benefits.

C. Useful Expressions

1. There are a few important factors to be considered when choosing a job or a career.

2. I would consider my desire to do the job for a long period of time, where the job is located, and what benefits I would receive.

3. So you want to evaluate whether it is something you are able and willing to do for an extended period of time.

4. On the other hand, if you love children and are patient enough to be around them all day long, then teaching is a good career option for you.

5. The second deciding factor is the location.

6. Likewise, an ice-water fishing career would not be a good choice if you don't want to be in cold climates.

7. Some jobs require us to travel, so these are also very important factors in choosing the right job for you.

8. Some companies or careers do not cover pregnancy under their basic healthcare packages.

9. So you have to watch out carefully for these minor details.

10. It would be detrimental to your future if you took a job where any of these important factors were not met or considered during the decision process.

Q200. If you had the opportunity to learn a musical instrument, what would you learn?

A. Essay Outline

Argument: If I had the opportunity to learn a musical instrument, I would want to learn the acoustic guitar.
Support 1: The most obvious reason, to me, why I want to learn the guitar is because I already have one.
Support 2: Next, I want to play music to my students and children.
Support 3: Finally, I feel that it will be a good challenge to me.
Thesis: Since I already have a guitar, it is something that will enhance my students' education, and it will be a great challenge to me, I want to learn the guitar if I am given the opportunity to do so.

B. Model Essay

If I had the opportunity to learn a musical instrument, I would want to learn the acoustic guitar. There are many other instruments I also want to learn, such as the piano, the violin, and the ukulele, but the guitar is the first one on my wish list. I have three reasons for my opinion: I already have one, I want to play it for others, and I want the challenge of mastering the chords.

The most obvious reason, to me, why I want to learn the guitar is because I already have one. Therefore, I would not incur any additional costs to purchase a new instrument. For my birthday two years ago, a friend of mine gave me her barely used guitar. I was so shocked that somebody would give me something that was worth so much money. Unfortunately, it has been sitting in my closet for the past two years and has not even been taken out of its box, except for one time when my boyfriend wanted to look at it. Because I already have an acoustic guitar, it makes the most sense to learn it if I'm given the opportunity to do so.

Next, I want to play music to my students and children. Throughout my years in education, the teachers who played music in the classroom are the ones whom I learned the most from. Therefore, I want to help my students and children to learn in a fun environment. In the classroom, we can sing songs that relate to the lessons. This will enhance the students' ability to retain information because it has been proven that songs increase our retention rate. Just think back on the ABC's song that we learn as children. Now, imagine we learn the Periodic Table through the use of a song, too. The options are limitless on what our brain will be able to hold on to over the years.

Finally, I feel that it will be a good challenge to me. I have already learned how to play the clarinet and it was a very simple instrument to learn. I want to challenge myself more by learning a more complex instrument. The guitar is just that. To the eye, it seems simple, but there are many chord progressions, and stylistic holdings that one can do. So it seems like the perfect adventure for me to partake in.

Since I already have a guitar, it is something that will enhance my students' education, and it will be a great challenge to me, I want to learn the guitar if I am given the opportunity to do so. The guitar offers me many options to perform, and I can still talk to others while playing this instrument, unlike the clarinet that I had previously learned as a child. After I master the guitar, then I want to move on to the next instrument, the ukulele.

C. Useful Expressions

1. There are many other instruments I also want to learn, such as the piano, the violin, and the ukulele, but the guitar is the first one on my wish list.

_____

2. I want the challenge of mastering the chords.

_____

3. Therefore, I would not incur any additional costs to purchase a new instrument.

_____

4. For my birthday two years ago, a friend of mine gave me her barely used guitar.

_____

5. Because I already have an acoustic guitar, it makes the most sense to learn it if I'm given the opportunity to do so.

_____

_____

6. Therefore, I want to help my students and children to learn in a fun environment.

_____

7. This will enhance the students' ability to retain information, because it has been proven that songs increase our retention rate.

_____

_____

8. The options are limitless on what our brain will be able to hold on to over the years.

_____

9. So, it seems like the perfect adventure for me to partake in.

_____

10. After I master the guitar, then I want to move on to the next instrument, the ukulele.

_____

Q201. Describe an experience of going on a picnic with your school.

A. Essay Outline

Argument: An experience I had going on a picnic during my schools days was my 6th grade class field trip in San Antonio, Texas at Candlewood Elementary School.

Support 1: All year, the 6th grade students look forward to the day off of school, in June.

Support 2: Then, we took a mile walk to the park where there were picnic tables with our teacher's names on them.

Support 3: When we arrived, we put our stuff down and started to play many different organized sports.

Thesis: We had such a great day that by the time we had to walk home, none of us wanted to go.

B. Model Essay

An experience I had going on a picnic during my schools days was with my 6th grade class for a field trip in San Antonio, Texas. Candlewood Elementary School, my school, hosts a party for the class that is moving up to middle school as congratulations for making it through elementary school. We get to go to a park that is nearby, eat yummy picnic foods, and play many fun team games.

All year, the 6th grade students look forward to the day off of school, in June. This is because all of the other students will be busy studying and learning, while we are out playing and having fun. On the day of the picnic, we, being the 6th grade class, all gathered at school wearing our school's colors and holding any sports equipment we wanted to use. We brought items such as footballs, soccer balls, and jump ropes. Our teachers took roll-call, lined use up, and gave us all a safety talk.

After we gathered at school, we then took a mile walk to the park where picnic tables were set up with our teacher's names on them. During the walk, we sang songs and talked about all the fun things we were going to do that day. I remember very clearly all the students having their clothing on backwards and singing to the song, "Jump" by Kris Kross. It was a silly thing to do then, and it makes me laugh even more thinking about it now. I wonder what my little brother's class will dress like and the music they will be listening to.

When we arrived at the park, we put our stuff, sports equipment, and food down. Then, we started to play many different organized sports. We played baseball, basketball, water balloon fights, tug-o-war, obstacle course races, and many other fun activities. The weather was perfect for this day, as it usually is in Texas. All the different classes competed against each other to see who the best 6th grade class was. Unfortunately, we had to wait until the end of the day to find out who the winners were.

We had such a great day that none of us wanted to go back to school or home. Our class was the biggest winner of the day, because we had the best runners in our grade and the strongest students too! It's fun to think about that day and all the good times we had together as a class on our picnic/field day.

C. Useful Expressions

1. An experience I had going on a picnic during my schools days was with my 6th grade class for a field trip in San Antonio, Texas.

_____

2. Candlewood Elementary School hosts a party for the class who is moving up to middle school as congratulations for making it through elementary school.

_____

3. All year, the 6th grade students look forward to the day off of school, in June.

_____

4. We get to go to a park that is nearby, eat yummy picnic foods, and play many fun team games.

_____

5. All year, the 6th grade students look forward to the day off of school, in June.

_____

6. On the day of the picnic, we, being the 6th grade class, all gathered at school.

_____

7. After we gathered at school, we then took a mile walk to the park where picnic tables were set up with our teacher's names on them.

_____

8. I remember very clearly all the students having their clothing on backwards and singing to the song, "Jump" by Kris Kross.

_____

9. I wonder what my little brother's class will dress like and the music they will be listening to.

_____

10. Unfortunately, we had to wait until the end of the day to find out who the winners were.

_____

Q202. Describe how you dress. Why do you dress this way?

A. Essay Outline

Argument: The way I dress is in a simple and modest style that is appropriate for teaching.
Support 1: First, while I am working, I wear loose fitting clothing that is very modest.
Support 2: My after work or free time clothing is less professional but still very modest.
Support 3: I usually wear most of my school clothing after work because it I often will see students or parents.
Thesis: Since clothing is a direct reflection of you, I dress in a modest style.

B. Model Essay

Clothing often times defines who you are, so I always try to dress in an appropriate manner. Therefore, the way I dress is in a simple and modest style. I have two slightly different styles; one for when I am working, and one for when I am out and about with my friends. Both of these styles are almost interchangeable.

First, while I am working, I wear loose fitting clothing that is very modest. I am a teacher, and I have many students who judge me, so I cannot wear the same clothing as the students, nor can I look inappropriate. Also, my clothing has to be more professional, since I am in a professional work environment. Some examples of what I wear to school are dresses, dress skirts, and blouses. I do have to admit that some days, I wear more relaxed clothing, like corduroy pants, but I still maintain my professional look.

On the other hand, my after work or free time clothing is less professional but still modest. I enjoy wearing long flowing skirts, tank-tops, and t-shirts to go eat dinner with my friends in downtown. I chose to dress this way because it is comfortable for all occasions. Also, it is respectful of the Korean culture's style of clothing. They are a very conservative society, so I try to never wear clothing that would be deemed inappropriate or upsetting to them, even though I might be a little hot during the summer time.

Furthermore, I can usually wear most of my work clothing after school because it is mostly all the same style. Most people classify my style of clothing as hippy or teacher-styled clothing. I don't mind this type of classification because it suits me well. Sometimes, while I am downtown having meals with my friends, I will encounter my students' and their families. So, I feel that I always have to look modest and semi-professional as to not give my school a bad name.

Since clothing is a direct reflection of you, I dress in a modest style. You never know when you will run into somebody and they will think differently of you based on your appearances. So it is very important to me, to always look appropriate to the Korean people and to my students.

C. Useful Expressions

1. Clothing often times defines who you are, so I always try to dress in an appropriate manner.

2. Therefore, the way I dress is in a simple and modest style. I have two slightly different styles; one for when I am working, and one for when I am out and about with my friends.

3. Both of these styles are almost interchangeable.

4. I do have to admit that some days, I wear more relaxed clothing, like corduroy pants, but I still maintain my professional look.

5. I chose to dress this way because it is comfortable for all occasions. Also, it is respectful of the Korean culture's style of clothing.

6. They are a very conservative society, so I try to never wear clothing that would be deemed inappropriate or upsetting to them, even though I might be a little hot during the summer time.

7. Most people classify my style of clothing as hippy or teacher-styled clothing.

8. I don't mind this type of classification because it suits me well.

9. Since clothing is a direct reflection of you, I dress in a modest style.

10. You never know when you will run into somebody and they will think differently of you based on your appearances.

Q203. Describe your favorite holiday. Why is it your favorite holiday?

A. Essay Outline

Argument: As a child my favorite holiday was always Halloween and still is to this day.
Support 1: The first thing to know is where the holiday Halloween originated from.
Support 2: In modern days, we do a hodge-podge of the traditions from the various ancient histories.
Support 3: My final reason why Halloween is my favorite holiday is because we can dress up and be somebody else for at least a few hours.
Thesis: Halloween is my favorite holiday because people get dressed up, parade around, receive candy, and get spooked by unknown events, and also the history is really interesting.

B. Model Essay

As a child my favorite holiday was always Halloween. As I grew up, I thought that I would grow out of the desire to dress up and scare people. However, this urge to frighten others never disappeared. I'm pretty sure that this passion comes from my own mother's love of Halloween. Halloween is often times only a holiday for the youth, but children and adults of all ages and nationalities can partake in this exciting and spooky holiday.

The first thing to know is where the holiday Halloween originated from. It happens every year on the 31st of October and is most notably celebrated in the United States, United Kingdom, Ireland, and Canada. The name Halloween originated from the shortening of the words 'All Hallows Evening.' Furthermore, it is actually a celebration from the Celtic times called Samhain. The ancient Gaels believed that every year on the 31st of October, when the harvest season was over, the worlds of the living and the dead would overlap, causing the deceased to come back to life and bring havoc upon the crops. Festivals were held, and costumes were worn to ward off the evil spirits. Bonfires would attract insects, which would attract bats, hence the bat as a symbol for Halloween. Another key point is the act of trick-or-treating. This came about from the Medieval Times, where beggars would go from door to door asking for food in return for prayers for their dead ancestors.

In modern days, we do a hodge-podge of the traditions from the various ancient histories. In America, we have many interesting activities during this time of year. One of my favorites is the haunted house. We willingly pay money to go inside of a dark and scary house, where the walls are moving, creatures will sneak up behind you and scare the living day lights out of you, and there are horrific looking scenes of bloody dismembered bodies strewn on a table. To many people, this might be too much for their stomachs to handle, but for me, I get a thrill out of it! One of my favorite haunted houses that I had the pleasure of experiencing was in Philadelphia, Pennsylvania. It is ordinarily called the Eastern State Penitentiary, but during the Halloween season it is called "Terror Behind the Walls." This place is a real jail where people have died and bad things have happened, so it makes the experience more realistic to the participants of the dark maze.

My final reason why Halloween is my favorite holiday is because we can dress up and be somebody else for at least a few hours. Throughout my childhood I have had the wonderful experience of being many different people and things. My mom was the creator of my costumes, as well as my two sisters' costumes. We were black cats, friendly witches, Peter Pan, cute ghosts, ballerinas, and princesses. But, as we got older, our minds changed and we grew up, and so did our costumes. In our teenage years, we were belly dancers, more vicious looking ghosts and witches, 1970's disco girls, and more. It's always fun to dress up and be somebody else because it feels like you are putting on a play for your friends. You have to act like the character you are dressed up as in order to get the sweet treats from the neighbors' candy bowls.

To conclude, Halloween is a very popular holiday around the world. It is a day where people get dressed up, parade around, receive candy, and get spooked by unknown events. It can be a frightening day for others, but for me it is an exhilarating feeling to feel the blood rush through my body when something jumps out in front of me in a dark maze. I look forward to the next Halloween where I will dress up as Alice-In-Wonderland!

C. Useful Expressions

1. As a child my favorite holiday was always Halloween.

_____

2. As I grew up, I thought that I would grow out of the desire to dress up and scare people.

_____

3. I'm pretty sure that this passion comes from my own mother's love of Halloween.

_____

4. Halloween is often times only a holiday for the youth, but children and adults of all ages and nationalities can partake in this exciting and spooky holiday.

_____

_____

5. The first thing to know is where the holiday Halloween originated from.

_____

6. Furthermore, it is actually a celebration from the Celtic times called Samhain.

_____

7. To many people, this might be too much for their stomachs to handle, but for me, I get a thrill out of it!

_____

8. It can be a frightening day for others, but for me it is an exhilarating feeling to feel the blood rush through my body when something jumps out in front of me in a dark maze.

_____

_____

9. I look forward to the next Halloween where I will dress up as Alice-In-Wonderland!

_____

> **Q204.** Describe how you learn a foreign language. Why do you learn this way and is it the best way for you to learn?

A. Essay Outline

Argument: German is a very difficult language to learn, so I learn it in a variety of ways.
Support 1: First, the best way to learn German is to make many friends who speak German.
Support 2: Second, I have a journal that I write a word or a phrase for the day in.
Support 3: Third, I attend a special after school academy where I usually spend four hours a night being taught grammar, reading, writing, and listening.
Thesis: By using a combination of these three learning techniques, I am able to learn German well.

B. Model Essay

Learning any language can be difficult feat, so I learn a foreign language in a variety of ways to make it less daunting and more interesting. Some examples are: I make many friends who speak German, I write in a journal to learn new words, and I attend an after school academy. Through the use of these three techniques, I hope that my German will improve.

First, the best way to learn German is to make many friends who speak this language. By doing this, I am forced to be exposed to the new language, and I have to learn it more quickly to communicate effectively. When I am around my German speaking friends, I am sometimes lost, because I don't always understand them. This might seem like a bad thing, but by being challenged, I am able to learn more things in a quicker amount of time.

Second, I have a journal that I write a word or a phrase every day in. Throughout the day, week, and month, I use these words as often as possible, until they are natural for me to use. For example, today's word was 'recommend.' So everywhere I went, I would use the word recommend in a sentence to become more fluent in its meaning and usage. I have learned many words and phrases this way.

Third, I attend a special after school academy, where I usually spend four hours a night being taught grammar, reading, writing, and listening. It is a very long day for me, but I know that I am improving my German skills every day! The other two ways are more of a self-learning technique, but this one is through the use of a professional teacher. I am able to ask questions to the teachers and get constructive feedback on my pronunciation, which is a great asset. While at the academy, I know that I am learning German well and that it is a guaranteed improvement to my skills.

By using a combination of these three learning techniques, I am able to learn German effectively, efficiently, and in a fun environment. I am able to learn through friends, through myself by writing in a journal, and through the use of a professionally-trained German teacher. I hope that in just a few years, I will be completely fluent in German.

C. Useful Expressions

1. Learning any language can be a difficult feat, so I learn a foreign language in a variety of ways to make it less daunting and more interesting.

_____

2. By doing this, I am forced to be exposed to the new language, and I have to learn it more quickly to communicate effectively.

_____

3. This might seem like a bad thing, but by being challenged, I am able to learn more things in a quicker amount of time.

_____

4. Throughout the day, week, and month, I use these words as often as possible, until they are natural for me to use.

_____

5. The other two ways are more of a self-learning technique, but this one is through the use of a professional teacher.

_____

6. I am able to ask questions to the teachers and get constructive feedback on my pronunciation, which is a great asset.

_____

7. While at the academy, I know that I am learning German well and that it is a guaranteed improvement to my skills.

_____

8. By using a combination of these three learning techniques, I am able to learn German effectively, efficiently, and in a fun environment.

_____

9. I hope that in just a few years, I will be completely fluent in German.

_____

Q205. Describe your favorite sport.

A. Essay Outline

Argument: I love all types of sports, but my favorite sport is soccer.
Support 1: The rules of the game are not very complicated to learn.
Support 2: The offensive teams and the defensive teams are in a constant battle back and forth.
Support 3: It is a physically challenging game, with minimal scoring.
Thesis: Because of the difficulty and the fast paced nature of the game, soccer is my favorite sport.

B. Model Essay

As a child, I loved playing football, tag, and basketball, but none of these are my favorite, soccer. Soccer is a very popular sport all around the world. Some places, such as England, call this sport football though. No matter what you call it, it is a fantastic sport requiring great skill and a body that is in excellent condition.

To begin with, soccer is a very simple game to learn based on the rules. It uses a ball with black and white hexagonal shapes on it. A soccer team consists of 10 players, plus a goalie for each team. These two teams are trying to either score a goal or to prevent a goal from being scored. You may not use your hands at all throughout the game, except for the goalie or if you are out of bounds and throwing the ball back in. Also, you cannot purposefully hit a player or grab a player, or you will receive a penalty.

Furthermore, the 10 players are divided into two teams: the offensive team and the defensive team. The offensive players are the players who shoot and score the goals. They pass and kick the ball towards the goal, where the goalie is waiting to block their shots. The defensive players, on the other hand, are the players who are trying to prevent the soccer ball from entering their goal. The goalie always stays within his rectangular space and does whatever he can to prevent the ball from entering his goal. I feel that the goalie is one of the most difficult positions because this player has the most pressure put on him or her.

In addition, the soccer field is very large, so the players have to be substituted out after they get tired. To many people, this sport is not very exciting due to the fact that not many goals are scored throughout the game. Actually, it is not uncommon for there to be no goals made by either team. This is because the sport is extremely difficult to play and it requires great skill to make a goal. To me, however, I think it is a very exciting game.

Because of the difficulty and the fast paced nature of the game, soccer is my favorite sport. Soccer players are some of the most physically fit athletes due to the constant motion of all of the players. I was fortunate to be able to play soccer in my school years, and it is the reason why I love the sport even more.

C. Useful Expressions

1. As a child, I loved playing football, tag, and basketball, but none of these are my favorite, soccer.

2. No matter what you call it, it is a fantastic sport requiring great skill and a body that is in excellent condition.

3. To begin with, soccer is a very simple game to learn based on the rules.

4. A soccer team consists of 10 players, plus a goalie for each team.

5. The goalie always stays within his rectangular space and does whatever he can to prevent the ball from entering his goal.

6. I feel that the goalie is one of the most difficult positions, because this player has the most pressure put on him or her.

7. In addition, the soccer field is very large, so the players have to be substituted out after they get tired.

8. To many people, this sport is not very exciting due to the fact that not many goals are scored throughout the game.

9. This is because the sport is extremely difficult to play and it requires great skill to make a goal.

10. Because of the difficulty and the fast paced nature of the game, soccer is my favorite sport.

12. There's the proof that you're doing something good right in front of your eyes.

13. That's why I would choose doing volunteer work over making a donation of money.

Q206. What is the most important subject you study at school?

A. Essay Outline

Argument: To me, the most important subject to study is math for a few reasons.
Support 1: Math is a subject that is guaranteed to be used outside of school.
Support 2: Math is required for many jobs.
Support 3: Too many people have become reliant on computers, calculators and cell phones.
Thesis: Since it is vital to our success in our lives, math is the most important to study in school.

B. Model Essay

There are many important subjects to study in school, such as math, science, art and music. To me, the most important subject to study is math for a few reasons. We will have to use it outside of school, it will be a requirement for our job, and people have become too reliant on technology.

First, math is a subject that is guaranteed to be used outside of school. An example would be estimating time and distance for a trip. If you want to be on time to your appointments, you need to be able to correctly judge what time you should leave your house to arrive at a certain destination that is far away. Also, we need to do calculations when shopping, fueling our gas tanks, and many other daily tasks. Without math, we would have a difficult time being at the right place, at the right time.

Next, many jobs and daily life activities require, at the minimum, basic math skills. For example, a job as a teacher requires a person to compute averages and to score papers. A job as a doctor requires a person to calculate the correct dosage. Throughout a person's life, he or she needs to be able to count money and know that they received the right amount of change back. If a person is not strong and well-trained in mathematics, then he will also struggle in achieving a good job.

Finally, too many people have become reliant on computers, calculators and cell phones to do their entire math calculations for them. What will happen when the technology doesn't work? Our future generations are going to be lost and they won't be able to work at their jobs properly without learning math in school. Sometimes power outages occur, and it causes many problems. This is because people cannot live without the use of a computer to help them complete their jobs tasks.

Since it is vital to our success in our lives, math is the most important to study in school. Math is needed in everyday life, unlike other subjects. Also, it is a requirement for many jobs. Finally, the current generation of children is too dependent on technology.

C. Useful Expressions

1. To me, the most important subject to study is math for a few reasons.

2. We will have to use it outside of school, it will be a requirement for our job, and people have become too

reliant on technology.

_____

_____

3. First, math is a subject that is guaranteed to be used outside of school.

_____

4. Without math, we would have a difficult time being at the right place, at the right time.

_____

5. Next, many jobs and daily life activities require, at the minimum, basic math skills.

_____

6. If a person is not strong and well-trained in mathematics, then he will also struggle in achieving a good job.

_____

_____

7. What will happen when the technology doesn't work?

_____

8. Sometimes power outages occur, and it causes many problems.

_____

9. Since it is vital to our success in our lives, math is the most important to study in school.

_____

10. Finally, the current generation of children is too dependent on technology.

_____

Q207. What has been your most important academic achievement?

A. Essay Outline

Argument: My most important academic achievement was earning all A's in my degree related college classes.

Support 1: It was the A's in the important classes that really mattered to me.

Support 2: I realized that my hard work paid off because I used the knowledge I worked hard to learn in my current profession.

Support 3: Getting A's showed me that I was capable of achieving more than what I was told I could achieve.

Thesis: Because I have learned many things in school and life, my obtaining a 3.95 GPA in college is my greatest academic achievement.

B. Model Essay

I have earned many academic achievements throughout my school years. My most important academic achievement was my receiving perfect grades in my degree related college classes. In college, I received a 3.95 GPA, earning all A's in my degree related classes, and two B's in History Fed/Form Republic and German.

My first point is that these two B's made me a little upset at first, but it was the A's in the important classes that really mattered to me. I studied hard to achieve the best grades and the best education I could possibly get in my Early Childhood and Elementary Education classes. I did numerous hours of practical field experience. Therefore, I received my best grades in these situations. So, it proved to me that I was in the right major.

Next, I realized that my hard work paid off because I have used the knowledge I worked hard to learn during my college years in my current profession. Every day, I have to think on my toes and my educational background has helped make this easier for me. An example would be when there is a change in the schedule and I need to think quickly about what to do with the students who are staring at me with curious eyes. I think of an activity I learned while in school and use that to make the class more exciting and not a waste of time.

Finally, receiving this level of education showed me that I was capable of achieving more than what I was told I could achieve. Throughout my life, I had to move many times, which caused me to repeat two different grades twice: Kindergarten (Germany and Pennsylvania) and 6th grade (Texas and Pennsylvania). It discouraged me for a while because people thought that since I was held back multiple times, I was not intelligent. It was actually quite the opposite and my college education proved it to me.

Because I have learned many things in school and life, my obtaining a 3.95 GPA in college is my greatest academic achievement. It has taught me that I am more capable than what I initially believed. Also, I have used this knowledge in my life towards my actual career.

174

C. Useful Expressions

1. I have earned many academic achievements throughout my school years.

2. My first point is that these two B's made me a little upset at first, but it was the A's in the important classes that really mattered to me.

3. So, it proved to me that I was in the right major.

4. Next, I realized that my hard work paid off, because I have used the knowledge I worked hard to learn during my college years in my current profession.

5. Every day, I have to think on my toes and my educational background has helped make this easier for me.

6. Finally, receiving this level of education showed me that I was capable of achieving more than what I was told I could achieve.

7. Throughout my life, I had to move many times.

8. It was actually quite the opposite and my college education proved it to me.

9. It has taught me that I am more capable than what I initially believed.

Q208. What type of music do you like the most?

A. Essay Outline

Argument: I like classical music the most.
Support 1: It is very calming and relaxing.
Support 2: I can learn a lot about other time periods from classical music.
Support 3: Listening to classical music helps me to study better.
Thesis: Because listening to classical music has so many benefits, it is my favorite musical genre.

B. Model Essay

I listen to many different types of music: jazz, rock, pop, and many others. While these are all good, I have to say that none of them is my favorite genre. Instead, my favorite musical genre has to be classical music without a doubt. I listen to classical music a lot because it is relaxing, because I can learn a lot about other time periods from classical music, and classical music helps me to study.

First, classical music is very calming. While rock, pop, and electronic music are usually very loud and stimulating, classical music beats are very soothing. Sometimes, I like to take a bath while I listen to classical music. They go very well together. The melodies of many famous composers can be upbeat while still tranquil. This is very true of Beethoven's Symphony No. 5. I listen to it every time I am feeling stressed from school or angry at somebody; it gets me out of my head for a little while so I can think about a situation more clearly.

Secondly, I can learn a lot about past European societies by listening to classical music. Since classical music is no longer the dominant genre on the planet now, it is in some ways very antiquated. Most of the pieces played by orchestras today were composed at least over two centuries ago. One of the things I learned from classical music was that all of the instruments were created by Europeans. The Europeans created the piano, the lute, and many other instruments played in traditional, classical music, but the Americans, including John Phillip Sousa, created the first marching band. I think this is a very fascinating part of musical history.

Lastly, classical music helps me to study. One of my worst subjects is math; sometimes, it will take me hours just to solve one problem. However, if I stop for a moment and play some classical music, it will almost instantly help guide me to the problem. There was also a study done in the U.S. on the effects of classical music while studying. They found that middle school students who listened to classical music before studying had higher test scores. This is just one of the many benefits of listening to classical music.

Because it is so relaxing and helps me to study, classical music is one of my favorite musical genres to listen to. Classical music not only helps me to learn more about subjects I currently study in school, for example, math, English, and history, but it also forces me to learn more about European musical instruments and the different waves of music. For these reasons, I will always cherish classical music.

C. Useful Expressions

1. While these are all good, I have to say that none of them are my favorite genre.

2. Instead, my favorite musical genre has to be classical music without a doubt.

_____

3. While rock, pop, and electronic music are usually very loud and stimulating, classical music beats are very soothing.

_____

_____

4. The melodies of many famous composers can be upbeat while still tranquil.

_____

5. This is very true of Beethoven's Symphony No. 5. I listen to it every time I am feeling stressed from school or angry at somebody.

_____

_____

6. It gets me out of my head for a little while so I can think about a situation more clearly.

_____

7. Since classical music is no longer the dominant genre on the planet now, it is in some ways very antiquated.

_____

8. Since classical music is no longer the dominant genre on the planet now, it is in some ways very antiquated.

_____

9. It will almost instantly help guide me to the problem.

_____

10. This is just one of the many benefits of listening to classical music.

_____

Q209. What expectations do you have of your parents?

A. Essay Outline

Argument: I expect my parents to support me in many different ways.
Support 1: I expect my parents to give me money until I am out of school and have a job.
Support 2: I expect my parents to support me when I am feeling sad.
Support 3: I expect my parents to tend to me when I am sick.
Thesis: Because parents are supposed to help their children, I expect my parents to support me when I need their help.

B. Model Essay

Some people have too great of expectations of their parents. They expect their parents to do their homework or help them cheat in school. Others have even more unreasonable expectations, perhaps even demanding their parents give them anything they want almost instantaneously. However, I am more reasonable; I simply expect my parents to help me while I cannot help myself. I need them to support me financially while I don't have a job, to cheer me up when I am sad, and to take care of me when I am sick.

First off, I expect my parents to support me when I am still in school. Because my parents brought me into life, I expect them to clothe and feed me, especially as I am still a child. There are many times when I cannot pay for things because they are too expensive even on my allowance. This includes regular meals or sometimes movies. Although I do not expect my parents to pay for all of my entertainment, I would definitely appreciate the gesture. More importantly, though, while I do not have a job, I need food, shelter, and clothing and I believe I am entitled to this at the very least.

Second, I believe that my parents should cheer me up when I am sad. One time in school, my friend made fun of me and my outfit that day. I felt like nobody could understand me at all because it was my best friend who made fun of me. When my mom saw me crying in my room, she immediately dropped everything and tried to cheer me up. She made my favorite meal and reassured me, telling me that everything would be alright in the end. My mom was right, and my friend and I made up the following week. I hope that all parents will give their children the emotional support they deserve.

Lastly, I expect my parents to take care of me when I am sick. This is because when I am sick, I cannot care for myself or make myself food. Then, I would need someone who will make sure I take my medicine or even take me to the hospital if I get worse. Just a couple of months ago, I had to get my wisdom teeth pulled. Because they put me under general anesthetic, I couldn't drive myself home. My mom drove me home from the oral surgeon's office, made me soup, and gave me ice cream because she knew that my mouth was sore. She filled my prescriptions and helped me to relax even as my entire mouth was in pain. My mother was very nice and I hope that she will still do this for me while I still need her.

In conclusion, I think that my expectations of my parents are very minimal. I expect my parents to help pay for me while I am still in school, to make me happy when I am feeling depressed, and to nurse me back to health when I am sick. I don't think these are unreasonable expectations at all, and all parents should do these things for their children.

C. Useful Expressions

1. Some people have too great of expectations of their parents.

_____

2. Others have even more unreasonable expectations, perhaps even demanding their parents give them anything they want almost instantaneously.

_____

_____

3. I simply expect my parents to help me while I cannot help myself

_____

4. Because my parents brought me into life, I expect them to clothe and feed me, especially as I am still a child.

_____

5. More importantly, though, while I do not have a job, I need food, shelter, and clothing and I believe I am entitled to this at the very least.

_____

_____

6. Lastly, I expect my parents to take care of me when I am sick.

_____

7. Just a couple of months ago, I had to get my wisdom teeth pulled.

_____

8. I expect my parents to help pay for me while I am still in school, to make me happy when I am feeling depressed, and to nurse me back to health when I am sick.

_____

_____

Q210. What would wish for if you had one wish?

A. Essay Outline

Argument: If I had one wish, I would wish for a giant mansion.
Support 1: I would have a place to live at for the rest of my life.
Support 2: I could impress my friends.
Support 3: I could learn how to be an interior designer and practice my skills designing rooms.
Thesis: Because there are so many benefits to having a big house, I would wish for mansion should I be granted one wish.

B. Model Essay

Although we can wish for many things in life, not all of them will come true. Wishes only come true when we work to achieve them. However, if I had one wish guaranteed to come true, I would wish for a mansion. I have three reasons to support this wish. First, I would have a place to live for the rest of my life. Second, I could impress my friends. Third, I would be able to practice interior design with the many rooms in my mansion.

The most important reason why I would wish for a mansion is because I would have a place to live for the rest of my life. One of the worst things in the world, I think, is moving. To me, it is a very stressful activity and it takes a lot of time. With a mansion, I would never have to move again; I would just have to move once into my mansion. That way, I would be less stressed and I would have more time to do the things I want to do like painting or playing video games. Also, it is really important to have some form of shelter, whether that be an apartment, a house, or even a cardboard box. It would be great if I didn't have to pay for a mortgage for a house; I wouldn't have to worry about making a monthly payment. If I forgot a payment, I would still have a roof over my head.

Second, with a mansion, my friends would be jealous of me and my life. Most of my friends live in simple, two-bedroom apartments with their parents. They might have an extra room or two, but for the most part, the places where they live are relatively small. If I had a mansion, especially all to myself, my friends would be impressed. I would have a lot of great things in my mansion: my own private movie theater, a swimming pool, and even a very big, well-stocked kitchen. They might even want to come live with me in my mansion, but I would only let them if they were nice to me. I think that my friends would tease me a lot less if they knew I lived in a big mansion.

Last, if I had a mansion, it would help me to realize my dream of becoming an interior designer. I've only studied interior design for about two years now, but I can now easily decorate a bedroom and my bathrooms are gorgeous. I really like a minimalist, modern aesthetic rather than something with a lot of grandeur. If I had a mansion, I could practice my interior design on many of the rooms in my mansion. Some of the rooms in my mansion could even be considered "test rooms" for me to test design ideas. I might even try to have different color rooms, like a plum room, a titanium room, and even a gray room, with a more grunge, industrial feel. I feel as if there is a lot of potential in a mansion and it would definitely be an asset to my career.

To sum up, if I had one wish, I would without a doubt wish for a brand new mansion. I would have a place to live until I die and I could certainly impress my friends. It would also help me to achieve my ultimate dream of becoming an interior designer. For these reasons, I think wishing for a big house would be the best way to use my one wish.

C. Useful Expressions

1. Although we can wish for many things in life, not all of them will come true.

_____

2. The most important reason why I would wish for a mansion is because I would have a place to live for the rest of my life.

_____

3. Also, it is really important to have some form of shelter, whether that be an apartment, a house, or even a cardboard box.

_____

4. They might have an extra room or two, but for the most part, the places where they live are relatively small.

_____

5. They might even want to come live with me in my mansion, but I would only let them if they were nice to me.

_____

6. Last, if I had a mansion, it would help me to realize my dream of becoming an interior designer.

_____

7. I really like a minimalist, modern aesthetic rather than something with a lot of grandeur.

_____

8. I feel as if there is a lot of potential in a mansion and it would definitely be an asset to my career.

_____

9. I would have a place to live until I die and I could certainly impress my friends.

_____

10. For these reasons, I think wishing for a big house would be the best way to use my one wish.

_____

Q211. Some parents give their children money on a monthly basis. At what age sho uld children receive an allowance and how much should they receive?

A. Essay Outline

Argument: Children should be allowed to receive an allowance at age 10 and they should receive $30 a month.

Support 1: Children should start getting an allowance at 10 because they are too irresponsible before then.

Support 2: Thirty dollars is just enough to get odd things like school supplies or snacks.

Support 3: If you give a child more than $30 a month, they will not spend the money wisely. They will buy too much junk food.

Thesis: Because it is appropriate, children should be allowed to receive an allowance of thirty dollars at age 12.

B. Model Essay

When I was in elementary school, there were some kids in my class who received an allowance. I never got an allowance, even now as I start the 12th grade. However, I think that kids should receive an allowance and they should be able to start getting an allowance starting at age 12. However, it should not be for any more than $30 a month. This is because kids should learn how to be responsible with money; if a child receives any more money than this, he will not spend the money wisely.

First off, some children need to have an allowance in order to pay for things that the need when parents aren't around. For example, after school, some students go to academy in order to study more things in depth, including English, math, or even chemistry. Although there are a lot of kids going to academy earlier in life, there aren't many children going to academy for long hours before the age of 12. Therefore, it makes sense that 12-year-olds should get an allowance. These kids need to be able to buy dinner when their parents aren't there so they can concentrate on studying and preparing for tests.

Secondly, thirty dollars is just enough for a 12-year-old. There aren't many things that a child needs to buy. They don't have to pay for rent, groceries, gas, electricity, or even Internet access. Most of them just need a little bit of pocket money to spend after school occasionally. I think that 20 dollars is too low; they should get about a dollar a day in case they need to buy snacks or dinner or even some school supplies on their own. That way, just in case, they can buy a little something every day. I think that $30 is just enough for a 12-year-old.

Last, but not least, although parents could give more money than 30 dollars a month, they shouldn't. Children need to learn how to spend money wisely and how to be responsible. If parents give more than $30 a month, children almost certainly will spend the money on things they don't need like on a Wii. Back in middle school, almost all of the kids I knew who had an allowance of more than 30 dollars just spent the money on junk food. I'm sure that most of them ended up getting fat later in life, which could be prevented if they just didn't eat candy and cookies all the time. Some of the other kids I know with big allowances started buying and playing a lot of video games. As a result, they didn't study for many tests and they're now at the bottom of the class. Therefore, it is important not to give children too much allowance money.

All in all, there's a lot of good to come out of allowance. It makes parents' lives a lot more comfortable and it gives children a greater sense of independence. However, parents shouldn't start giving an allowance until their child is 12 and even then, they should only give the child $30 a month. That way, children will spend the money wisely and they will not become lazy or fat.

C. Useful Expressions

1. However, I think that kids should receive an allowance and they should be able to start getting an allowance starting at age 12.

_____

2. First off, some children need to have an allowance in order to pay for things that they need when parents aren't around.

_____

3. For example, after school, some students go to an academy in order to study more things in depth, including English, math, or even chemistry.

_____

_____

4. Therefore, it makes sense that 12-year-olds should get an allowance.

_____

5. Most of them just need a little bit of pocket money to spend after school occasionally.

_____

6. That way, just in case, they can buy a little something every day.

_____

7. I think that thirty dollars is just enough for a 12-year-old.

_____

8. If parents give more than thirty dollars a month, children almost certainly will spend the money on things they don't need like on a Wii.

_____

_____

9. I'm sure that most of them ended up getting fat later in life, which could be prevented if they just didn't eat candy and cookies all the time.

_____

_____

10. All in all, there's a lot of good to come out of allowance.

_____

_____

Q212. Who do you like the better, athletes or entertainers?

A. Essay Outline

Argument: I prefer entertainers to athletes.
Support 1: Entertainers are creative, whereas athletes are not.
Support 2: I don't really like sports, so I don't much care for athletes.
Support 3: Entertainers give more money to charity than athletes.
Thesis: Because entertainers are so much better than athletes, I prefer entertainers to athletes.

B. Model Essay

Many people follow celebrity news in the media; it is all around us. Among the people we follow in the tabloids are entertainers and athletes. Entertainers, including singers, actors, and movie stars, are just some of the people I read about online or in magazines. However, I don't much care for the many athletes these magazines talk about, including figure skaters, runners, and soccer players. On the whole, I simply prefer entertainers to athletes.

First, I think that entertainers are more creative than athletes. Although both entertainers and athletes work hard, I don't think that athletes are generally creative in the sports arena. Playing soccer takes more skill than creativity; you need to be able to pass and shoot the ball in quick situations before being "creative." On the other hand, many entertainers have to be creative: for many of them, it is simply their job. For example, everyone thinks that Madonna is very creative: she reinvented the pop music genre by adding elements of other genres like electronica. When Madonna took a long hiatus between two of her albums, people thought that she was done with her career. Simply put, they thought her music was just too old to survive in a new generation. However, instead of pumping out the same music she had be doing for decades, she came back strong and released a very modern album. Madonna had to be very creative in order to create vastly different types of music herself.

Secondly, I don't much care for sports and as a result I don't much care for the people who play them. While some people are die hard about a particular sport or even some sports, I do not consider myself a sports fan. While I do enjoy watching some sports like tennis, I don't consider myself a fan at all. Because of that, I don't really follow up on how athletes do in their respective sports or know anything about their personal lives. However, I care a lot about music and movies. I go to the movie theater all the time and I always carry my headphones and mp3 player wherever I go. I read up on many of my favorite movie stars like Johnny Depp and Brad Pitt all the time and I watch movies with them every time I can. They just interest me more than athletes.

Last, I think that of the famous people who give to charity, the majority are people in the so-called entertainment industry. I've heard a lot, for example, about how George Lucas, the creator of the Star Wars franchise, has donated millions of dollars to his charity, the George Lucas Educational Foundation, to help students achieve their dreams. Additionally, actress Barbra Streisand has also donated a lot to her charity, the Barbra Streisand Foundation, in order to find cures for various diseases, including HIV/AIDS and breast cancer. However, I haven't heard about many athletes doing the same; I haven't heard about Michael Jordan donating any of his recent winnings to charity. Because entertainers seem more generous than athletes, I like entertainers more.

In conclusion, there are three reasons why I prefer entertainers to athletes. Entertainers are more creative and more generous than athletes and as a whole, I am apathetic when it comes to sports. Although I think athletes are important and we can read about them in the newspapers frequently, entertainers will always have a special place in my heart.

C. Useful Expressions

1. Many people follow celebrity news in the media; it is all around us.

_____

2. Among the people we follow in the tabloids are entertainers and athletes.

_____

3. However, I don't much care for the many athletes these magazines talk about, including figure skaters, runners, and soccer players.

_____

_____

4. On the other hand, many entertainers have to be creative: for many of them, it is simply their job.

_____

5. When Madonna took a long hiatus between two of her albums, people thought that she was done with her career.

_____

6. Simply put, they thought her music was just too old to survive in a new generation.

_____

7. While some people are die hard about a particular sport or even some sports, I do not consider myself a sports fan.

_____

8. While I do enjoy watching some sports like tennis, I don't consider myself a fan at all.

_____

9. I read up on many of my favorite movie stars like Johnny Depp and Brad Pitt all the time and I watch movies with them every time I can.

_____

10. Because entertainers seem more generous than athletes, I like entertainers more.

_____

Q213. Describe your most unforgettable day. Why will you never forget this day?

A. Essay Outline

Argument: My most unforgettable day was my sixteenth birthday.
Support 1: All of my friends were there for my great birthday party.
Support 2: I got a lot of great gifts from my friends.
Support 3: When I drove the car, that night, I got into an accident.
Thesis: Because my sixteenth birthday was so bittersweet, it is a day I will never forget.

B. Model Essay

My sixteenth birthday was both the best and the worst day of my life; it was such a mixture of both extreme happiness and intense sadness. In short, I had an amazing birthday party except right at the very end.

First, my parents held me a great birthday party. All of my friends from school were at my birthday party. They put on their best clothes and we ended up having lots of fun. First, we went to a very fancy steakhouse. We ordered a lot of big steaks that were cooked just perfectly. There were also lots of good side dishes. I also remember having the best piece of cheesecake I ever had. Even though someone at another table complained that there was a fly in his soup, we didn't let that bother us. We kept laughing and giggling with our own conversation. After the restaurant, we went to a karaoke room. Even though I can't sing, my friends didn't say anything. We had lots of fun just trying to sing "Girls Just Wanna Have Fun."

After we were done at the karaoke room, my parents took all of my friends and me back to our house to open my presents and have some more cake and coffee. I loved all of the gifts that I got from my friends: lots of clothes, perfume, lotions, and even a cute little bracelet that my friend Amber gave me. Some of the gifts were even quite expensive; one of my best friends, Tiffany, got me an mp3 player and my other best friend, Nicole, gave me a fur coat. However, they saved the best gift for last. When I was finished with my presents, I was a little sad. My father didn't give me a present and I was worried that he had procrastinated and couldn't get me a gift at the last minute, like he usually does. However, we heard a sound from outside. It sounded like an ice cream truck; my dad told me to go outside with him to investigate. As soon as I got outside, there was a car I didn't recognize in the driveway. It was brand new and my parents said that it was mine. I jumped up and down, screaming with excitement. I hugged and thanked my dad. It felt so great to have a new car.

However, that's when the fun stopped and the misery began. I wanted to drive the car as soon as I saw it. I got my driver's license just that day, so I knew that I could drive the car confidently. I got into the car and started it up. I looked out my window and I moved my foot on the gas. As soon as I did, I realized I did something very, very wrong. I put the car in forward instead of in reverse. My friend was in front of the car and I hit her and the garage door. My beautiful new car now had a big dent in the front. I instantly started crying my eyes out. My car was gone and I was probably not going to get a new one for a while. My dad got angry at me for crashing the car and my mom tried to console me. I later found out that there was no insurance on the car, and so, my dad had to take out a loan to fix the damage to the house and the car. My friend, Kristen, though, had to go to the hospital. She recovered, but never talked to me again after that. I think that was the day I lost both my car and my friend.

To sum up, my birthday was the most unforgettable day in the world to me. I had so much fun until the moment I crashed the car and hurt my friend Kristen. Since then, I learned an important lesson: always double check you put the car in reverse when you're backing out of the driveway.

C. Useful Expressions

1. My sixteenth birthday was both the best and the worst day of my life.

2. Even though someone at another table complained that there was a fly in his soup, we didn't let that bother us.

3. Some of the gifts were even quite expensive.

4. However, they saved the best gift for last.

5. My father didn't give me a present and I was worried that he had procrastinated and couldn't get me a gift at the last minute, like he usually does.

6. It sounded like an ice cream truck; my dad told me to go outside with him to investigate.

7. However, that's when the fun stopped and the misery began.

8. I instantly started crying my eyes out.

9. I later found out that there was no insurance on the car, and so, my dad had to take out a loan to fix the damage to the house and the car.

10. I had so much fun until the moment I crashed the car and hurt my friend Kristen.

Q214. Who will you remember the most after you finish school, your friends or your teachers?

A. Essay Outline

Argument: I will remember my friends more than my teachers after I finish school.
Support 1: I will still hang out with my friends after I finish school.
Support 2: I spend more time talking to my friends compared to teachers.
Support 3: My friends support me all the time; my teachers have not done that.
Thesis: Because my friends mean so much to me, I will remember them more than teachers after I finish school.

B. Model Essay

I have a lot of teachers in high school and they are all very great. Mr. Johnson is really funny, Mrs. Smith is really smart, and I learn a lot in Mr. Cooper's English class. However, if I had to pick which I would remember more about high school, my friends or my teachers, I would say my friends. This is because my friends and I hang out a lot after school, because I spend more time talking to my friends compared to my teachers, and because my friends support me 100%.

To start off, I hang out with my friends a lot after schools. Sometimes we go to the movie theater and watch a movie or sometimes we go to the mall and buy some cute clothes. However, I can never do this with a teacher; my teachers are just too busy reading papers and grading my essays. My friends are always up for doing something, even if there is a quiz or test the next day. We just have so much fun talking, shopping, and laughing together. I will always remember that time and I hope that we continue to hang out after we finish high school.

Secondly, I will remember my friends more than my teachers because I simply spend more time talking to my friends. Most of the time, when I talk to my teachers, it is because they want something for me or I want something for them. Just the other day, I tried to talk to Mr. Cooper. However, the only reason why I talked to him was because I was having trouble with my English class. We didn't really talk about anything except the class. Even though he told me I was still doing well, I didn't really get the chance to talk to Mr. Cooper about anything other than English, so I really don't know much about him other than his interest in English. However, I talk to my friends all the time, especially during lunchtime and we talk about everything and anything: boys, music, flowers, and even cake. I wish my teachers were more like my friends; if they were, I would remember them more.

Thirdly, my friends always support me no matter what I do. If I am in a bad situation, my friends will always be there for me and never leave my side. For example, there was one time when I got into an accident. My friend, Caitlin who had just gotten a car, tried to start the car. She didn't really know how to drive and so when she meant to go backwards, she went forwards and hit me. I was in the hospital for a really long time. I never talked to Caitlin after that, but my other friends were nice enough to visit me in the hospital. One of them brought me soup and another one of my friends gave me a bouquet of flowers. My teachers, however, didn't come see me when I was in the hospital; they just gave my friend Tiffany all of this homework to give to me. It hurt to see them be so mean to me.

In conclusion, I will absolutely remember my high school friends more than my high school teachers. We just do so many more things together and spend more time talking to them in and out of class. I hope that I keep in touch with my friends after we go our own ways in life.

C. Useful Expressions

1. However, if I had to pick which I would remember more about high school, my friends or my teachers, I would say my friends.

_____

_____

2. This is because my friends and I hang out a lot after school, because I spend more time talking to my friends compared to my teachers, and because my friends support me 100%.

_____

_____

3. However, I can never do this with a teacher; my teachers are just too busy reading papers and grading my essays.

_____

_____

4. My friends are always up for doing something, even if there is a quiz or test the next day.

_____

_____

5. Secondly, I will remember my friends more than my teachers because I simply spent more time talking to my friends.

_____

_____

6. However, I talk to my friends all the time, especially during lunchtime and we talk about everything and anything: boys, music, flowers, and even cake.

_____

_____

7. If I am in a bad situation, my friends will always be there for me and never leave my side.

_____

8. One of them brought me soup and another one of my friends gave me a bouquet of flowers.

_____

9. We just do so many more things together and spend more time talking to them in and out of class.

_____

10. I hope that I keep in touch with my friends after we go our own ways in life.

_____

_____

Q215. Describe your idea of a happy life.

A. Essay Outline

Argument: My idea of a happy life involves three things: a good job, a happy family, and lots of money.
Support 1: I need to be happy with my co-workers at my good job.
Support 2: I want my family to be happy, both in life and with me.
Support 3: I want to have a fair amount of money, so we never have to worry about our basic necessities.
Thesis: My idea of a happy life involves surrounding myself with positive people and lots of money.

B. Model Essay

There are many things that go into a happy life, but I have reduced that down to three, basic things: a good job, a happy family, and a decent amount of money. I have many reasons and several examples to support my opinion.

First, a good life starts with a good job. You can do a lot of things in life: you can be a businessman, an engineer, or even a garbage collector. However, the most important thing about your job is not that you make a lot of money or become famous; rather, you just have to be content with your job. For me, I would like to have a job where I know I am making an important contribution to society. I want to be able to help people, perhaps through a non-profit organization like the Red Cross or Doctors without Borders. In addition, I would like a job knowing that I am valued; for me, that means my boss and my co-workers should be nice and pleasant to work with. It also means that they should be just as hardworking as me, so that we can help as many people as possible.

Also, I want my family to be happy. I want to be able to settle down with someone in the future and start a family with her. One of my biggest fears in life is that I will grow old with no one to talk to. If I find someone, I will want to marry her and have kids. I want to have two children, but I could also deal with having just one. Not having at least one child will make me very sad. My family should also be happy. I want to be able to provide for them, but they should want me to be around. We should be able to go to the movies together and have a good time. I don't want to argue a lot with my family at all.

Last, I want to have a fair amount of money to live off of for the rest of my life. Although I said that how much money you make from your job is not that important, it is important that you have enough money to live on. For example, I would not be happy if I couldn't pay rent on an apartment or afford to eat everyday. In that way, money does matter, but money doesn't matter so much to me once my family and I have our basic needs met. I want to be able to live fairly comfortably too; I want to be able to own a house one day and take vacations to Europe occasionally, but I don't really care if I earn a lot more other than that. I just want enough to make me and my family happy after I finish working.

To sum up, I don't want a lot out of life; I don't expect to become very rich or famous. However, I want my happy life to include a good job, a happy family, and enough money for me and my family to live off. With that, I would be content and could die happy.

C. Useful Expressions

1. There are many things that go into a happy life.

2. I have reduced that down to three basic things.

3. However, the most important thing about your job is not that you make a lot of money or become famous; rather, you just have to be content with your job.

4. However, the most important thing about your job is not that you make a lot of money or become famous; rather, you just have to be content with your job.

5. One of my biggest fears in life is that I will grow old with no one to talk to.

6. I want to have two children, but I could also deal with having just one.

7. Last, I want to have a fair amount of money to live off of for the rest of my life.

8. In that way, money does matter, but money doesn't matter so much to me once my family and I have our basic needs met.

9. To sum up, I don't want a lot out of life; I don't expect to become very rich or famous.

10. With that, I would be content and could die happy.

Q216. Which genre of books do you enjoy reading the most? Why?

A. Essay Outline

Argument: My favorite genre of books is fantasy.
Support 1: Fantasy novels always have really impressive worlds, like in Lord of the Rings.
Support 2: I really like the idea of magic.
Support 3: I really like stories about good versus evil.
Thesis: Because there are so many things I like about fantasy books, I enjoy reading them the most.

B. Model Essay

I am an avid reader; I like to read a lot of books in my free time. I read a lot of different kinds of books too, ranging from romance to science fiction to even political books. However, I enjoy reading fantasy books the most for three reasons. First, fantasy novels have really impressive worlds, like in Lord of the Rings. Second, I really like how the authors incorporate magic into their stories. Finally, I love the traditional story of good versus evil.

To start off, fantasy novels always incorporate great and diverse worlds. Take, for example, Lord of the Rings. Lord of the Rings takes place in a world called Middle Earth. There are many different kingdoms in Middle Earth, including the Elf Kingdom, where all the elves live and Mordor, where there is nothing but evil. The protagonist, Frodo, comes from the Shire, which looks like a quaint little village in the English countryside. In Lord of the Rings, there are also a big forest with tree spirits and the Misty Mountains, where there are lots of rocks and goblins. In general, the worlds in fantasy novels are so impressively described; there is just so much detail, you feel as if you are actually there. Middle Earth especially seems like a great place to have an adventure and I would love it if I had the chance to actually live in these fantasy worlds.

Next, I really like the idea of magic. It's something I always wanted to do ever since I was a little kid and something that still sticks with me today. Even though it's not real, I can do the next best thing: read fantasy novels. This is because there is always some magical element in fantasy novels. Take, for example, Harry Potter. Harry Potter was an ordinary boy who lived a miserable life in England. When he got older, he learned that he was a wizard. It is there that he starts his adventure and gets entrapped in a magical world, where he can play soccer on flying broomsticks (Quidditch) and make magic potions that can heal people or make them sick. Fantasy novels help me to escape my mundane world and let me live a fantasy, even if it's only for a couple hours.

Last, I really like fantasy novels because most of them deal with the battle between good and evil. This is a tried and true method of talking about a lot of things and it works very well; it always catches my interest. For example, in Lord of the Rings, Frodo battles many creatures who lust after his ring. The ring, made of gold, is meant to represent greed and thus, the battle for good against evil is truly a battle between greed vs. generosity. Harry Potter has the battle of Harry versus Lord Voldemort. J.K Rowling, the author of Harry Potter, has even said that Voldemort represents Adolf Hitler, and so when Harry fights Lord Voldemort, he is fighting against needless cruelty and violence. Because the triumph of good over evil is so meaningful in the fantasy genre, I love to read fantasy books.

In conclusion, the fantasy genre is my favorite among many genres. It is just one of the best because of the cool worlds created, the magic used, and the stories developed by the authors. I hope that everyone reads at least one fantasy novel before they die.

C. Useful Expressions

1. I am an avid reader; I like to read a lot of books in my free time.

_____

2. I read a lot of different kinds of books too, ranging from romance to science fiction to even political books.

_____

3. To start off, fantasy novels always incorporate great and diverse worlds.

_____

4. The protagonist, Frodo, comes from the Shire, which looks like a quaint little village in the English countryside.

_____

5. Next, I really like the idea of magic. It's something I always wanted to do ever since I was a little kid and something that still sticks with me today.

_____

6. Even though it's not real, I can do the next best thing: read fantasy novels

_____

7. Last, I really like fantasy novels because most of them deal with the battle between good and evil.

_____

8. Because the triumph of good over evil is so meaningful in the fantasy genre, I love to read fantasy books.

_____

9. In conclusion, the fantasy genre is my favorite among many genres.

_____

10. I hope that everyone reads at least one fantasy novel before they die.

_____

Q217. Which fruit do you like the most? Why?

A. Essay Outline

Argument: Avocados are my favorite fruit.
Support 1: Avocados are really delicious.
Support 2: Avocados come from Mexico, a country I really want to visit.
Support 3: Avocados are an unusual fruit; they're not like apples or bananas.
Thesis: Because they are unique, avocados are my favorite fruit.

B. Model Essay

Some people prefer to eat a fruit that is very sweet, like a pear, an apple, or a banana. However, I am a very different kind of person and my favorite fruit is the avocado. Not only are avocados absolutely delicious, but they come from Mexico, which is a country I really want to visit when I get older. Also, avocados are an unusual fruit, which I really like about it. Avocados are my most favorite fruit out of so many great fruits.

First of all, avocados are really delicious. They are green, but they are really creamy. They are used for a lot of different things, but my favorite thing they are used for is guacamole. Guacamole is basically a bunch of mashed up avocados with some onion, some chilies, lime juice, and cilantro. It is really delicious and it is one of the best side dishes when you go to a Mexican restaurant. Avocados are really great; because they are so creamy, some people even make ice cream out of them instead of using eggs. They make the ice cream green, but they're so good. I wish they had more avocados in Korea.

Next, avocados come from Mexico, so when I eat them, I am reminded of how much I want to go to Mexico when I am older. Even though there aren't a lot of Mexicans living in Korea right now, I have always been fascinated by Mexican culture. One of the best things that happens in Mexico is "Dia de los Muertos" or in English, "Day of the Dead." It is a time when Mexican families go to graveyards and have parties with their dead relatives. I have never been to Mexico, but this seems absolutely unique and great. Also, Dora the Explorer is from Mexico. Dora the Explorer is a very popular kid's program in the U.S. When I saw it, I was instantly hooked. Dora, the main character in Dora the Explorer, helps kids learn Spanish. Because avocados come from Mexico, one country I hope to visit when I am older, they are my favorite fruit.

Last, avocados are a very unique fruit. Unlike apples, oranges, strawberries, or bananas, avocados aren't really sweet. In fact, some people even think they are a vegetable because they are used so much in savory cuisine. Most people don't think about eating avocados after dinner. However, that is something I really like about avocados: they in some way defy traditional boundaries of what a fruit is. Even though biologically they are a fruit, it only has one massive seed that you cannot eat. They are also kind of ugly and brown on the outside, but absolutely delicious on the inside. Because the avocado is special, it is my favorite fruit.

To sum, avocados area a really great fruit that have a lot of uses. They are so different, unique, and delicious that I just love them. Plus, avocados are really great in Mexican cuisine and whenever I eat an avocado, I am reminded of Mexico. I hope to have a fiesta with my Mexican friends one day and eat a lot of avocados with them.

C. Useful Expressions

1. However, I am a very different kind of person and my favorite fruit is the avocado.

_____

2. They are used for a lot of different things, but my favorite thing they are used for is guacamole.

_____

3. Guacamole is basically a bunch of mashed up avocados with some onion, some chills, lime juice, and cilantro.

_____

_____

4. It is really delicious and it is one of the best side dishes when you go to a Mexican restaurant.

_____

5. Next, avocados come from Mexico, so when I eat them, I am reminded of how much I want to go to Mexico when I am older.

_____

_____

6. Even though there aren't a lot of Mexicans living in Korea right now, I have always been fascinated by Mexican culture.

_____

_____

7. I have never been to Mexico, but this seems absolutely unique and great.

_____

8. Dora the Explorer is a very popular kid's program in the U.S. When I saw it, I was instantly hooked.

_____

9. In fact, some people even think they are a vegetable because they are used so much in savory cuisine.

_____

10. However, that is something I really like about avocados: they in some way defy traditional boundaries of what a fruit is.

_____

_____

Q218. What is your favorite TV show and why?

A. Essay Outline

Argument: My favorite TV show is Downton Abbey.
Support 1: The show is about the British aristocracy in the early 1900's.
Support 2: There are many characters, and they are all very interesting.
Support 3: The costumes are very well done.
Thesis: Because Downton Abbey is a well-made TV series, it is my favorite TV show of all time.

B. Model Essay

I don't watch a lot of television, but when I do, I try to make it count. My favorite TV show at the moment is Downton Abbey; I just started watching it and I love watching and rewatching episodes. It has quickly become my favorite show for three reasons. First, it is about the British aristocracy in the early 1900's, which to me is really fascinating. Second, there are so many three-dimensional characters, and they are all are put in very interesting circumstances. Last, the costume designers are great; their works deserve to be in a museum.

Downton Abbey is primarily a show about aristocrats in the United Kingdom before, during, and after World War I. The series takes place in an estate called Downton Abbey and follows the lives of the rich and poor as they continue their lives in the estate. I find this time period really fascinating: it was a time of great transition in Britain, moving from an older, more hierarchical society into a more equal one. The war changed a lot of things about Britain, including the role of women in society. By watching the show, I also have gotten the chance to learn a lot more about the time period and some of the events that occurred then. I learned about the Spanish flu and British politics at the time. The series talked a lot about women's suffrage in Europe and how it affected many of the women on the show. Truly, Downton Abbey is a really interesting show and it made me very interested to learn more about British history.

In addition, there are a lot of characters on Downton Abbey, including aristocrats and many servants and they are all very interesting. First, there is the Earl of Grantham. He is an old man, but he is very kind. He married an American woman for her money, but he still loves her. There are also their three daughters: Lady Mary, Lady Edith, and Lady Sybil. They are all very attractive, but they have very different personalities. Lady Edith, the middle child, doesn't know what to do with her life. Lady Sybil has a very strong will and Lady Mary wants to follow in her grandmother's footsteps and basically be a princess. There are a lot of servants too, like Thomas, the footman, and Mr. Bates, Lord Grantham's valet. They do not like each other at first, but they eventually learn to like each other. Mr. Bates also falls in love with Anna, one of the housemaids. They have a very beautiful, but humble, wedding. There are so many characters; it is so fascinating to see them interact with one another.

Most importantly, though, the costumes for every episode of Downton Abbey are just fantastic. They are period pieces, true, but they look so very real and so true to what was worn back in the day. For example, Lady Mary's grandmother, the Dowager Countess of Grantham, wears a cute little tiara, while by the third season, Lady Edith starts to wear flapper dresses. My favorite, though, is the elegant black dress that Lord Grantham's wife wore. It had such a simple cut, but had lots of sparkle. It was so pretty! In truth, all the costumes are very impressive; it just looks like the costume designer had a lot of fun designing, sewing, and making all of the costumes.

Because of the wonderful characters, costumes and story material, Downton Abbey is simply a marvelous show and absolutely my favorite show on television currently. Everything about this TV show is just done perfectly. I hope everyone gets the chance to watch this great show.
.

C. Useful Expressions

1. I don't watch a lot of television, but when I do, I try to make it count.

_____

2. Second, there are so many three-dimensional characters, and they are all are put in very interesting circumstances.

_____

3. The series takes place in an estate called Downton Abbey and follows the lives of the rich and poor as they continue their lives in the estate.

_____

4. The series talked a lot about women's suffrage in Europe and how it affected many of the women on the show.

_____

5. I find this time period really fascinating: it was a time of great transition in Britain, moving from an older, more hierarchical society into a more equal one.

_____

6. By watching the show, I also have gotten the chance to learn a lot more about the time period and some of the events that occurred then.

_____

7. Most importantly, though, the costumes for every episode of Downton Abbey are just fantastic.

_____

8. They are period pieces, true, but they look so very real and so true to what was worn back in the day.

_____

9. In truth, all the costumes are very impressive; it just looks like the costume designer had a lot of fun designing, sewing, and making all of the costumes.

_____

10. Everything about this TV show is just done perfectly.

_____

Q219. What is your favorite movie and why?

A. Essay Outline

Argument: Spirited Away is my favorite movie.
Support 1: It was directed by Hayao Miyazaki, who is a great animator and director.
Support 2: It is beautifully animated; I love all of the colors in the film.
Support 3: The story is great, interesting, and thought-provoking.
Thesis: Because Spirited Away is such a great movie, it is my favorite movie.

B. Model Essay

Spirited Away is one of the best movies made in the 21st century. Directed by Hayao Miyazaki, it tells the story of a little girl named Chihiro who gets lost in an alternate universe where spirits run and inhabit a magical bathhouse. The film, made in 2001, won many awards; it even won Best Animated Feature at the 75th Annual Academy Awards. Because it is beautifully animated, tells a great story, and was directed by the great Hayao Miyazaki, Spirited Away is my favorite film ever made.

One of the greatest animators ever, Hayao Miyazaki, wrote and directed this masterpiece of cinema. Miyazaki was known before Spirited Away for some great works like Laputa: Castle in the Sky, Princess Mononoke, My Neighbor Totoro, and Kiki's Delivery Service. Miyazaki always makes animated films featuring children, but adults can definitely enjoy the films as well. His films always have some sort of magical element, either ghosts or spirits or magical, talking animals. They take place in magical worlds where curiosity and idealism are rewarded. At the same time, many of the children have to face difficult challenges like saving an entire forest or people. Because Miyazaki is such a brilliant director, his touch transforms Spirited Away from a good film to one of my favorites.

Another reason I love Spirited Away is the fact that it is animated with such craft. Unlike Miyazaki's earlier films, which were limited by technology, Spirited Away is really the first film by Miyazaki where the colors shine and the figures float so easily. There is so much detail paid to everything from hair to simple objects. Even compared to Miyazaki's earlier films, the faces have so much more emotion and depth. Even the images seem to move with such grace; to a certain extent, it doesn't even feel like we're watching a series of images, but an authentic, real video. Because Spirited Away is so well-made and every character and image is so great, it is my absolute favorite film.

All of this pales in comparison to the basic story of Spirited Away. Spirited Away revolves around a girl named Chihiro. She and her parents are moving to a new place and Chihiro is not excited to go. They end up at an abandoned amusement park; Chihiro's parents eat at a restaurant stand and are instantly turned into pigs. It then becomes Chihiro's task to try and save them from forever being pigs in the spirit world. Without revealing too much more of the story, Chihiro metaphorically has to learn to become an adult. She has to face many more difficult tasks along with way, including cleaning up a very smelly, polluted river spirit. Spirited Away is a highly fascinating coming-of-age tale that makes you think about what it means to become an adult and the future of the world.

In conclusion, Spirited Away is a fantastic movie that makes you think about a lot of things. It was directed by the great Hayao Miyazaki, known for many different great films. It is a very beautiful film too, with so many lush colors and seamless transitions, but these only help the fact that the story is so magnificently written and wonderfully understated. It is for these reasons that Spirited Away is my most cherished movie. I hope that everyone can see this movie one day.

C. Useful Expressions

1. One of the greatest animators ever, Hayao Miyazaki, wrote and directed this masterpiece of cinema.

_____

2. His films always have some sort of magical element, either ghosts or spirits or magical, talking animals.

_____

3. They take place in magical worlds where curiosity and idealism are rewarded.

_____

4. Because Miyazaki is such a brilliant director, his touch transforms Spirited Away from a good film to one of my favorites.

_____

_____

5. Another reason I love Spirited Away is the fact that it is animated with such craft.

_____

6. There is so much detail paid to everything from hair to simple objects.

_____

7. Even the images seem to move with such grace; to a certain extent, it doesn't even feel like we're watching a series of images, but an authentic, real video.

_____

_____

8. They end up at an abandoned amusement park; Chihiro's parents eat at a restaurant stand and are instantly turned into pigs.

_____

_____

9. Without revealing too much more of the story, Chihiro metaphorically has to learn to become an adult.

_____

10. Spirited Away is a highly fascinating coming-of-age tale that makes you think about what it means to become an adult and the future of the world.

_____

Q220. Compare the advantages and the disadvantages of Smart Phones.

A. Essay Outline

Argument: Smart Phones have changed the world we know in some positive ways, but they have also affected the world in some negative ways.

Support 1: Let me begin with the positives aspects of the Smart Phone: convenience, emergency use, and information tool.

Support 2: Now, I will discuss the negatives that come from the Smart Phone usage: distractions while operating machinery, addiction, and health risks.

Support 3: In my opinion, Smart Phones are a vital tool in this technologically advanced world.

Thesis: To summarize, Smart Phones have both detrimental factors and advantageous factors.

B. Model Essay

Nowadays, almost everyone in the USA has some sort of mobile phone. However, a large percentage of people use what is now known as a Smart Phone. Smart Phones have changed the world we know in some positive ways, but they have also affected the world in some negative ways. These intelligent phones provide us not only with a source of calling people, but also a way to browse the Internet, to take photos, and to save important information all at our fingertips.

Let me begin with the positives aspects of the Smart Phone. The most obvious plus to this tool is that it is more convenient to get a hold of somebody. In the past, we had to call somebody's home and leave a message for them. However, nowadays, we are able to call their cell phone and reach them immediately. Also, in an emergency situation, Smart Phones are a vital tool for fast response. The biggest factor that sets the Smart Phone apart from regular mobile phones is the fact that we can stay in the know about many things. All Smart Phones have the ability to access the Internet, and as you know, the Internet has a plethora of information.

Now, I will discuss the negatives that come from the Smart Phone usage. The biggest and most troublesome downside of the Smart Phone is that it is distracting. While people are driving, they will talk on their phone, text their friends, or post a recent update on their Facebook account. These distractions often times lead to vehicular accidents or people walking into a hazard. Another adverse effect is that they become highly addictive. As students, we want to text our friends or play a game during class, instead of focusing on our teacher's instructions. Furthermore, it distracts us from doing our necessary tasks in life, because we want to beat a game, or to always update our friends through our desired social media network. Probably the most unknown negative is the medical hazards it can pose to us. Research has been conducted on the increased use of technology, specifically Smart Phones, and it has shown that they cause bad posture, poor eyesight, and they even can impair younger children's thinking skills.

In my opinion, Smart Phones are a vital tool in this technologically advanced world. However, I do think that the Smart Phone is taking over too much. Recently I bought my first Smart Phone, and I have now become one of those addicted people, too. I always feel I have to have my cellphone next to me, just in case something important happens. On the other hand though, I love the fact that my Smart Phone is my camera, phone, calendar, and my clock all in one. So despite the negatives, I would never give up my Smart

Phone. I can recall a time when I had to carry around multiple devices or tools to accomplish all those tasks. So, I am not completely opposed to the intelligent phone's usage. I just feel that our brains should be the ones doing the thinking, not the phone.

To summarize, Smart Phones have both detrimental factors and advantageous factors. The negatives range from being a distraction to being harmful to our health. The positives range from giving us a multiple-device-tool-in-one to having a first responder at our fingertips in an emergency situation. Over the next decade, I am sure that the Smart Phone will continue to change. I just hope that we can maintain our own intelligence and not allow the phone to do all the work for us.

C. Useful Expressions

1. Nowadays, almost everyone in the USA has some sort of mobile phone.

_____

2. However, a large percentage of people use what is now known as a Smart Phone.

_____

3. The most obvious plus to this tool is that it is more convenient to get a hold of somebody.

_____

4. The biggest factor that sets the Smart Phone apart from regular mobile phones is the fact that we can stay in the know about many things.

_____

_____

5. The biggest and most troublesome downside of the Smart Phone is that it is distracting.

_____

6. Another adverse effect is that they become highly addictive.

_____

7. However, I do think that the Smart Phone is taking over too much.

_____

8. So despite the negatives, I would never give up my Smart Phone.

_____

9. So, I am not completely opposed to the intelligent phone's usage.

_____

10. The negatives range from being a distraction to being harmful to our health.

_____

> ## Q221. Which option is healthier, eating three large meals a day or eating four to five small meals a day?

A. Essay Outline

Argument: Eating many smaller meals throughout the day is better than eating a few larger meals.

Support 1: Eating smaller meals is healthier, if and only if they are properly balanced meals

Support 2: By eating a small meal every four hours during the day time, our bodies can be supplied with a constant flow of energy.

Support 3: Eating four to five well-balanced meals throughout the day can curb your hunger and lead to maintaining a healthy weight.

Thesis: Eating smaller meals more often throughout the day has been proven to make us feel less sleepy, maintain a balanced weight, and it curbs our desire to eat more.

B. Model Essay

In life, we have many decisions to make that affect our health. One of the decisions is about what we eat, how much we eat, and how often we eat. According to a study conducted in 1989, by David Jenkins, M.D., Ph.D., and Tom Wolever, M.D., Ph.D., of the University of Toronto, it is better for our health to eat five or six meals a day, rather than to eat three meals a day. So, I must agree with the doctors that eating many smaller meals throughout the day is better than eating a few larger meals for various reasons: it reduces our calorie intake, keeps our level of insulin up, and controls our hunger.

First, let me explain what the smaller meals should consist of, in order to make it clear why eating these types of meals is healthier for us. Eating smaller meals is healthier, if and only if they are properly balanced meals, such as apples and peanut butter, versus a candy bar and milkshake. To achieve this proper balance, each smaller meal should include a low-fat or lean protein, a fiber, and at least one fruit or vegetable. An unusual thing that should be implemented into this type of meal is a healthy fat. This may sound quiet odd, but some examples of healthy fats are avocados, nuts, and fatty fish. Eating a balanced meal is the key to why the smaller meal diet works as a healthier option.

Secondly, I will explain what eating four to five smaller meals can do to our chemical make-up inside of our bodies. To begin with, many people often get sleepy around three to four in the afternoon. Why is this? It's because our glucose levels have dropped, which lowers our insulin level. Most people go for six hours without eating, so it's no wonder we feel lethargic by the time the afternoon reaches us. By eating a small meal every four hours during the day time, our bodies can be supplied with a constant flow of energy. Also, multiple meals have been proven to lower our cholesterol, which is why many doctors suggest a diet, such as this, to reduce our cholesterol levels.

Finally, I will discuss how eating four to five well-balanced meals throughout the day can curb your hunger and lead to maintaining a healthy weight. It is mostly due to the fact that eating more often makes us feel less hungry. This is because we have a constant flow of food in our bodies. This then in return helps to increase our metabolism, which is one of the factors to maintaining a healthy weight. The smaller meal more frequently regime also helps reduce our calorie intake, because if we feel full for a longer period of time, then we are less likely to snack on the 'unhealthy' foods in-between our regular more frequent meals.

Despite the fact that eating more frequently could actually mean less nutrition and more calories if you don't carefully plan out your snacks and meals, it still provides our bodies with the needed energy and numerous benefits. Eating smaller meals more often throughout the day has been proven to make us feel less sleepy, maintain a balanced weight, and it curbs our desire to eat more. My suggestion to everyone is to follow this method if they want to live a long and happy life. Also, who doesn't want to eat more delicious food more often!

C. Useful Expressions

1. According to a study conducted in 1989 by David Jenkins, M.D., Ph.D., and Tom Wolever, M.D., Ph.D., of the University of Toronto, they have proven that it is better for our health to eat five or six meals a day, rather than to eat three meals a day.

_____

_____

2. So, I must agree with the doctor that eating many smaller meals throughout the day is better than eating a few larger meals for various reasons; it reduces our calorie intake, keeps our level of insulin up, and controls our hunger.

_____

_____

3. First, let me explain what the smaller meals should consist of, in order to make it clear why eating these types of meals is healthier for us.

_____

_____

4. Eating smaller meals is healthier, if and only if they are properly balanced meals, such as apples and peanut butter, versus a candy bar and milkshake.

_____

_____

5. Most people go for six hours without eating, so it's no wonder we feel lethargic by the time the afternoon reaches us.

_____

_____

6. Also, multiple meals have been proven to lower our cholesterol, which is why many doctors suggest a diet, such as this, to reduce our cholesterol levels.

_____

_____

7. Finally, I will discuss how eating four to five well-balanced meals throughout the day can curb your hunger and lead to maintaining a healthy weight.

_____

_____

Q222. If you could win a lot of money, how much would you want to win and why ?

A. Essay Outline

Argument: If I were given a lot of money, I would want to win 200 million dollars.
Support 1: The first reason I would want 200 million dollars is because I would want to use half of my winnings by donating it to a local charity or orphanage.
Support 2: Second, I would use a large portion of the remaining 100 million dollars to travel around the world for an entire year.
Support 3: Finally, I would want just a small chunk of money for my own personal gain, maybe 50,000 dollars.
Thesis: Having too much money would be overwhelming, and having too little money would be a disappointment; therefore by receiving 200 million dollars, I could do great things for others, while also getting a little benefit for myself.

B. Model Essay

If I were given the chance to win a lot of money, I would want to win 200 million dollars. I would want this much money because I could donate my money to a local charity. Then, I could travel around the world while volunteering at needy schools and hospitals. Finally, I would want to do something for myself, such as buying a new computer.

The first reason I would want 200 million dollars is because I would want to use half of my winnings by donating it to a local charity or orphanage. I know that there are many places that could use more resources to do good things for others. So why do I need to be having excess amounts of money when there are needy people out there? There are many orphanages and soup kitchens here in Daegu, and I know that their visitors and residents will benefit greatly from the donation. If I received only a small amount of money, I couldn't do as much good for this specific community.

Second, I would use a large portion of the remaining 100 million dollars to travel around the world for an entire year. I want to go to Australia, Asia, and Europe the most. While in these new countries, I would do volunteer work and donate my time and money to help them build more schools or hospitals. I have done volunteer work already at local schools in America that needed a lot of help. It was very tough work, but it was also very rewarding to see those students' faces light up when they saw how their run down school was completely changed. So, by winning a large sum of money, I could do more beneficial work around the world.

Finally, I would want just a small chunk of money for my own personal gain, maybe 50,000 dollars. My computer is very old and it does not have enough memory for all of the photos I take. By buying a new computer, I would be able to take more pictures and organize them better. I love taking photos, so it would brighten my life greatly. I could also update my wardrobe, buy some new books, and fly my family to Korea to see me.

Having too much money would be overwhelming, and having too little money would be a disappointment. So by doing by receiving 200 million dollars, I could do great things for others, while also getting a little benefit for myself. We are all entitled to a little splurge once and a while, so why not dream big, and do random acts of kindness for others at the same time?

C. Useful Expressions

1. The first reason I would want 200 million dollars is because I would want to use half of my winnings by donating it to a local charity or orphanage.

_____

_____

2. There are many orphanages and soup kitchens here in Daegu, and I know that their visitors and residents will benefit greatly from the donation.

_____

_____

3. Second, I would use a large portion of the remaining 100 million dollars to travel around the world for an entire year.

_____

_____

4. It was very tough work, but it was also very rewarding to see those students' faces light up when they saw how their run down school was completely changed.

_____

_____

5. Finally, I would want just a small chunk of money for my own personal gain, maybe 50,000 dollars.

_____

6. I love taking photos, so it would brighten my life greatly.

_____

7. Having too much money would be overwhelming, and having too little money would be a disappointment.

_____

_____

8. We are all entitled to a little splurge once and a while, so why not dream big, and do random acts of kindness for others at the same time.

_____

_____

Q223. We are continuously learning and doing new things in life and often times we fail at our first attempt. Describe your first attempt to gain something new.

A. Essay Outline

Argument: A very funny experience happened to me during my first attempt to gain knowledge about cooking potatoes by myself.
Support 1: My mother entrusted each of her young children to cook dinner for the rest of the family.
Support 2: Something went very wrong though in the process of trying to cook potatoes.
Support 3: I learned a few great lessons from this.
Thesis: So my first attempt to learn how to cook something as simple as potatoes, also taught me other important life lessons.

B. Model Essay

A very funny experience happened to me during my first attempt to gain knowledge about cooking potatoes for myself. Usually, scary cooking experiences don't happen until around the high school ages, but mine happened when I was much younger, in elementary school. I definitely gained something from this experience that I will never forget.

To start with, I was eight years old and at home with my two sisters, who were six and ten. My mom always trusted us to cook dinner and to have it ready for her when she came home. She felt that it was a very good trait for children to have for us to be independent. Plus, my mom was very busy working in order to afford raising her three children on her own. So, it was my turn to cook the potatoes for the first time. I turned on the oven and put the potatoes in, just like my mom had shown me many times.

However, something went horribly wrong. The potatoes suddenly burst into flames. I was very nervous at first. However, I calmly and quickly called my mom hoping she wasn't going to be angry. She told me in her soothing, motherly voice, to carefully pour baking powder onto the flames. The flames immediately went out and I cleaned up the mess before my mom came home.

Even though this was a frightening experience, I learned some very important lessons. I learned how to remain calm, and to think clearly in a time of panic. It has helped through many of my life's challenges. I am very thankful for my mother's encouragement of independence. I have used many of the skills as an adult that I had learned as a child.

So my first attempt to learn how to cook something as simple as potatoes also taught me other important life lessons. I still don't know why the potatoes burst into flames. It will forever be a mystery to us all. The most valuable lesson to take away from this experience was to remain calm, call for help, and to not make the same mistake again.

C. Useful Expressions

1. A very funny experience happened to me during my first attempt to gain knowledge about cooking potatoes for myself.

_____

_____

2. Usually, scary cooking experiences don't happen until around the high school ages, but mine happened when I was much younger, in elementary school.

_____

_____

3. I definitely gained something from this experience that I will never forget.

_____

4. She felt that it was a very good trait for children to have for us to be independent.

_____

5. I turned on the oven, and put the potatoes in, just like my mom had shown me many times.

_____

6. However, something went horribly wrong.

_____

7. I was very nervous at first.

_____

8. Even though this was a frightening experience, I learned some very important lessons.

_____

9. I learned how to remain calm, and to think clearly in a time of panic.

_____

10. It will forever be a mystery to us all.

_____

Q224. Describe your ideal holiday resort.

A. Essay Outline

Argument: My ideal holiday resort would have to be in a place that is hot and tropical, such as the Grand Cayman Islands.

Support 1: It is located in the Caribbean Sea near Jamaica, so the weather is perfect.

Support 2: Besides the weather, the scenery is beautiful.

Support 3: There are many interesting places to visit.

Thesis: The warm waters and the perfect weather make the Grand Cayman Islands my ideal holiday resort.

B. Model Essay

There are many locations to construct a holiday resort at, such as Japan, China, South Korea, and the USA. However, my ideal holiday resort would have to be in a place that is hot, tropical, and not somewhere I've lived for a long time already at. Therefore, the best place for me to stay at a holiday resort would be the Grand Cayman Islands.

To start with, the Grand Cayman Island is a fairly small island located in the Caribbean Sea, near Jamaica. Therefore, the weather there is perfect. When I visited these islands last December to help babysit my cousin's three children, I found this fact out for myself. The temperature only differs by no more than 10 degrees from the day time to the night time. Plus, there is always a cool breeze blowing that acts as an air-conditioner to warm sun heated air.

Besides the weather, the scenery is also beautiful! The crystal clear blue water meets a clean white sand beach. Usually, I don't like going into the ocean or sea because it is so cold. However, the water surrounding the Grand Cayman Islands is like bath water! The main attraction is the seven mile beach, where most of the hotels are built. It gives almost every visitor a great view of the tropical serenity. I like to enjoy my holiday by sitting on the beach, with a nice cool drink, and watching the scenery change throughout the day.

On top of the great weather and beautiful scenery, there are interesting places to visit. Since it is a British colonized tropical island, there is a lot of history to learn and to see around the island. Plus, it is the perfect place to go scuba diving, where you can swim with the stingrays and tour the underwater ship wrecks. Also, you can go on a pirate ship and be treated like one of the crew, having to clean the deck with a toothbrush. The Grand Cayman Island is not a big island, but it offers so many great things to do.

The warm waters and the perfect weather make the Grand Cayman Islands my ideal holiday resort. The island has a great many of places to see, and also many exciting things to do. I know that if I had the chance to go again, I would leave immediately with no hesitations!

C. Useful Expressions

1. When I visited these islands last December to help babysit my cousin's three children, I found this fact out for myself.

_____

2. The temperature only differs by no more than 10 degrees from the day time to the night time.

_____

3. Plus, there is always a cool breeze blowing that acts as an air-conditioner to warm sun heated air.

_____

4. Besides the weather, the scenery is also beautiful! The crystal clear blue water meets a clean white sand beach.

_____

5. The main attraction is the seven mile beach, where most of the hotels are built.

_____

6. On top of the great weather and beautiful scenery, there are the interesting places to visit.

_____

7. Since it is a British colonized tropical island, there is a lot of history to learn and to see around the island.

_____

8. The Grand Cayman Island is not a big island, but it offers so many great things to do.

_____

9. The island has a great many of places to see, and also many exciting things to do.

_____

10. I know that if I had the chance to go again, I would leave immediately with no hesitations!

_____

Q225. What is your biggest ambition in life?

A. Essay Outline

Argument: My biggest ambition in life is to open my own early childhood education center.
Support 1: I love being around children and I have had a lot of experience with early childhood.
Support 2: I hope to nurture the children at their most formidable ages.
Support 3: It will take a lot of work to make this dream come true.
Thesis: Because it will be so rewarding, I want to open my own early childhood education center.

B. Model Essay

I have many ambitions in life to do many great things, such as get married and have a family, win the lottery, travel the world, and eat live octopus. However, my biggest ambition in life is to open my own early childhood education center. This will be a big feat to me because it will take a lot of time, preparation, finances, and other resources to make it run successfully. However, it is something I am willing to put a lot of hard work into because teaching children is my passion.

First, I have this ambition because I love to be around children. Also, my educational specialty is in dealing with early childhood aged children. Ever since I was young, I have always babysat or taught children in some manner. I started to teach at my church when I was 13 years old and immediately fell in love with it. So by doing this, I will be continuing on with my life's passion.

Next, by opening this education center, I hope to nurture the children at their most formidable ages. In this type of environment, the children will learn to have manners and to respect others. They will also learn the basic life skills needed in life, such as brushing their teeth, cleaning the dishes, and sharing with others. These vital skills of how to treat others will guide my future students a long way in their lives. Just imagine what properly raised and educated children could do to change our world, versus the children who are raised without ever hearing the word 'no'.

However, in order to achieve this great ambition of mine, I will have to save a lot of money, and also start to network with people. These people will be able to help support me financially and in many other ways. I'm already starting to save money, and I hope that by the time I am in my 40s or 50s, I will have enough money to make my dream come true.

Hard work is usually involved when you have great ambitions to do something. So it is no surprise to me that opening my own education center will take a lot of work on my part. In the long run, I know that it will be a great experience for the children who will attend my education center. I hope that with the right support and through the right people, I can accomplish this grand goal.

C. Useful Expressions

1. This will be a big feat to me because it will take a lot of time, preparation, finances, and other resources to make it run successfully.

_____

2. However, it is something I am willing to put a lot of hard work into because teaching children is my passion.

_____

3. Ever since I was young, I have always babysat or taught children in some manner.

_____

4. Next, by opening this education center, I hope to nurture the children at their most formidable ages.

_____

5. These vital skills of how to treat others will guide my future students a long way in their lives.

_____

6. Just imagine what properly raised and educated children could do to change our world, versus the children who are raised without ever hearing the word 'no'.

_____

7. However, in order to achieve this great ambition of mine, I will have to save a lot of money, and also start to network with people.

_____

8. Hard work is usually involved when you have great ambitions to do something.

_____

9. So it is no surprise to me that opening my own education center will take a lot of work on my part.

_____

> **Q226. Which family member has influenced you the most? Why is this person a positive or negative role model in your life?**

A. Essay Outline

Argument: The person who has influenced me the most is my older sister for many reasons.
Support 1: She is the person I have been around the most since the day I was born.
Support 2: She was not necessarily a good influence on my life though.
Support 3: I learned from those mistakes that she made and decided to never do them myself,
Thesis: My older sister taught me what not to do and I will forever be grateful for her guidance to stay out of trouble.

B. Model Essay

Many superior people have influenced me positively and negatively throughout my life. However, the family member who has influenced me the most is my older sister. She influenced me in an unusual way though.

Firstly, my older sister is the person I have been around since the day I was born. Therefore, she is naturally the person who would have the most power and influence over my life. For the first 15 years of my life, we lived in the same room, went to the same school, and went everywhere else together. I was called her 'mini-me' because we never left each other's side. Sometimes, I didn't like this type of attention because I never felt like my own person next to her.

Normally, this closeness would bring about a positive influence, but she had quite the opposite effect on me. Actually, she taught me all the bad things not to do because I saw her make many mistakes. She would stay out late, talk back to our parents, and just push every limit that was set by any authority. Most children would follow in their big sisters footsteps and do the same things that their 'role-model' does. For me, if I followed in her footsteps, I would have been in an enormous amount of trouble too.

However, I learned from those mistakes that she made and decided that I should never do them too. This is because I did not like the punishments and treatment she had received from our parents. I had seen how severely she was punished for doing all those bad things, and it made me do the opposite of everything she did. One example was when she came home late, which happened often. This time, our mother caught her and she was grounded for 2 months. I loved hanging out with my friends, so I never came home late because my older sister set the example of what not to do.

It is unusual to think that the person who has influenced me the most is not a positive influence. Sometimes, negative things in our lives teach us more than the positive things in our lives. My older sister taught me what not to do and I will forever be grateful for her guidance to stay out of trouble.

C. Useful Expressions

1. Many superior people have influenced me positively and negatively throughout my life.

2. Therefore, she is naturally the person who would have the most power and influence over my life.

3. Sometimes, I didn't like this type of attention because I never felt like my own person next to her.

4. Normally, this closeness would bring about a positive influence, but she had quite the opposite effect on me.

5. She would stay out late, talk back to our parents, and just push every limit that was set by any authority.

6. For me, if I followed in her footsteps, I would have been in an enormous amount of trouble too.

7. I had seen how severely she was punished for doing all those bad things, and it made me do the opposite of everything she did.

8. I loved hanging out with my friends, so I never came home late, because my older sister set the example of what not to do.

9. Sometimes, negative things in our lives teach us more than the positive things in our lives.

10. My older sister taught me what not to do and I will forever be grateful for her guidance to stay out of trouble.

Q227. Where do you see yourself in twenty years?

A. Essay Outline

Argument: In twenty years, I hope to see myself with a family, settled down in a home somewhere, and teaching.
Support 1: To me, having a family is the most important thing that I want in my future.
Support 2: Having my own place will increase my level of happiness.
Support 3: Having a stable teaching job is something that I long for.
Thesis: In twenty years, I hope to see myself with a family, settled down in a home somewhere, and teaching, because by having all of these things, I will have achieved my perfect life and level of happiness.

B. Model Essay

I don't know what my future really holds for me but I hope that it will be just as good as or even better than the life I have now. In twenty years, I hope to see myself with a family, settled down in a home somewhere, and teaching. By having all of these things, I will have achieved my perfect life and level of happiness.

To begin with, having my own family is the most important thing that I want in my future. Currently, I am not dating anybody, but I hope that one day that will change for me. Having a family of my own is something that I have desired to have for a long time and I know it will eventually come with patience. I want a family that is close and supportive of each other. Also I want a family who shows unconditional love but also shows tough love. A family is the group of people who will guide you in the right direction, but will always take you back if you stray from the path.

Next, having my own place will increase my level of happiness. This is because I won't have to share my living space with other people who don't respect shared living spaces. Also, I won't feel like I always have to clean up after people who are not my own family. When I have my own family, I will have no issues cleaning up after them. However, I will teach them to clean the dishes after using them, to wipe off the counter if they spill, and to take out the trash on a regular basis. These basic skills are very useful when we become adults who are living on their own or in a shared living experience at college.

Lastly, I hope to be teaching in twenty years. I love teaching and it is something I know I am good at. When you are good at something, why not continue doing it? Therefore, I will continue to work hard at my special skill and improve upon my techniques through various classes and courses that will be offered to me. I hope to be in a university professor position by then or running my educational business. It is an achievable goal, but it will take time to make it happen.

We don't know exactly what the future really holds for us, but I hope that mine will be just as good as or even better than the life I have now. In twenty years, I hope to see myself with a family, settled down in a home somewhere, and teaching. By having all of these things, I will have achieved my perfect life and level of happiness.

C. Useful Expressions

1. I don't know what my future really holds for me but I hope that it will be just as good as or even better than the life I have now.

_____

_____

2. In twenty years, I hope to see myself with a family, settled down in a home somewhere, and teaching.

_____

3. Currently, I am not dating anybody, but I hope that one day that will change for me.

_____

4. Also I want a family who shows unconditional love but also shows tough love.

_____

5. A family is the group of people who will guide you in the right direction, but will always take you back if you stray from the path.

_____

_____

6. Also I won't feel like I always have to clean up after people who are not my own family.

_____

7. When you are good at something, why not continue doing it?

_____

8. Therefore, I will continue to work hard at my special skill and improve upon my techniques through various classes and courses that will be offered to me.

_____

_____

9. It is an achievable goal, but it will take time to make it happen.

_____

Q228. What quality or qualities do you look for in a best friend?

A. Essay Outline

Argument: A best friend should have some specific qualities; honest and trustworthy, understanding, and supportive.

Support 1: Without having an honest friend, there can be no trust.

Support 2: The next, understanding, is also a very important quality to have in a best friend.

Support 3: The last quality I want in a best friend is support.

Thesis: Since honesty and trust, understanding, and support are all essential aspects of a long lasting and strong friendship, I want a best friend that possesses all of the aforementioned characteristics.

B. Model Essay

Throughout our lives, we meet many people who come and go. Some of them become friends, some become mistakes, and some become best friends. No matter what happens between these relationships, they all teach us lessons. However, a best friend should have some specific qualities; she should be honest and trustworthy, understanding, and supportive. Without these qualities, there isn't much of a friendship, let alone a relationship that is one of the closest we have in our lives.

First and foremost, honesty and trust go hand in hand. Without having an honest friend, there can be no trust. For example, if Sue knows something that could prevent John from being hurt, she should tell John immediately, no matter how hurtful it could be. If Sue doesn't say something and he finds out that his friend knew about it, it will be detrimental to their friendship's trust. How can you trust somebody who isn't fully honest with you? Often times, so-called-friends withhold information in fear of it hurting you, but it hurts more when it was something trivial that should have been told in the first place.

The next, understanding, is also a very important quality to have in a best friend. A best friend is supposed to be the person that knows you the most and is by your side at all times. So, they should be able to understand that you are going through a difficult time and give you the space and understanding that you need. Sometimes, something negative happens between friends, and all they need is just a little bit of distance. But, when a friend continues to leave notes and pester the person, it leads to even more resentment towards the person who did wrong in the first place. Best friends understand this balance, and they don't continue to pressure you into talking, until you are ready to do so.

The last quality I want in a best friend is support. When we are being faced with challenging decisions in life, we need a rock to lean on. Your best friend is supposed to be that rock. They are somebody who can talk to, cry to, and laugh with about all the pros and cons of that decision. For example, when deciding to move to a foreign country, the best friend might want to be selfish to keep their friend in the same country as them. However, they will be supportive and give them an open ear to bounce off their ideas and thoughts to.

I have many friends, but only two of them I consider to be a best friend. They all possess these basic qualities; honesty and trust, understanding, and support. I couldn't imagine a life without my best friends or a life with friends who didn't stand by my side, even while I'm thousands of miles away in a foreign country for an extended period of time.

C. Useful Expressions

1. Some of them become friends, some become mistakes, and some become best friends.

_____

2. No matter what happens between these relationships, they all teach us lessons.

_____

3. Without these qualities, there isn't much of a friendship, let alone a relationship that is one of the closest we have in our lives.

_____

_____

4. First and foremost, honesty and trust go hand in hand.

_____

5. If Sue doesn't say something and he finds out that his friend knew about it, it will be detrimental to their friendship's trust.

_____

6. Often times, so-called-friends withhold information in fear of it hurting you, but it hurts more when it was something trivial that should have been told in the first place.

_____

_____

7. But, when a friend continues to leave notes and pester the person, it leads to even more resentment towards the person who did wrong in the first place.

_____

_____

8. When we are being faced with challenging decisions in life, we need a rock to lean on.

_____

9. They are somebody who can talk to, cry to, and laugh with about all the pros and cons of that decision.

_____

10. However, they will be supportive and give them an open ear to bounce off their ideas and thoughts to.

_____

> ## Q229. Parents should be required to pay for their children's university education. Do you agree or disagree with this statement?

A. Essay Outline

Argument: Parents should not pay for their children's university education.
Support 1: Paying for one's higher education teaches students who have entered adulthood to be financially responsible.
Support 2: A university student can be more academically responsible.
Support 3: Parents can still choose to support their child financially later.
Thesis: Despite the negatives of being overwhelmed by the financial burden of loans, paying for one's own university education has many positives.

B. Model Essay

In many countries, parents pay for their children's higher education in its entirety. In other countries, the university student must take out numerous loans. Which of this is the correct point of view? It's a rather difficult question to answer because I feel it should be a balance between the two. However, if I had to choose to agree or disagree with the statement, 'parents should pay for their children's university education', I would choose the latter.

In the first place, paying for ones higher education teaches students who have entered adulthood to be financially responsible. While students are in universities, they are still able to reach out to their parents for assistance, as well as after their graduation. However, here they are eligible for low-interest loans, scholarships, and other sources of income. So, by having a university student pay for education, they can build their credit score, as well as their confidence to survive in a financial environment.

Second, a university student can be more academically responsible. I paid for my own degree, and I worked very hard to get all A's in my classes. So I know from first-hand experience that it teaches academic responsibility to people. When somebody pays for something on their own, they are more apt to treat it well. The same goes for paying for one's university degree. Many times, university students view college as a party place, and not much of an academic environment. However, having responsibility for the bill ensures that they take their classes seriously, attend them all, and complete all of the requirements for their courses.

Third, parents can still choose to support their child financially later. After a student graduates with a university degree, the parents can give their child a check for a graduation gift to help with the overwhelming loans that built up over the last four years. I know people who have over 100,000 dollars in college loans, and this can be very stressful to them when they are required to start paying it back. I fortunately worked hard and paid off all of my college loans because I had a few jobs while I attended my university.

In summary, despite the negatives of being overwhelmed by the financial burden of loans, paying for one's own university education has many positives. It teaches financial responsibility, as well as academic responsibility. The financial responsibility learned in the college years will last long into the adult years. Also, just because the parents don't pay for the university education for their children while they attend college, it doesn't mean that they can't help out after they have graduated and after their child has learned the vital lessons that come from these formidable years.

C. Useful Expressions

1. In many countries, parents pay for their children's higher education in its entirety.

_____

2. However, if I had to choose to agree or disagree with the statement, 'parents should pay for their children's university education', I would choose the latter.

_____

3. While students are in universities, they are still able to reach out to their parents for assistance, as well as after their graduation.

_____

4. So, by having a university student pay for their education, they can build their credit score, as well as their confidence to survive in a financial environment.

_____

5. So I know from first-hand experience that it teaches academic responsibility to people.

_____

6. When somebody pays for something on their own, they are more apt to treat it well.

_____

7. The same goes for paying for one's university degree.

_____

8. Many times, university students view college as a party place, and not much of an academic environment.

_____

9. The financial responsibility learned in the college years will last long into the adult years.

_____

10. Also, just because the parents don't pay for the university education for their children while they attend college, it doesn't mean that they can't help out after they have graduated, and after their child has learned the vital lessons that come from these formidable years.

_____

_____

Q230. Describe the qualities of a good citizen.

A. Essay Outline

Argument: There are three very important qualities that I deem to be required in a good citizen; they should be a faithful voter, they should never break the law, and they should always pay their expected taxes.

Support 1: First off, they should be a faithful voter.

Support 2: Second, a good citizen is someone who never breaks the law.

Support 3: The third quality to be considered as a good citizen is that a person should pay their taxes and pay them on time.

Thesis: Since the above mentioned qualities are all supportive of making a better community, I feel that voting, being a law abiding citizen, and paying our required taxes show that we are good citizens.

B. Model Essay

We are all citizens in a country somewhere, but what makes us good citizens? There are three very important qualities that I deem to be required in a good citizen. They are that they should be a faithful voter, they should never break the law, and they should always pay their expected taxes.

First off, they should be a faithful voter. What does being a faithful voter mean? It means that they should vote in every election. This ensures that their voice is heard and the right officials are being elected into office. If they do not vote in an election, then I feel that they don't have the right to speak their mind about the elected officials because they didn't vote for anybody. It frustrates me when somebody who didn't vote complains about their government. I always say to them, "Vote and do something about it. It's our right as citizens!"

Second, a good citizen is someone who never breaks the law. What I mean by this is that they should never cheat, steal, kill, or damage anybody else's property. Good citizens should be moral role models for the youth in the community. If they break the laws, then they are setting an immoral example for future generations. The future generations will think it is ok to behave badly, and then the community will turn into a dangerous place to live. If we are good role models for future generations, then we can build a great country to live in.

The third quality to be considered a good citizen is that a person should pay their taxes and pay them on time. By paying taxes on time, we are giving money back to the community. This tax money, in theory, goes to the schools, the police force, parks, etc. If we don't pay them or don't pay them on time, then our communities will not have ample resources to provide the best possible place to live. I know it seems like paying taxes is a burden and unfair sometimes, but they do truly help our communities become a better place.

Since the above mentioned qualities are all supportive of making a better community, I feel that voting, being a law-abiding citizen, and paying our required taxes show that we are good citizens. We should all strive to be good citizens, and these three aspects are just simple ways we can be exactly that. If we do not follow these simple guidelines, then we are doing the opposite and should be punished appropriately by the law.

C. Useful Expressions

1. There are three very important qualities that I deem to be required in a good citizen.

_____

2. This ensures that their voice is heard and the right officials are being elected into office.

_____

3. If they do not vote in an election, then I feel that they don't have the right to speak their mind about the elected officials because they didn't vote for anybody.

_____

4. What I mean by this is that they should never cheat, steal, kill, or damage anybody else's property.

_____

5. If they break the laws, then they are setting an immoral example for future generations.

_____

6. If we are good role models for future generations, then we can build a great country to live in.

_____

7. This tax money, in theory, goes to the schools, police force, parks, etc.

_____

8. I know it seems like paying taxes is a burden and unfair sometimes, but they do truly help our communities become a better place.

_____

9. Since the above mentioned qualities are all supportive of making a better community, I feel that voting, being a law abiding citizen, and paying our required taxes show that we are good citizens.

_____

10. We should all strive to be good citizens, and these three aspects are just simple ways we can be exactly that.

_____

Q231. What are the most important qualities of a good teacher?

A. Essay Outline

Argument: I think back to my best teacher and he had three specific qualities; he was always fair and consistent, he was never rude or condescending, and he was easy to approach.
Support 1: The first of the most important qualities a good teacher should have is being fair and consistent.
Support 2: The next most important quality of a good teacher is to never be rude or to be condescending.
Support 3: The final quality that I hold to be important of a good teacher is to be approachable.
Thesis: A teacher who is fair and impartial, who is not rude or condescending, and who is open and welcoming is a good teacher in my opinion.

B. Model Essay

We have hopefully all had a good teacher that we remember in our lives. Thinking back to the best teacher I have ever had, Mr. Hillshire possessed three specific qualities. He was always fair and consistent, he was never rude or condescending, and he was easy to approach. Because he had all of these qualities, I saw him as a good teacher, and so did all of the other students.

The first of the most important qualities a good teacher should have is being fair and consistent. Mr. Hillshire never had favorites and he held all the students to the same level of discipline and love. If you were an A+ student, but forgot your homework, you got the same punishment as the C student. This might seem unfair, but in actuality, it is very fair. It showed me that he kept to his rules consistently in the classroom, which made it very easy to know what his expectations of you were.

The next most important quality of a good teacher is to never be rude or to be condescending. Teachers who make us cry, or make us feel bad about ourselves are not good teachers in my eyes. If I did something wrong in class, Mr. Hillshire corrected me on it, but he didn't do it in a way where it lessened my desire to learn and to make mistakes. Students often make mistakes because it is a part of the learning process. But, if a teacher harshly criticized me or embarrassed me in front of the other students, I would not be as willing to answer a question in the future.

The final quality that I hold to be important of a good teacher is to be approachable. If students find the teacher to be unapproachable, they will not be able to ask for help if they are confused on a specific topic or skill that was discussed in the class. Mr. Hillshire was not best friends with the students, but rather, he granted an open and welcoming opportunity for the less confident students, like me, to ask for clarification in the classroom. There is a very careful balance between being too friendly and being approachable.

A teacher who is fair and impartial, who is not rude or condescending, and who is open and welcoming is a good teacher in my opinion. Possessing these qualities affords all students an equal chance to excel in the classroom, not just the ones who are considered to be the teacher's pets or favorites. I will never forget Mr. Hillshire because he had all of these qualities.

C. Useful Expressions

1. Thinking back to the best teacher I have ever had, Mr. Hillshire possessed three specific qualities.

---

2. He was always fair and consistent, he was never rude or condescending, and he was easy to approach.

---

3. This might seem unfair, but in actuality, it is very fair.

---

4. It showed me that he kept to his rules consistently in the classroom, which made it very easy to know what his expectations of you were.

---

5. He was always fair and consistent, he was never rude or condescending, and he was easy to approach.

---

6. This might seem unfair, but in actuality, it is very fair.

---

7. It showed me that he kept to his rules consistently in the classroom, which made it very easy to know what his expectations of you were.

---

8. Mr. Hillshire was not best friends with the students, but rather, he granted an open and welcoming opportunity for the less confident students, like me, to ask for clarification in the classroom.

---

9. There is a very careful balance between being too friendly and being approachable.

---

10. Possessing these qualities affords all students an equal chance to excel in the classroom, not just the ones who are considered to be the teacher's pets or favorites.

Q232. What qualities does a good student have to have?

A. Essay Outline

Argument: Being a good student means always being prepared, managing time well, and asking for help when it's needed.
Support 1: One of the most essential qualities a student should possess is to be hard working and motivated.
Support 2: The next important quality of a good student is to have a good sense of time management.
Support 3: Finally, not being timid in the classroom is a great quality of a good student.
Thesis: Having these three qualities will benefit a student academically.

B. Model Essay

Often times, we are under great pressure by our parents, teachers, and peers to be a good student. But what does being a good student mean? It means being a hard worker and having the motivation to finish all the assigned tasks properly. It means managing your time well. It also means not being afraid to ask for help if you don't understand something. Having possessed all of these skills made me a very successful student in school.

One of the most essential qualities a student should possess is to be hard working and motivated. What exactly does hard working and motivated mean? It means that the student should always do their homework, and they should pay attention in the classroom to the instructor. A good student will successfully complete all of their assigned tasks, and they will do it by putting their best effort forward. Also, they will not have to be told to study on their own; they will be intrinsically motivated to study themselves.

The next important quality of a good student is that they have a good sense of time management. Schools require a lot of time to accomplish their assignments, so a student needs to be able to properly manage the time that it will take to finish these assigned tasks. They will know how far out they should start preparing for their ten-page essay assignment, and they will also know how much time they need to study for the big final exams next week. They will not be a procrastinator and wait until the last minute to start their assignments.

Finally, not being timid in the classroom is a great quality of a good student. If you are timid in the classroom, then you will not be willing to ask for clarification when you don't understand something the teacher says, leaving you lost and confused. I'm not saying that the student needs to ask a lot of questions to be a good student. I'm only stating that if they are unsure of something or confused about a specific topic, they should be unafraid to ask the teacher for more of an explanation.

In school, students should have many qualities to be academically successful. These three qualities are that they should be hard working and motivated, have a good sense of time management, and not be timid about asking for clarification. Having these three qualities will benefit a student academically, as they did for me.

C. Useful Expressions

1. Often times, we are under great pressure by our parents, teachers, and peers to be a good student.

2. Having possessed all of these skills made me a very successful student in school.

_____

3. One of the most essential qualities a student should possess is to be hard working and motivated.

_____

4. A good student will successfully complete all of their assigned tasks, and they will do it by putting their best effort forward.

_____

_____

5. They will know how far out they should start preparing for their ten-page essay assignment, and they will also know how much time they need to study for the big final exams next week.

_____

_____

6. They will not be a procrastinator and wait until the last minute to start their assignments.

_____

_____

7. I'm not saying that the student needs to ask a lot of questions to be a good student.

_____

_____

8. I'm only stating that if they are unsure of something or confused about a specific topic, they should be unafraid to ask the teacher for more of an explanation.

_____

_____

9. Having these three qualities will benefit a student academically, as they did for me.

_____

_____

Q233. What would you change about your country if you were given the opportunity?

A. Essay Outline

Argument: I would love to see three things change in the U.S.A.: more diversity and acceptance in all parts of the country, less arguing between politicians, and no reporting of negative news.

Support 1: The first thing I would change is to have more diversity and acceptance in all parts of the country.

Support 2: The second item that I would love to see changed in the USA is for there to be less arguing between the politicians, including the disputes received by the public.

Support 3: The last item I would make amendments to in America is the media's reporting of negative news.

Thesis: To conclude, if Americans could see more diversity and acceptance, more civil political settings, and more positive media influences, then the "Land of the Free and the Home of the Brave" would be an even better country to live in.

B. Model Essay

To many Americans, the United States of America is a great country with very few problems. To others, the country has many flaws that they would fix. I fall in between these two opinions. I love America and feel very fortunate to have been born there, but I would love to see three things change in the U.S.A.: more diversity and acceptance in all parts of the country, less arguing between politicians, and no reporting of negative news.

The first thing I would change is to have more diversity and acceptance in all parts of the country. America has come a long way since the Civil Rights Act and the Emancipation Proclamation, but it has a lot more it can grow. America is viewed as an equal opportunity country by many, yet there are still many racist and prejudiced people, whether it is against race, gender, nationality, or religion. The great thing about America is that you are supposed to have the freedom to possess your own beliefs, just as long as they don't break the constitutional rules, such as killing other humans.

The second item that I would love to see changed in the USA is for there to be less arguing between the politicians, including the disputes received by the public. I would encourage the politicians to bridge the gap between the right-wing (Conservative) and the left-wing (Democrat) politicians. Making a defined three-party system might help to alleviate some of these tensions between the current two-party system. If we can take away the constant battles and political back-lashings, then maybe, just maybe, our country might be able to move forward, instead of backward, like its current track.

The last item I would make amendments to in America is the media's reporting of negative news. Too often, the media only reports deaths, shootings, and other negative things. But, wouldn't it be nice if we could see a story about people helping each other, instead of hurting each other? Having positive role-models and media would greatly affect our country. Imagine how much respectable actions would be done, if we saw other's good actions being reported. They too would want to be rewarded for their positive contributions in life, rather than the 'bad' people in the country being glorified by the news.

To conclude, if Americans could see more diversity and acceptance, more civil political settings, and more positive media influences, then the "Land of the Free and the Home of the Brave" would be an even better country to live in. Americans have it so good, compared to other countries in the world, yet Americans want more. How about we, as Americans be thankful for all that we have and learn to make what we have been given an even better place to live?

C. Useful Expressions

1. To many Americans, the United States of America is a great country with very few problems. To others, the country has many flaws that they would fix. I fall in between these two opinions.

2. I love America and feel very fortunate to have been born there, but I would love to see three things change in the U.S.A.

3. America has come a long way since the Civil Rights Act and the Emancipation Proclamation, but it has a lot more it can grow.

4. The great thing about America is that you are supposed to have the freedom to possess your own beliefs, just as long as they don't break the constitutional rules, such as killing other humans.

5. I would encourage the politicians to bridge the gap between the right-wing (Conservative) and the left-wing (Democrat) politicians.

6. Making a defined three-party system might help to alleviate some of these tensions between the current two-party system.

7. But, wouldn't it be nice if we could see a story about people helping each other, instead of hurting each other?

8. Having positive role-models and media would greatly affect our country.

9. Americans have it so good, compared to other countries in the world, yet Americans want more.

10. How about we, as Americans be thankful for all that we have and learn to make what we have been given an even better place to live?

Q234. Do you agree or disagree with the following statement? An eye for an eye. Why or why not?

A. Essay Outline

Argument: Despite my human instincts to react negatively back toward others, I do not agree with this statement.
Support 1: To begin, there are other options to resolve this conflict.
Support 2: Next, you should be the better person in this situation.
Support 3: Lastly, hitting them will only cause further harm to you in the future.
Thesis: Since retaliating back only causes more harm than good, I do not agree with the statement of "an eye for an eye."

B. Model Essay

The saying "An eye for an eye" means that if someone does something negative to you, you should do something negative back to them. Despite my human instincts to react negatively back toward others, I do not agree with this statement. There are other options to resolve conflicts, you should be the better person and not resort to their childish actions, and they are not worth the negative backlash you'd receive for doing wrong to them. I will use one specific example to demonstrate my reasoning: somebody physically harming you by hitting you.

To begin, there are other options to resolve this conflict. When somebody hits you, your first instinct is to want to hit them back. However, this is not the best option. The best option is to avoid them in the future and to cut off all contact with them. This type of person is not somebody you want or need in your life. Another approach would be to talk to them about their rude, violent, childish act of resorting to physical violence for their own anger problems. One more final option is to leave them a note expressing your feelings about their physical assault. However, I find notes to be an elementary-aged thing to do. So, I do not recommend this option.

Next, you should be the better person in this situation. If you follow the eye-for-an-eye rule in life, then you are just as negative of a person as they are. Just because somebody hits you, or steals from you, or even spreads negative rumors about you, it doesn't mean you should stoop down to their level by doing the same immature acts. As early as elementary school, we can control our feelings and choose who we want to surround ourselves by. So this means that we do not need to be around those that are negative or bring us down. So, instead of being on their destructive level, we can choose to avoid them and be the better person in the situation.

Lastly, hitting them will only cause further harm to you in the future. If you resort to physically harming them back, it will only prove that you are a violent person too. This then will get you in trouble at school, at your job, with your friends, or with your family. It will most likely make you look bad to those that care about you, and in return, you might lose people you care about because of your rash decision making skills.

In conclusion, I do not agree with the statement of "an eye for an eye." Retaliating towards those that do negatives to you is of no benefit to you in your future. You should be the better person, try to resolve the conflict through another means, and learn from the mistakes that got you in that position in the first place. If you live by these simple rules, you will have a happy life without resorting to revenge upon others that will only fill your heart with hate and pain.

C. Useful Expressions

1. There are other options to resolve conflicts, you should be the better person and not resort to their childish actions, and they are not worth the negative backlash you'd receive for doing wrong to them.

_____

2. I will use one specific example to demonstrate my reasoning: somebody physically harming you by hitting you.

_____

3. When somebody hits you, your first instinct is to want to hit them back.

_____

4. Another approach would be to talk to them about their rude, violent, childish act of resorting to physical violence for their own anger problems.

_____
_____

5. Just because somebody hits you, or steals from you, or even spreads negative rumors about you, it doesn't mean you should stoop down to their level by doing the same immature acts.

_____
_____

6. As early as elementary school, we can control our feelings and choose who we want to surround ourselves by.

_____
_____

7. This then will get you in trouble at school, at your job, with your friends, or with your family.

_____

8. It will most likely make you look bad to those that care about you, and in return, you might lose people you care about because of your rash decision making skills.

_____
_____

9. Retaliating towards those that do negatives to you is of no benefit to you in your future.

_____

10. If you live by these simple rules, you will have a happy life without resorting to revenge upon others that will only fill your heart with hate and pain.

_____
_____

Q235. What is the most important job or task you have ever had? Why was it important?

A. Essay Outline

Argument: The most important task that I was assigned was being the Barracks NCO (Non-commissioned Officer) for one and half years in Daegu, South Korea.
Support 1: I had to keep everything well-organized.
Support 2: Second, people relied on me to do my job properly.
Support 3: Third, I had to conduct presentations to the top officials of the US Army in the Daegu area.
Thesis: Since it taught me valuable lessons of organization, people skills, and presenting in front of high-ranking officials, being the Barracks NCO was my most important task or job that I was given.

B. Model Essay

Some important tasks or jobs that I have had were being a manager of a food stand at an amusement park, teaching Sunday school to Kindergarten-aged children for 10 years, and assisting in raising another woman's baby for two years as a nanny. These jobs were all important for various reasons, but the most important task that I was assigned was being the Barracks NCO (Non-commissioned Officer) for one and half years in Daegu, South Korea. Barracks are military housing for soldiers who live with one other roommate on the military base, and an NCO is a leader in the US Army who is responsible to various tasks.

First of all, the reason that my job was important was that I had to keep everything well-organized. My job entailed the issuing out of keys and storage lockers, the assignment of roommates and cleaning duties, and the rotating of mattresses. It also involved keeping a painstakingly precise inventory of all the furniture items in the four-story building. Because of my organization skills, the almost 180 residents had bug-free rooms, well-maintained furniture, as well as a safe room to stay in due to the strict key control regulations.

Second, people relied on me to do my job properly. My job was not just about me, but about taking care of others. So, if one of my tasks slipped through the cracks, it would send a harmful ripple-effect to all of the incoming soldiers who were brand new to Korea. I had to always make sure that everything ran smoothly, and that I was never off my game when it came to running the soldiers' dorm-like housing. If I forgot to collect a key from a soldier before they left the country, the current resident soldier would have to share one key with their incoming soldier roommate. This would cause a lot of stress to the newbie, which was not helpful to the already unfamiliar surroundings.

Third, I had to conduct presentations to the top officials of the US Army in the Daegu area. These were the leaders of the Army bases who were much higher than me in the promotion scale. I had a lot of pressure to ensure that I had accurate rosters of all incoming personnel and out-going personnel, the appropriate work-order requests (repair of furniture) from the soldiers documented, and a wide variety of other information on colorful spreadsheets. I remember one time when my boss, known as a First Sergeant, was asked a difficult question, and he was unsure of the answer, but I stepped in as a lower ranking soldier and saved him. This made my First Sergeant relieved, because he knew he could rely on my for all the difficult situations that were presented to me.

Running a building of over a hundred and seventy soldiers was not an easy task. I was a little nervous about taking on such a large project, but I knew it was an important job that needed to be done. So, I took on the important challenge of successfully maintaining the organization of the soldier dormitories. It taught me valuable lessons of organization, people skills, and presenting in-front of high-ranking officials. So, this is why it was my most important task or job that I was given.

C. Useful Expressions

1. Some important tasks or jobs that I have had were being a manager of a food stand at an amusement park, teaching Sunday school to Kindergarten-aged children for 10 years, and assisting in raising another woman's baby for two years as a nanny.

_____

2. Barracks are military housing for soldiers who live with one other roommate on the military base, and an NCO is a leader in the US Army who is responsible to various tasks.

_____

3. My job entailed the issuing out of keys and storage lockers, the assignment of roommates and cleaning duties, and the rotating of mattresses.

_____

4. It also involved keeping a painstakingly precise inventory of all the furniture items in the four-story building.

_____

5. Second, people relied on me to do my job properly.

_____

6. So, if one of my tasks slipped through the cracks, it would send a harmful ripple-effect to all of the incoming soldiers who were brand new to Korea.

_____

7. I had to always make sure that everything ran smoothly, and that I was never off my game when it came to running the soldiers' dorm-like housing.

_____

8. I had a lot of pressure to ensure that I had accurate rosters of all incoming personnel and out-going personnel, the appropriate work-order requests (repair of furniture) from the soldiers documented, and a wide variety of other information on colorful spreadsheets.

_____

9. I remember one time when my boss, known as a First Sergeant, was asked a difficult question, and he was unsure of the answer, but I stepped in as a lower ranking soldier and saved him.

_____

10. Running a building of over a hundred and seventy soldiers was not an easy task.

_____

Q236. What are the advantages and disadvantages of studying abroad?

A. Essay Outline

Argument: Studying abroad has both many advantages and disadvantages of studying abroad that range from financial burdens, to excelling in a new language.

Support 1: Some disadvantages of studying abroad are that the parents might become overwhelmed financially, and the students will get frustrated by the language barrier.

Support 2: Some advantages of studying abroad are that the student will develop a more open mind, their language skills will improve, and they can earn credits towards their college degree.

Support 3: I would have loved to been given the opportunity to have traveled abroad so that I could have made more friends from all around the world.

Thesis: To summarize, studying abroad has some highly desirable aspects, but it also has some less desirable aspects.

B. Model Essay

Studying abroad has always been a popular desire for students wishing to learn a new culture and to improve upon their language skills of their destination's mother-tongue. There are both many advantages and disadvantages of studying abroad. These range from financial burdens to excelling in a new language.

Let me begin with discussing the disadvantages of studying abroad. First, the parents will be overwhelmed with a large financial burden. Traveling is not cheap, and on top of that, the cost of living can be outrageous in the foreign country. In addition, the student might become more frustrated with themselves. This is partly due to their lack of language skills or maybe the extreme cultural differences.

On the contrary, there are numerous advantages. The foreign-bound student will develop a more open-mind to other cultures, all while they are able to experience traveling around the world. Also, the student will create a higher level of independence and will have many opportunities to improve their language skills. Often times, college credits can be earned towards their degree at some universities.

I was never given the amazing chance to travel abroad during my school years. So even though I would miss my family and friends during the holidays, I would love to been given the opportunity to travel abroad and to study. On top of the many advantages listed above, I could make new friends and business contacts for future jobs. Networking is a vital tool when it comes to competing in the job-market of today. Who knows, one of the people I meet through my travels could be my open door into obtaining my dream job!

To summarize, studying abroad has some highly desirable aspects, but it also has some less desirable aspects. It is a difficult predicament to be in, but the positives far outweigh the negatives when it comes to this specific situation. A lifetime of knowledge while being fully immersed in a language is far more beneficial to me in my future than the possibility of missing my family for a short period of time.

C. Useful Expressions

1. Studying abroad has always been a popular desire for students wishing to learn a new culture and to improve upon their language skills of their destination's mother-tongue.

2. There are both many advantages and disadvantages of studying abroad. These range from financial burdens, to excelling in a new language.

3. Let me begin with discussing the disadvantages of studying abroad.

4. This is partly due to their lack of language skills or maybe the extreme cultural differences.

5. The foreign-bound student will develop a more open-mind to other cultures, all while they are able to experience traveling around the world.

6. Often times, college credits can be earned towards their degree at some universities.

7. So even though I would miss my family and friends during the holidays, I would love to been given the opportunity to travel abroad and to study.

8. Networking is a vital tool when it comes to competing in the job-market of today.

9. To summarize, studying abroad has some highly desirable aspects, but it also has some less desirable aspects.

10. It is a difficult predicament to be in, but the positives far outweigh the negatives when it comes to this specific situation.

> **Q237. Describe your dream job. Why is it your dream job?**

A. Essay Outline

Argument: My dream job is work at an all English immersion program for infants through Kindergarten.
Support 1: To begin with, I have been teaching for 17 years now.
Support 2: Furthermore, I truly enjoy the rewards I receive from the light-bulbs clicking on in young learners.
Support 3: Finally, it has been scientifically proven that learning a new language at a young age is easier for the 'student,' so I want to help encourage this behavior for the future native English speakers.
Thesis: As you can see, I have the experience, the knowledge, and the passion for teaching young children, which is why working in an all English immersion program for young children is my dream job.

B. Model Essay

I love my current job of being an elementary/middle school/high school/university-aged English Language teacher, but it is not my dream job. My dream job still entails working with children, but just in a different environment. I would love to work at an all English emersion program for infants through Kindergarten. First, it is what I am best at and have more experience in. Second, I can enjoy the rewards of the environment. Third, it is the most appropriate age level to expose children to learning a new language.

To begin with, I have been teaching for 17 years now. I started assisting my step-mother when I was 13 years old in her Sunday school classes and fell in love with teaching. Through this experience, I was able to grow and learn as a teacher and to learn my preferences. I graduated from my university with a teaching degree in early childhood and elementary education; however, my specialty was in the early childhood portion. I excelled in all of my classes and received top marks for my experience and knowledge of the younger children's mentalities. So, working in a younger learners' environment is definitely my dream job.

Furthermore, I truly enjoy the rewards I receive from the light-bulbs clicking on in their young minds. In teaching, we call it the 'a-ha' moment. It's the moment when somebody finally understands something, or they finally use something properly. I'll never forget an 'a-ha' moment I experienced in my current school with a Kindergarten-aged child. Throughout the past few months, she always had a candy, and she always wanted her candy to be opened. So, I kept reinforcing the words, "Open my candy, please." Well, one day, I was downstairs in the lobby waiting for someone, and this little girl was with her mom. She had a piece of candy in her hand as usual, and the long awaited moment happened! She said in a sweet and confident voice using English, to her Korean mother, "Open my candy, please." I was so shocked and excited at the same time. These are the moments that teachers live for, that reward us, and that show us our students do listen to us!

Finally, it has been scientifically proven that learning a new language at a young age is easier for the 'student'. I struggle in learning a new language because I am constantly trying to translate the unfamiliar language into my own familiar language. This takes time, brain power, and causes a great deal of frustration to me. On the other hand, an infant through Kindergarten-aged child doesn't translate words. Rather, they learn the context of a word and use it in a trial and error process, until they realize the pattern the word should be used in. For example, young children learn the word 'cat' and then they see a dog. They call the dog a 'cat' because they don't know any better. That is until somebody corrects them. Now, all four legged animals are cats and dogs to them. They continue this pattern throughout their early life learning new words and making mistakes. So, I want to help encourage this behavior for the future native English speakers.

As you can see, I have the experience, the knowledge, and the passion for teaching young children. Through my numerous years of experience in educating the youth, I hope that one day in the future, I will be able to work in a full immersion English as a Second Language program. I am very happy with my current job, but I hope that in 20 years or so, I can achieve my dream job.

C. Useful Expressions

1. First, it is what I am best at and have more experience in.

_____

2. Second, I can enjoy the rewards of the environment.

_____

3. Through this experience, I was able to grow and learn as a teacher and to learn my preferences.

_____

4. So, working in a younger learners' environment is definitely my dream job.

_____

5. It's the moment when somebody finally understands something, or they finally use something properly.

_____

6. I'll never forget an 'a-ha' moment I experienced in my current school with a Kindergarten-aged child.

_____

7. Finally, it has been scientifically proven that learning a new language at a young age is easier for the 'student'.

_____

8. On the other hand, an infant through Kindergarten- aged child doesn't translate words. Rather, they learn the context of a word and use it in a trial and error process, until they realize the pattern the word should be used in.

_____

_____

9. So, I want to help encourage this behavior for the future native English speakers.

_____

10. Through my numerous years of experience in educating the youth, I hope that one day in the future, I will be able to work in a full immersion English as a Second Language program.

_____

_____

Q238. At what age is it appropriate to allow a child to stay at home alone?

A. Essay Outline

Argument: I will state that a child, who is responsible and has some other variables included, can be left home alone at the age of ten.

Support 1: The first reason is based on the child's personality.

Support 2: This leads me into my next point that it depends on why the child needs to be left alone in the first place.

Support 3: Lastly, the length of time affects the age that is appropriate for a child to be alone in their home.

Thesis: To sum up my thoughts, a child at the age of ten can be left unattended, but only meeting certain conditions.

B. Model Essay

This is a very challenging question; at what age is it appropriate to allow a child to stay at home alone? I strongly believe that it depends on the child's personality, the reason the child needs to be left alone, and the length of time the child is left unattended. No one child is the exact same as another, so to give an exact age is not accurate. So, I will state that a child, who is responsible and has some other variables included, can be left home alone at the age of ten.

As stated above, there are a variety of factors that determine whether a child can be left home alone or not. The first reason is based on the child's personality. In my case, I was left home alone as early as eight years old. My mother felt that I was independent enough to take care of myself and responsible enough to do what was right. I was able to cook microwaveable meals, brush my teeth and get ready for bed, all on my own.

This leads me into my next point that it depends on why the child needs to be left alone in the first place. Again, in my situation, my mother had to work, and she couldn't afford to pay for a babysitter. Sometimes, circumstances arise that make it difficult to provide for your children successfully, but my mother did the best she could. She did ask a neighbor to keep an eye on me from her house, by just observing me and calling me once and a while. So, I was not completely unattended.

Lastly, the length of time affects the age that is appropriate for a child to be alone in their home. At the age of ten, a child can be left alone for a few hours and should not have any major catastrophes occur, just as long as strict guidelines are observed. A ten year old child should not be left alone for more than five hours though, because they might have difficulty preparing their meals or going to bed on time.

To sum up my thoughts, a child at the age of ten can be left unattended, but only after following the suggestions listed above. They should have set rules to follow, contact numbers to call, and somebody to observe them from a distance. By being left alone at a younger age, children learn a great deal of independent skills that will be vital to them in their adult lives.

C. Useful Expressions

1. I strongly believe that it depends on the child's personality, the reason the child needs to be left alone, and the length of time the child is left unattended.

2. Not one child is the exact same as another, so to give an exact age is not accurate.

3. So, I will state that a child, who is responsible and has some other variables included, can be left home alone at the age of ten.

4. As stated above, there are a variety of factors that determine whether a child can be left home alone or not.

5. The first reason is based on the child's personality.

6. This leads me into my next point that it depends on why the child needs to be left alone in the first place.

7. Again, in my situation, my mother had to work, and she couldn't afford to pay for a babysitter.

8. Lastly, the length of time affects the age that is appropriate for a child to be alone in their home.

9. At the age of ten, a child can be left alone for a few hours and should not have any major catastrophes occur, just as long as strict guidelines are observed.

10. To sum up my thoughts, a child at the age of ten can be left unattended, but only after following the suggestions listed above.

> **Q239. Some people say that the quality of a product is more important. Others say that the price of a product is more important. Which statement do you agree with and why?**

A. Essay Outline

Argument: I believe quality is more important than its price tag.
Support 1: For starters, cheap prices usually mean a cheap quality product.
Support 2: Next, I can have trust in the product that it will work properly.
Support 3: To conclude, if my product did break down, I have a guaranteed warranty with higher quality products.
Thesis: Since money is of no importance when it comes to the functioning capabilities of a product, I prefer quality over price.

B. Model Essay

Imagine you are in the market to buy a computer. You have the choice between a high quality laptop, and a less pricy computer. Which would you choose? I without a doubt would buy the higher quality laptop for the following three reasons: cheap prices usually mean cheap quality, trust in the product to work properly, and guaranteed warranty.

For starters, cheap prices usually mean a cheap quality product. In the case of the laptop, a cheap computer doesn't come with some of the desired programs. I just bought a laptop myself, and the cheaper computers did not have the programs I wanted. So I went for a more expensive product that had higher quality.

Next, I can have trust in the product that it will work properly. When it comes to quality versus price, the price doesn't matter when it comes to my product functioning properly. In the example of the laptop, if I bought a cheap computer, it would most likely break down in a few short months. The cheaper products are generally made from cheaper quality products. Therefore, cheap prices mean a lower quality computer.

To conclude, if my product did break down, I have a guaranteed warranty with higher quality products. Most high quality products are produced by a name-brand. Because of this, they almost always come with a warranty on their products. Mistakes can happen, and something might happen to my computer, so I want to be ensured that my money spent on something is not wasted.

Since money is of no importance when it comes to the functioning capabilities of a product, I prefer quality over price. I don't want to lose out on my money due to faulty materials used in the production of a cheap product. To me, my time in fixing a broken cheap product is more of a hassle and frustration than buying a more expensive product that I know will work.

C. Useful Expressions

1. Imagine you are in the market to buy a computer. You have the choice between a high quality laptop and a less pricy computer. Which would you choose?

2. I without a doubt would buy the higher quality laptop for the following three reasons: cheap prices usually mean cheap quality, trust in the product to work properly, and guaranteed warranty.

3. For starters, cheap prices usually mean a cheap quality product.

4. In the case of the laptop, a cheap computer doesn't come with some of the desired programs.

5. When it comes to quality versus price, the price doesn't matter when it comes to my product functioning properly.

6. In the example of the laptop, if I bought a cheap computer, it would most likely break down in a few short months.

7. Because of this, they almost always come with a warranty on their products.

8. Mistakes can happen, and something might happen to my computer, so I want to be ensured that my money spent on something is not wasted.

9. Since money is of no importance when it comes to the functioning capabilities of a product, I prefer quality over price.

10. I don't want to lose out on my money due to faulty materials used in the production of a cheap product.

Q240. How will you help a foreigner learn about your country?

A. Essay Outline

Argument: I feel that the best way to help a foreigner learn about America is through three things: sightseeing, movies and music, and socializing with my friends and family.

Support 1: The first way I can help a foreigner learn about my country is my taking them around the various tourist spots in America.

Support 2: Secondly, I can introduce them to American movies and music.

Support 3: Finally, socializing with my friends and family will be the best way for the out-of-towner to see my culture.

Thesis: Since using a variety of tactics will be the best options for a foreigner to learn about my country, I would show them tourist spots, movies and music, and my friends' and family's lifestyles.

B. Model Essay

There are so many ways to assist a foreigner in learning about my country. America has a large variety of places to see and things to do. I feel that the best way to help a foreigner learn about America is through three things: sightseeing, movies and music, and socializing with my friends and family.

The first way I can help a foreigner learn about my country is my taking them around the various tourist spots in America. Through these different locations, the foreigner will be able to learn the history and culture of my country. For instance, if I take a foreigner to New York City, I would show them the Statue of Liberty. By doing this, they can see how many people have come to America from other countries.

Secondly, I can introduce them to American movies and music. I feel that music and movies show a skewed version of our culture, but it will still be an entertaining experience for them. Movies, such as American Beauty, and Precious show a more realistic side of the American society. If we can expose the foreigner to just a taste of the American music and movies, then they can better understand our differences and similarities to their own cultures.

Finally, socializing with my friends and family will be the best way for the out-of-towner to see my culture. When I was in a new country, South Korea, hanging out with native people from that country helped me greatly to learn about the Korean culture. If I had solely relied on movies and music or books, I would have not learned as much of the little nuances of this conservative, yet complex culture. One example was that I gained knowledge about the things that are taboo in the Korean society.

Since using a variety of tactics will be the best options for a foreigner to learn about my country, I would show them tourist spots, movies and music, and my friends' and family's lifestyles. By doing a mixture of all of these things, a person who is unfamiliar with the American culture will gain a better view of how people from the USA live, work, and play.

C. Useful Expressions

1. There are so many ways to assist a foreigner in learning about my country.

2. I feel that the best way to help a foreigner learn about America is through three things: sightseeing,

movies and music, and socializing with my friends and family.

_____

_____

3. Through these different locations, the foreigner will be able to learn the history and culture of my country.

_____

_____

4. For instance, if I take a foreigner to New York City, I would show them the Statue of Liberty.

_____

_____

5. I feel that music and movies show a skewed version of our culture, but it will still be an entertaining experience for them.

_____

_____

6. If we can expose the foreigner to just a taste of the American music and movies, then they can better understand our differences and similarities to their own cultures.

_____

_____

7. Finally, socializing with my friends and family will be the best way for the out-of-towner to see my culture.

_____

_____

8. If I had solely relied on movies and music or books, I would have not learned as much of the little nuances of this conservative, yet complex culture.

_____

_____

9. Since using a variety of tactics will be the best options for a foreigner to learn about my country, I would show them tourist spots, movies and music, and my friends' and family's lifestyles.

_____

_____

10. By doing a mixture of all of these things, a person who is unfamiliar with the American culture will gain a better view of how people from the USA live, work, and play.

_____

_____

ABOUT THE EDITOR

LIKE TEST PREP

Free Bonus 1

Preview of '240 Speaking Topics with Sample Answers'

240 SPEAKING TOPICS

WITH SAMPLE ANSWERS

LIKE TEST PREP

Q121. Which season – winter, spring, summer, or fall – is your favorite?

_____

_____

_____

_____

_____

_____

A. Sample Answer

My favorite season is winter because of two reasons. First, Christmas is in winter and I always love getting presents from my family. Usually, on Christmas, I get toys from my sister and chocolate from my mother. We always have a great time together on Christmas. Second, I love to play in the snow. When I was younger, I made a snow angel or a snowman every year on the first day it snowed. I still do it today. In winter, I also get to see my little brother throw a snowball at my dad. It's very funny. Since it is a great season to spend with my family, I think winter is my favorite season.

B. Create new sentences using the expressions below.

(1) one's favorite

_____

(2) love … ing (cf. love to + verb)

_____

(3) have a good time ~ing

_____

(4) a wonderful place to visit

_____

C. Find an error in each sentence.

(1) At Christmas, we get together and sing Christmas carol.

(2) We had a great time to play hide and seek in the woods.

(3) On the first day it snowed last year, we made snowballs and threw them for each other.

(4) I still remember to play in the snow with my sisters when I was very young.

Free Bonus 2

Visit www.liketestprep.com and www.sunshinebooks.co.kr And sign up for our email services on new books and free e-books!!!

Free Bonus 3

Visit www.liketestprep.com and www.sunshinebooks.co.kr And get free Audio mp3 files and more downloads!!!

LIKE TEST PREP Series

Advanced Reading, Writing, and Grammar for Test Prep

1. Teaches you how to do better on reading and writing tests
2. Tips based on reading, writing, and grammar research
3. Vocabulary, Sample Questions, and Question Type Analysis

480 Model Essays

480 Challenging Essay Questions and Sample Essays

480 Model Critiques

480 Model Critiques on 480 Model Essays

480 Writing Topics with Sample Essays

480 Essay Questions and Sample Essays

480 Speaking Topics with Sample Answers

480 Speaking Questions and Sample Answers

480 Writing Summaries

480 Reading/Listening Summary Questions & Sample Summaries

480 Speaking Summaries

480 Speaking Questions and Sample Summaries

240 Basic Writing Topics

480 Basic Essay Questions and Sample Essays

240 Basic Speaking Topics

480 Basic Speaking Questions and Sample Answers

Meet Amazing Americans Workbook Series

Meet Amazing Americans Workbook for http://www.americaslibrary.gov/aa/

LIKE/Sunshine Publishing

200 Korean Dialogues

Master Basic and Intermediate level daily conversations

Korean for Children 1-3

Children can learn Basic and Intermediate level Korean.

Open Door to English Book 1-6

Pre, K-6, or ESL/EFL K-6 students can enjoy learning Basic level English through musical dialogues. Videos (DVDs and downloads) and Audios are available.

English for Kids Book 1-4

Pre, K ESL/EFL students can enjoy learning Basic level English through fun songs.

Videos (DVDs and downloads) and Audios are available.

English for Children 1-3

Pre, K-6 ESL and EFL Children can learn Basic level English.

Aesop's Fables 1-4

K-6, ESL and EFL students can learn Intermediate level English through Aesop's Fables and songs.

200 English Dialogues

Master Basic and Intermediate level daily conversations in English.

Great for ESL (English as Second Language) Learners

Proverbs for Preschoolers

Young Children can learn good moral values through proverbs for Pre, K-6

All True Stories: 33 Life Lessons

Heart touching short stories told by In-hwan Kim, Ph.D.

Made in the USA
San Bernardino, CA
03 November 2015